COMMUNITY

A Journey into the Heart of Community

ELIZABETH CLARE PROPHET

THE SUMMIT LIGHTHOUSE LIBRARY

COMMUNITY
A Journey into the Heart of Community
by Elizabeth Clare Prophet
Copyright © 2002 The Summit Lighthouse Library
All rights reserved

For information, please contact The Summit Lighthouse Library, PO Box 5000, Corwin Springs, MT 59030-5000.
Tel: 1-800-245-5445 or 406-848-9500.
E-mail: tslinfo@tsl.org
Web site: www.tsl.org

THE SUMMIT LIGHTHOUSE LIBRARY™

Library of Congress Control Number: 2001091653
ISBN: 0-9720402-0-X

Pearls of Wisdom, Keepers of the Flame and Summit University are registered trademarks.

Readings from *New Era Community* Copyright © 1951 Agni Yoga Society, 319 W. 107 St., New York. Used by permission.

Design and production: Lynn Wilbert
Cover: James Bennett
Cover image Copyright © 2002 Larry Stanley

Printed in the United States of America

06   05   04   03   02   5   4   3   2   1

Today I was contemplating the mystery of community, and I knew in my heart that along with Mother Mary's teaching on the birth of the Manchild, the next most important step was to form the cradle in which to place the Manchild.

Without question, I would lay down my life a thousand times for the community to endure, and the only way it will endure is through living people who have become the essence of the master.

If we do not leave the continuity of the Great White Brotherhood's name, its organization and its teaching upon the planet for those who follow us, we will not have retained an open door for the traveler.

Elizabeth Clare Prophet

Contents

Acknowledgment

We wish to express our thanks to Daniel Entin of the Agni Yoga Society for his kind permission to quote extensively from the timeless work, *New Era Community,* a book dictated by the ascended master El Morya to his messengers Nicholas and Helena Roerich early in the twentieth century.

We are profoundly grateful for the pioneering spirituality of the Roerichs and hope that the publication of these lectures by Elizabeth Clare Prophet, also a messenger of El Morya and the Great White Brotherhood, will lead to a greater understanding and appreciation of the Roerichs' work and mission.

Introduction

*"What life have you if you have not life together? There
is no life that is not in community."*

—T .S. ELIOT

One has only to consider man's
highest dreams, hopes and longings to realize there is a soul
remembrance of a home and a life, a shared life, that once were
ours and to which we aspire in our earthly sojourn as we find our
way back to this golden, fabled existence.

From the earliest ages of the world emerge images of the
paradise that was Eden—God and man walking and talking in
surroundings of breathtaking perfection that outpictured ideals
of beauty in the divine mind. "The earth is holy and wholly
God's,"[1] as we have been told, and what more magnificent illustration than this.

The Garden of Eden, far from being a myth or just a symbol
of better things, was the first mystery school, a community provided for souls of light to worship God, to show themselves ap-
proved unto God and return Home. While this focus was indeed
lost, humanity has yearned across time for a return to this pure
existence, to this pristine sacred receptacle of the light of God.

In *New Era Community,* the ascended master El Morya
asks, "Have not the best people understood the community?"[2]
Historically, yes, the best have understood. Spiritual pioneers
past and present have sought to offer a chalice into which God
may pour his light for a needy world, for dedicated disciples seeking his face. They have perceived community as a "cosmic cradle
for the entire goals of civilization."[3]

The great spiritual teachers of the past established commu-

nities for those who wished to practice their teachings. Jesus had
his circle of apostles and holy women. Gautama Buddha had his
sangha, or community, of disciples. Pythagoras established his
city of the elect at Crotona. Hypatia had her inner circle of students and initiates. Saint Francis of Assisi gathered his band of
brothers and Saint Clare her Poor Ladies.

Camelot, the mystical, not mythical, kingdom, was a once-
and-future community of initiates "questing in the world and in
the world of the Spirit"[4] for the Holy Grail—symbol of the
Christ consciousness. The community founded by the ascended
masters through Mark and Elizabeth Clare Prophet, their
anointed messengers in this age, is Camelot come again.

In 1978, this contemporary Camelot was established in California's Santa Monica Mountains. Camelot was the home of
Summit University and Montessori International. It was a unique
experiment in community life, where parents, children and
people of all ages could come together to share in the joys and
challenges of the spiritual path. A larger vessel nestled in the
peace and majesty of nature's surroundings was needed to hold
the flame, and, in 1986, the community completed its move to its
present home at the Royal Teton Ranch on the northern border
of Yellowstone National Park. It is a mountain retreat, rising
from the valley of the Yellowstone River to snow-covered peaks.
There are pine forests, wildflower meadows and alpine lakes.
And the fire in the heart of the mountain speaks of other dimensions, just beyond the outer awareness. The ascended masters
have formally dedicated this physical focus as a modern-day
mystery school.

Here, spiritual seekers can reconnect with the original edenic
mystery school and discover and define the inner Camelot on the
altar of their hearts through ascended master teaching, especially on the mystical paths of the world's religions—in reality,
the one path that has appeared in different outer forms. The
masters come to us in the tradition of the saints of the West and
the sages of the East, seeking disciples, or chelas, dedicated to

keeping the flame of life on earth.

Community is a legacy of the spiritual questing at the Camelot focus in California. It contains a series of lectures delivered by Elizabeth Clare Prophet at Summit University, a retreat at which seekers study ascended master wisdom and dip into the flame of community. The students who heard these talks came to sit at the feet of the masters and to be with the messenger, who represents the guru in this sangha.

Her talks—which were based on *New Era Community,* a book of El Morya's dictations given early in the twentieth century through his messengers Nicholas and Helena Roerich—present new teaching from the masters on community and offer her own commentaries on the original teachings and her unique insights as a spiritual leader on the alchemy of spiritual community.

As we offer these lectures to a wider audience, it is with the hope that many others will catch the flame and the vision of community and will be inspired to pursue a guru-chela relationship with the ascended masters.

THE EDITORS

CHAPTER 1

The Dream of Community

In the name of the Christ, in the name of the Holy Spirit, I call forth the light of beloved El Morya, beloved Saint Germain, beloved Lanello and all who have served the great communities of the Holy Spirit in all ages. I call forth the light of our own Mother Mary, who is the very heart of our community.

I call forth the light of Helios and Vesta and of the Great Central Sun. I call for the intensification of the love flame within us. I call for the intensification of the light of truth. I call for the diamond jewel from the heart of El Morya to focus the action of the Holy Spirit to precipitate our community.

Let this be the nucleus, then, of the light of God that never fails to manifest within us our home of light, our endeavor for the Brotherhood. Let it be the fulfillment of our alchemy and of the sacred fire in the heart of Saint Germain. In the name of the Father, the Mother, the Son and the Holy Spirit, Amen.

What we are about to take up today is the sacred flame of community and the flame of the Holy Spirit. The flame of community is something Mark* and I have held in our hearts very intently, and so have the members of our family and the members of the board of directors. It has been the dream of our souls for many years and the dream of the Great White Brotherhood for

---
*Mark Prophet, now the ascended master Lanello.

centuries. Through his messengers Nicholas and Helena Roerich, the master El Morya wrote a book called *New Era Community*. Nicholas ascended, Helena reincarnated, and so they hold the balance of their twin flames in the Spirit-Matter cosmos.

The Importance of Community

This book on community gives the fundamental teaching that makes us realize that we give our lives for the continuity of community. Through the various trials and burdens that have been upon this organization, my experience has taught me that the community is the most important thing in my life. Without The Summit Lighthouse on this planet, life here would not be worth living.

Therefore, when we have had crises and lawsuits and on-slaughts, without any reservation I have gone before the Lord of the World to offer my life and my balanced karma to God to use for the victory over the momentary crisis. I have seen it accepted, and I have seen the Brotherhood use the light to sustain the activity.

Perhaps I needed a crisis such as that to make me realize that the community was more important than the messenger. I truly believe that. I feel that the world could sooner do without me than it could without the community. Therefore, my life was not worth having if the community was going to be lost and the messenger was going to survive.

Your love for God will ultimately manifest in a similar love and the same sense of sacrifice. For the community, which is the opportunity for all chelas to be together and to be one with the guru and receive the teachings, is more important than the survival of any one of its members.

The community Morya is talking about is really the white-fire core of the Israelite nation. We are that white-fire core, so our inner community is a disciplined guru-chela relationship. We are the white-fire core of America.

The larger community of the United States of America has a

stepped-down version of that relationship. There are laws that the people must obey. For the people of America are still held to standards, and, when they are disobedient, they receive the punishment of the law. Therefore, the law is operable, even though it is not such an intense action as in the white-fire core.

I would like us to study this book. It is very precious to me, because I see community as the most precious thing in the world. You might think that being a messenger is the most precious, or having chelas, but a mother bird needs a nest for her young. A mother is concerned for the ultimate safety and well-being of her young. And without a nest in which to lay her eggs, the eggs will not hatch and the little birds will not come forth.

There can be no guru-chela relationship without community, and, therefore, the teaching, the Word, the messenger and the students will not survive. The more we know about community as the white cube in the heart, and then as its ramification in the outer, the more we stabilize an outer forcefield of the Great White Brotherhood.

The Brotherhood needs a home on earth and a permanent physical forcefield. A piece of land does not make a forcefield. Hearts make a forcefield, but without a piece of land, how can hearts unite?

A Worldwide Antahkarana

Community challenges us to master the interaction of spiritual-material energies. The concept of a community that stretches worldwide is *antahkarana,* or the web of life. Wherever the chelas are, the community exists, but unless the chelas and the guru are together in one place, there is not a duplicate of the Great Central Sun Magnet to hold the balance for the earth.

An outer focus of the Great White Brotherhood with a living messenger and living chelas is something that has not succeeded in a long time. Today I was contemplating the mystery of community, and I knew in my heart that along with Mother Mary's teaching on the birth of the Manchild, the next most important step was to form the cradle in which to place the Manchild.

Without question, I would lay down my life a thousand times for the community to endure, and the only way it will endure is through living people who have become the essence of the master. Each of us must have such deep love for El Morya or for any of the brothers of light that we recognize that our reason for being is to transfer this torch of community.

If we do not leave the continuity of the Great White Brotherhood's name, its organization and its teaching upon the planet for those who follow us, we will not have retained an open door for the traveler—the traveler who needs a hostel when he is weary. And we read about the traveler on the first page of the book, *New Era Community.*

Setting Forth the Blueprint of Community

Let us open the book to the page following the title page. Here, on an unnumbered page, El Morya sets forth the blueprint of the community:

> Wayfarer, friend, let us travel together. Night is near, wild beasts are about, and our campfire may go out. But if we agree to share the night watch, we can conserve our forces.
>
> Tomorrow our path will be long and we may become exhausted. Let us walk together. We shall have joy and festivity. I shall sing for you the song your mother, wife and sister sang. You will relate for me your father's story about a hero and his achievements. Let our path be one.
>
> Be careful not to step upon a scorpion, and warn me about any vipers. Remember, we must arrive at a certain mountain village.
>
> Traveler, be my friend.

Let us look at what El Morya is saying here. I would like you to see that this writing is a glyph. It is just like taking a grid of the master's mind. He has decided that he is going to convey certain energies that are keys on the points of a grid, where vertical meets horizontal, Alpha meets Omega, at the point at which the lines cross. El Morya has selected certain key points on the grid, and he wants to superimpose them upon our consciousness.

These first four paragraphs of the book contain the entire matrix of community. First, the community is based upon divine friendship. Second, it is based upon a common journey. So the Zen master El Morya says, "Wayfarer, friend, let us travel together."

The purpose of friendship is for the journey, for movement on the Path. El Morya mentions movement in this book at the very start. By the fifth word in the book, you know that you are moving with the Mercurian master. Then he gives you the reasons for moving together: "Night is near, wild beasts are about, and our campfire may go out."

He is establishing the whole purpose of friendship and community. "If we agree to share the night watch, we can conserve our forces." Conservation of cosmic forces is the purpose of community. We can do better together than we can alone because we have a common foe and limited resources. If we pool our resources, we can arrive at the mountain village.

The image of that mountain village keys right into our soul— the archetypal pattern, the Himalayan fastnesses, a place somewhere in the vast beyond, where you finally arrive at a village. In the heart of the village is a rustic sort of a little house, and in that house is the master.

You sense the crudity of the surroundings, which denotes that the value of this master is on inner planes. That is not to say that the master could not be found in a palace, but these are archetypal patterns, like finding Babaji and his disciples in the midst of nowhere or finding Kuthumi and El Morya hiking up a mountain trail.

The archetypal pattern is of the soul on a quest. It is part of every spiritual story that has ever been told. It is this archetypal pattern of the soul that makes our young Americans go to India and, of course, we know that we could all go to India, yet we would not necessarily be there in consciousness.

The first paragraph keys into the etheric body and sets forth the blueprint of the community. The second paragraph expresses the mental body, and we notice that it is longer than the first one: "Tomorrow our path will be long and we may become exhausted." This is the reasoning mind, the mental body.

"Let us walk together. We shall have joy and festivity." The emotional body enters here, right within this paragraph. We understand from this that the community is based on human relationships, which in turn are focal points for divine relationships; so the emotional body begins with "joy and festivity." Notice that the mental body must plan for joy and festivity. It must allow the emotional body to express itself.

"I shall sing for you the song your mother, wife and sister sang." It is the song of the feminine ray, the song of the culture of the Mother. It is a folk song, a national song. It is a joyous song. It may be a love song or a romantic song or poetry that extols chivalry, knighthood and the heroes of the land.

"You will relate for me your father's story." We must include in community all the tenderness and interaction with life that we feel at the desire-body level. In fact, community becomes the forcefield for the expression of the soul through the four lower bodies. Community becomes the larger matrix of our four lower bodies and the extension of our mastery of the self.

"Let Our Path Be One"

"Let our path be one." Here you will notice that Morya's style does not include the long, involved statements that you sometimes find from yellow-ray masters. He reduces everything to the simplicity and common denominator of soul awareness.

Our souls are very direct, but the path that leads to the heart of the soul is often tortuous and winding. It is a winding path, and it winds through the understanding of the mental body, the etheric body, and so forth. At the physical level comes the warning of danger: "Be careful not to step upon a scorpion." Travelers need to warn each other, so "warn me about any vipers." The scorpion represents the misuse of Scorpio on the ten o'clock line. Vipers come with revenge, the eleven o'clock line. So in order to make it to the village, we have to pass through the treacherous traps and trials that are set for us by the false hierarchy.

"Remember, we must arrive at a certain mountain village. Traveler, be my friend." When you read stories about the rugged travels and experiences of people in the jungles or the mountains, you will find that many explorers travel together and that community is formed when necessity involves survival. If the necessity for survival and survival of the mission were not present, people would have no reason to surrender their selfishness.

Perhaps a hundred years ago we would have not seen the need for community. But one of the reasons we want community is that at a very basic level, way down here in the solar plexus, we have a need for survival—spiritual survival and material survival. In the face of the threat of world upheaval, a crumbling economy, an unstable way of life, we band together in community.

Our common understanding of the adversity we face is probably what the Great White Brotherhood conceived to be the most fertile soil in which to plant the seed of community. If all our needs were met today, spiritually and materially, I doubt very much that we would have found each other or that we would have sensed the urgency of this cause—a cause that would make us live for it night and day.

So, from what I just gave you, reflect on what motivates people to come together for community. And then review what Morya has talked about on this very first page of the book.

The Yellow-Ray Purpose of Community

We are dissipating superstition, ignorance and fear. We are forging courage, will and knowledge.

Every striving toward enlightenment is welcome. Every prejudice, caused by ignorance, is exposed.

Thou who dost toil, are not alive in thy consciousness

the roots of cooperation and community?

If this flame has already illumined thy brain, adopt the signs of the Teaching of Our mountains.

Thou who dost labor, do not become wearied, puzzling over certain expressions. Every line is the highest measure of simplicity.

Greeting to workers and seekers!

The opening page has a blue-ray thrust to it, a very Zen thrust. This one succinctly sets forth the yellow-ray purpose of the community: to dissipate superstition. Saint Germain once told us that superstition is the greatest enemy of the consciousness of humanity. He told us that he would like to free the energy held in pockets of superstition in the mass consciousness and use that energy to free the children of the world.

If people were able to redirect the same amount of energy they put into superstition into decreeing for the children, we could change the face of the earth—there is so much of mankind's energy invested in supersitition. Thus, we are dissipating all forms of superstition, including black magic, witchcraft, voodoo, psychicism—everything from the use of the pendulum to fear of the number thirteen is superstition. Any belief that is not based and founded upon cosmic law or the Christ consciousness becomes superstition. Although scientists believe in their theories, many of our scientific hypotheses today are mere superstition.

We are dissipating the three great enemies of man—superstition, ignorance and fear. If you want to remember them, think *s, i, f*—superstition, ignorance and fear. In their place "we are forging courage, will and knowledge"—*c, w, k*—the flames that dissipate the previous three. Courage replaces superstition, will replaces ignorance and knowledge replaces fear. Knowledge also replaces ignorance and will replaces fear.

"Every striving toward enlightenment is welcome." The purpose of community is enlightenment. "Every prejudice, caused by ignorance, is exposed." Prejudice and ignorance are the things we must guard against.

Our Sacred Labor

"Thou who dost toil, are not alive in thy consciousness the roots of cooperation and community?" El Morya is speaking here to workers who understand the concept of the sacred labor.

Jesus' understanding of the flame of work was, "My Father worketh hitherto and I work."[1] The people Morya has in mind are those who have a similar understanding and a similar flame. To them we can say, "Are not alive in thy consciousness the roots of cooperation and community?" Those who work without that sense within do not have the Holy Spirit. Their work will be based on pride and ambition, gain and amassing things of this world.

There are two different types of workers in the vineyard of the world. One is amassing his private wealth, and the other is working for the commonweal. This becomes a point to ponder for the community member. If you are a toiler, is your toil for cooperation and community?

"If this flame has already illumined thy brain, adopt the signs of the Teaching of Our mountains." "Of Our mountains" means of our highest consciousness.

"Thou who dost labor, do not become wearied, puzzling over certain expressions. Every line is the highest measure of simplicity." If you have the virtue of labor, then let labor be the movement and the wheel that keeps on turning. Don't let this movement of your labor be stopped by a lack of understanding of the teaching, because you will come to know the lines of simplicity.

"Greeting to workers and seekers!" There is no room for any other type of person in community. As you read *New Era Community,* you will find it astounding how much this is stressed. I was glad to have confirmation of it because Mark and I and Morya have always stressed work.

Some have complained that they are driven and must work night and day. They have said that there is something wrong with us or that this kind of discipline simply won't work. However, the very core of this book on community says that if a person isn't willing to work, he is not a part of community. Love of the work is the sign of the person who is a part of the mandala.

Now we come to the first numbered paragraph.

> 1. Family, clan, country, union of nations—each unit
> strives toward peace, toward betterment of life. Each unit of
> cooperation and communal life needs perfecting. No one
> can fix the limits of evolution. By this line of reasoning a
> worker becomes a creator.

A worker becomes a creator, and then a co-creator with God.

> Let us not be frightened by the problems of creativeness. Let
> us find for science unencumbered paths. Thus, thought
> about perfectionment will be a sign of joy.

This is like savoring very rich morsels, isn't it? I won't comment on every line because the meaning is there. It's intrinsic, although some of it yet bears commentary. We need moments to think about perfectionment, but more importantly, we need moments for the attainment of perfection in a handiwork. This is why work is the necessary element of the community.

Depression

> 2. Depression is the enemy of each improvement.

Depression causes the chakras to become concave and then collapse. They collapse by the pressure of the mass consciousness and the astral plane. The depressing of the chakras makes people weak-spined and makes their brains fuzzy and confused. It allows them to misqualify the heart chakra and put themselves completely out of attunement.

Thus, depression needs to be met with a thrust of energy to force out the substance in the chakras that is depressing them. If you find depression in your consciousness, you need to realize that it takes an enormous effort to thrust it out. You have to stop everything you are doing and get rid of it.

You may be depressed because of a biochemical imbalance in your physical body—the acid/alkaline balance and the balance of minerals. This can cause you to be unable to deal with the astral energies that are causing your chakras to be depressed. We need to treat depression from the physical as well as from the astral level. When we solve the depression there, we can usually cause the mental and etheric conditions to swing back as well.

Fear and Doubt

There can be no constructive building in doubt. There will be no learning under fear. Observation is a step toward justice. Selfhood is betrayal of self-renunciation. Without achievement there is no path.

People in our midst who have fear and doubt can become betrayers of the community, especially when they let their fear and doubt grow into a sense of injustice on the opposite side of the clock, the eight o'clock line.[2] When they have a sense of injustice about community life, they swing from the eight o'clock line of the earth sign, Virgo, into twelve o'clock criticism, condemnation and judgment based on their sense of injustice and ultimately to rebellion on the four o'clock line.

Seeds of doubt and fear are enemies of the community. In the writings of Kuthumi given to Blavatsky,[3] we have the teaching that there will always be the moment when the chela must face the great test of the doubt of the teacher. If the chela can overcome the test of doubt of the teacher as well as the fear of the teacher, he can remain on the path of chelaship.

Develop a Study System

3. Monasteries were often called communities. The communal life has long been a sign of cooperation and of mutual respect. So too each workshop can be a cell of a community in which everybody contributes his skill. Altruism is a requisite if one is to devote one's talent to the common work.

I have found in the study of the Roerich material that unless you develop a study system for these books, you will not retain what you read. They contain concentrated doses of teaching that are matrices of light, fohatic keys. These little books are like Bibles. Once you have read them, reread them and underlined them, keep them close at hand. Then, when you pick them up again, you will recall what you read before and you will reinforce the subconscious matrix.

There is a key for you in each of these numbered sections. There might also be an obvious subject to the section that you will want to underline. You might ask yourself: What is the thrust of the author in each paragraph? What does he want to get across? And secondly, what stands out to you as something very important?

You will want to underline this last point, not just because it sounds nice but because it really has that point of penetration for your being. Then, when you go back to the book because you need something to restore your soul, it will be there. You will already have gone through the process of distilling it, so you just pick up the book and you see those passages that meant so much to you.

A Community of Friends

Number 4 is on unity and the fact that community may consist only of friends.

> 4. Unity is pointed out in all beliefs as the sole bulwark of success. Better attainments can be affirmed if the unity of coworkers is assured. One may cite a great number of examples when mutual trust among the coworkers helped in lofty solutions. Let people, from home and hearth up to the spacial preordinations, remember about the value of cooperation. The seed of labor withers without the moisture of reciprocity.

Reciprocity—give and take—is the concept of unity and friendship in the community.

Let us not look backward too much.

Looking backward is looking back to old human ties, which cannot endure in the community. I think this is one of the most difficult parts of the Path for many people. Fortunate are you if you are not in this position. Many people have difficult decisions to make about the worth of associations that cannot survive in a community setting.

Those associations were not based on the principles of community, yet many times they often form a deep part of our subconscious and of our energy spirals. To remove them in order to be in the community, we have to go through the agony of a certain surgery of the removal, let us say, of a cancer upon the self.

That's why El Morya says, "Let us not look backward too much." Looking backward to the old enjoyments, the old relationships, the old ties can completely cut you off from community.

The Meaning of Friendship

We hastening fellow-travelers shall become weary if we jostle each other. We shall realize a beautiful meaning if we can introduce the great concept—friend. Community may consist only of friends.

5. The path of life is one of mutual help.

To me, the real meaning of friendship is understood only in the context of mutuality of discipleship on the Path. Every other type of friendship seems to be motivated by lesser standards, for people do have motives in friendships—let us not say all people, but let us say that it is something to be wary of in the world. I think we have all been disappointed by such friendships, realizing that we have been used thereby instead of deeply loved.

I think we feel the greatest love for fellow souls who are going through the same process of overcoming as we are, for then we can share understanding and help. A change in the relationship between Jesus and his disciples occurred when he said, "Henceforth, I call you not servants but friends."[4] He made them his equal by declaring that they were his friends.

When we have served the Brotherhood century after century, a time comes in our lives when we know in our heart, as Abraham did, that we are friends of God. We are not just children, and we are not just servants. We have attained the status of friend, and we have trust in that sense of friendship.

For example, my mother asked me this morning, "What are you going to do about establishing your headquarters?" And I replied, "I don't know, but God knows. He has never let me down. I have never let him down, and I trust, by his grace, I never will." That's what friendship is—knowing that your friend will not let you down.

I think of my relationship with God as a relationship with someone whom I adore and worship, someone whom I know also in the various persons of Father, Mother, Son and Holy Spirit—and above all, friend. God is my friend, so he will secure a home for my children. He is everything else, of course, that we can name in a relationship.

Friendship is based on trust, so "community may consist only of friends." If we are not friends, we cannot be in community together.

When is true friendship broken? For me, it is broken when an individual betrays my master. I cannot bear to be with anybody who betrays my master. My whole life is in the service of my King, my Lord, the chohans. If I see someone betray their purposes, I must immediately put him out of the community. The friendship is broken, the trust is broken and the person himself is no longer a vessel of the Brotherhood.

"The path is one of mutual help." This is an important point because as soon as you see the point of mutual help, you realize that if I am not helping you or you are not helping me, then one of us must be a parasite. Either I am a parasite on you, or you are a parasite on me. Mutual help eliminates the parasite.

The teaching is that we cannot have parasites in the community. Yet one does have them. They will do their token work, but they are really here because they have their daily bread, a place to sleep, friendship and light on which to live. Yet at the core of the person, there's no commitment and no sincerity. These are usually quiet and unobtrusive people who can hang around a long time. And you do not realize that you have parasites in your midst except by a certain drained feeling in body and mind. You feel drained of energy because someone in the community has stopped the flow.

Mark's Rule

I would like to tell you about one of Mark's rules. When a person betrayed the master or the messengers and broke the trust of the community to the extent that he was no longer a friend but was a rebel in our midst, Mark would see to it that that person was out of the community by sundown. He would not allow a two-week transition period or give the person time for a leisurely leaving.

Mark would not sleep in the same house with someone whose consciousness was tied to the false hierarchy. The person had to be removed, and until they were removed, there was discord and there was an opening into the astral plane and a rending of the garment and forcefield of the community.

We have to do the same thing in our households, in our families. I was talking to a prominent attorney not long ago who had to remove his daughter from his house because she had become a heroin addict and was becoming very vicious and violent in the home. He told me he would have done it long ago, but the child's mother was unable to make that decision. But it had to be done for the good of the other children and the rest of the family, and it became quite a large crisis.*

We have to do the same with our own family members. We even have to do it in our own body temple and consciousness, or we will destroy the community of our soul with God. Our soul

---

*Of course, all other avenues of counseling and professional assistance need to be tried before taking such a step.—Ed.

with God is a community that will be destroyed if we harbor energies in our emotional body or our mental body that are incompatible with our absolute harmony with God.

This is the cause of disease, insanity, mental and emotional imbalance, neurosis and psychosis. If an individual is not exorcising from his own consciousness the foreign elements, the parasites, elements that have broken trust with the whole, he will not remove them from his family. Families can go on for years in a state of discord because one element of that family is allowed to remain and drag down the whole. From the family it goes to the neighborhood and then the community.

In a dictation many years ago, Archangel Uriel said that it took only one person aligned with evil to completely pollute a city and bring it down.[5] Even though one person of darkness in a city seems so few, Uriel was explaining that when our culture originally turned away from the light, it took just one dark soul in a community to do it.

Mark was very zealous in guarding the community, and I have come to realize that I must also be zealous. I must remove all persons who do not have a one-hundred-percent commitment to the Path (with the exception of students who come and go, of course). But the permanent community members need to be considered in that light.

Therefore, community may consist only of friends. And the definition of friend tells us who may and who may not live within the community.

The Humanity-Haters

Participants in the great task cannot be humanity-haters. This term denoting a shameful hatred is a long one. But perhaps people will the better remember it and be ashamed.

This may come as a surprise to you, but there are an awful lot of people-haters. Some people-haters come to the Path because they have rejected the common people and want to be among the elite. They will try to be part of the community, and yet they do not want to have anything to do with people. They do not want to help others. They just want to withdraw and make their ascension.

You might take the word *humanity-hater* and translate it into the hatred of the Mother* and her children, and we know that this is the most stubborn type of hatred on the earth. It is a cancer on the body of the earth. The hatred of the Mother and her children can manifest as the intense insanity that is the ripening of rebellion. If rebellion is allowed to ripen over many incarnations, its consequence is insanity, and this insanity will be exposed when you attempt to have community. To remove this unwanted substance requires a painful process of the surgery of parting with this substance that is unwanted and yet so intertwined with the self that it cannot help but be an enormous emotional upheaval to remove it.

Jesus exorcised and healed many possessed and insane people. There were a number of cases around him, and I want to tell you, not from the record but from what I know, that Jesus did attract to himself insane people.

The demons understood the presence of the light and the core of the demon is God, and that core wants to be set free. Therefore, demons will pursue representatives of the Brotherhood through the people whom they possess. The demons in the people will actually recognize the master before the people do. "We know thee, thou holy one of God. Torment us not,"[6] is what they said.

The defense of community and the defense of the Mother and her children, then, come right down to the need to be in the center of the circle and sword of Astrea for the constant removal of the humanity-haters. Who are the humanity-haters? They are the demons and discarnates who attach themselves to the children of God.

---

*The Mother of the World

An Encounter with the Humanity-Haters

Here is an example of an encounter with the humanity-haters. In Aimee Semple MacPherson's *The Story of My Life* we are told of an incident at a meeting. Aimee's tent was set up near a football field. Some young college boys, who were also football players, were harassing her to the point of viciousness and malicious mischief, so much so that she could not sing or conduct her service.

By the instruction of her Christ Self, Aimee began to praise the Lord. And as the praise swelled up from the congregation, she saw with her inner eye that demons with intertwined bat-like wings had surrounded these football players. As she continued to praise God, the demons began to retreat, and in their place the angels came forward with their wings intertwined.

What is so important about this is that at the conclusion of this praise and then the stillness that followed, these football players came forward to join the meeting. They came to the altar, were converted and they joined with the others in carrying the sick to the altar.[7]

This shows us that the most vicious opposition to the Path and the masters manifests through the humanity-haters. Without a clearer understanding, we would mark these college boys as humanity-haters. But because of the inner sight that Aimee was given that showed them to be simply the victims of the humanity-haters and that they themselves were not the humanity-haters, we are given great insight into how to liberate the children of God.

When we see an extreme attack upon our person and upon our movement, it is the time for us to do intense decrees for the people who are involved to be stripped of the humanity-haters. What the demons want us to do is to give up, turn our backs and say, "Oh, well, these people aren't meant for the Path, anyway. We will go somewhere else." Instead, we have to go in and exorcise those demons and release their hold on people.

The Inner Stream of Community

Our Community of the Holy Spirit is the repository of all efforts toward community that have ever been made by any group of souls anywhere on the face of the earth. It is the repository of the twelve tribes of Israel, of Camelot, of the people of Tibet, of the people of China, of the mystery school of Pythagoras.

Every effort toward community that has ever been made and then attacked and destroyed has suffered the destruction of its outer structure. But the inner stream, the confluence of that stream, is here and now in this forcefield. That stream is the great River of Life, and all the rivulets have come together to incarnate in this focal point. These are El Morya's words to us. This is the heart of the message of community.

I have the good fortune to tell you that in the last several days, precious treasures from other activities have come to me, such as pictures and photographs that have never been seen or published. These treasures have been given to me personally to use. They include autographed copies of books and other items that were part of the establishment of Saint Germain's earlier movement on this continent.

To me, they are symbols of the ascended masters' intent to use us for the resurrection and the life of the effort of the community that was once America and that we intend to make America again. In this sense, *New Era Community* is a book of patriotism as it aims to enshrine the individual peoples of the earth in their individual communities.

Archangel Michael's decree (see p. 273) gives us the ability to call for the protection of all the communities of the Holy Spirit that are springing up throughout the earth for the Aquarian age. We want to see these communities happen over and over again until the islands of lightbearers finally join and create a vast continent of lightbearers.

When we assimilate the jewels contained in this book, and when we give our lives to become the matrix that Morya has set forth, we will not be simply an experimental community. We will be the fullness of the alchemy of the victory—the living community.

The word Jesus used for his community, the Greek word *ecclesia,* was translated as "church" but literally means "the assembly of the called-out ones." And the true meaning of his statement to Peter is, "Upon this rock will I build my community of the called-out ones."[8] Jesus did not found a building, and he did not found a hierarchy of doctrine and dogma. He founded a community of the called-out ones—those who would be separate from the mass consciousness.

This is a revolutionary concept of church, and it has remained hidden from us because of the mistranslation from the Greek. The term *ecclesiastical,* which comes from the same root, does not mean in English today what the root means. I want you to be able to say wherever you go that *ecclesia* really means the community or the assembly of the called-out ones. This is what we are restoring. We are the restorers of the cathedral. We are the artisans in the temple. This is the purpose to which we have been called.

The Problem of Malice

6. Also let us not forget that realization is simplified through clear consciousness. But let us not lose the shortest Path. Time is precious. We should not deprive anyone because of our sluggishness. Laziness and ignorance sleep in the same cradle.

7. Malice admits leprosy and pestilence. Malice can transform a peaceful fireside into a swarm of snakes. Qualities of malice are not befitting the community. The common task is General Welfare.

8. Cooperation must be based upon sound rules.

Malice, or malicious animal magnetism,[9] can erode the etheric blueprint of the community. Those in our midst who have had malice bear a visage of outer conformity, but beneath that visage is a smoldering cruelty and hatred that may turn into one final act of betrayal or one sudden burst of energy. All of a sudden, the aura is turned inside out and the "swarm of snakes" at the subconscious level will be revealed and exposed.

The only one who can force out these snakes is the guru. The guru within the community will make a seemingly ridiculous request of the chela. The chela, in his pride, does not consider that the request is worthy of him, and then he will suddenly turn upon the guru because the guru has hit him at his weak point.

This happens because the ascended masters use the messengers to do this. The messengers themselves are not prone to disturb people or attack them at their weak points, for their weak points are hidden from us. It is not until the masters make a request or give an assignment that you have the explosion and the resulting exposure.

I trust that when you see the word *malice* you will associate it with malicious animal magnetism.

Continuous Labor

8. Cooperation must be based upon sound rules. This teaches orderliness—that is, it helps the acquirement of a rhythm. Thus even in daily work are expressed the great laws of the Universe. It is especially needed to become accustomed from childhood to continuous labor. Let the better evolution be built upon labor as the measure of value.

Rules equal orderliness. Orderliness equals rhythm. Rhythm is a reflection of the great laws governing the universe. From childhood, we should pattern ourselves after orderliness. We should let children become accustomed to it as a continuous expression of the sacred labor. We cannot have children in the midst of our community grow up in the ways of the world, in idleness and in the need to be constantly entertained.

The greatest destruction of the potential of the soul is to allow children to spend their free time seeking entertainment from without instead of from within. It is like quicksand because children gravitate toward entertainment like ants toward honey. Not like bees, because bees belong in honey, but like ants, who go after honey in the same way that kids go after entertainment. If a child is not encouraged to be creative, you can see it as life-threatening to the soul.

"Let the better evolution be built upon labor as the measure of value." By the grace of God, I had parents who saw work as a measure of virtue. I don't know what I would have done without that foundation for community. I always had to be industrious, doing something with my hands, doing something with my mind. We did not believe in continuous entertainment.

Labor Must Be Voluntary

9. And another absolute condition must be fulfilled. Labor must be voluntary. Cooperation must be voluntary. Community must be voluntary. Labor must not be enslaved by force. The condition of voluntary agreement must be laid into the foundation of advancement. No one may bring dissolution into the new house. Workers, builders, creators, can be likened to high-soaring eagles. Only in a broad flight does the dust and rubbish of decay fall away.

This section, number nine, totally invalidates Communism and the welfare state. Communism, in the theories taught by Marx and Engels, is the diabolical counterfeit of the Community of the Holy Spirit. America should long ago have been a Community of the Holy Spirit, but the beast of selfishness and sensuality has torn the essence of community from America.

Today we have more parasites in the land than we have ever had, and one problem is motivation. Motivation by the threefold flame in the heart is missing in America. We are counting upon our students, upon the Girl Scouts and the Boy Scouts and the minute-men and -women of Saint Germain to go out and motivate the community, motivate the people back to offering the voluntary services that they love to give. We especially need to motivate them to apply the ethic of work.

This nation was built on the ethic of work and the desire for excellence and the elimination of mediocrity. When mediocrity is tolerated, it is so sickening to the soul that it destroys even the desire for work or for a sacred labor. Mediocrity intrudes as a poison in the water, and it is water with a stench. It begins to smell like a sewer, and then no one wants to become part of the great River of Life.

Workers, builders, high-soaring eagles—images of flying and birds relate to the mind and to consciousness. Whenever you come across images like this, relate them to consciousness. It means that while our bodies are engaged in the sacred labor, our consciousness must be high soaring.

> 10. A lofty quality will enter into pure labor through love of a favorite craft. A beautiful quality will be affirmed throughout life. Nothing will remain in darkness. Ignorance will be a shameful offence. Darkness is infectious but Light is attractive.

This is a very interesting use of those two words—the infection of darkness and the attraction of light.

Hence, let us affirm the love of a favorite craft, which uplifts the life.

We all need projects, including our children. They need something to turn to, to weave their energies into, to pass the hours and pass the days.

> Science should indicate the best quality. Science should attract the strongest energies. Let the knowledge of the spirit shine over every workbench.

Isn't that sweet? It's like all the ascended master focuses in our offices!

> 11. Many falsehoods have been piled around the concept of labor. Only recently was labor scorned and considered harmful for health. What an outrage this is—this

regarding of labor as harmful! Not labor is injurious but the ignorant conditions surrounding labor.

Ignorant animal magnetism destroys the integration of the mind of God with the physical body—the figure-eight pattern between the mental and the physical bodies. When you have ignorance in the mental body, you have sloth in the physical body. When you have sloth in the physical, it turns back and becomes ignorance in the mind because there is no flow. You find that people who do not exercise or work with their bodies get very stodgy in their minds.

Conscious Cooperation

Only conscious cooperation can render healthy the sacred labor.

"Conscious cooperation." When Saint Germain introduces his work on alchemy, he says your motive in alchemy must be for the service of humanity. Otherwise, your alchemy will not work.

Not only must the quality of labor be high, but there must be strengthened the mutual desire to make the conditions of labor clearly understood. One must not curse labor, one should set forward the better worker.

To curse labor is to curse the Holy Spirit. This is the crisis we have in America. The sacred labor, the virtue of work, is right there on the nine o'clock line. It must not become an end in itself or a driving force without the Spirit so that the individual does not tie into God or dedicate his labor to God's glory. We have to have a rhythm of work, a twenty-four-hour spiral of work, but we must insert and infuse intervals of cosmic consciousness into it that reestablish a connecting point, a common purpose of labor.

America is in her initiation of the Holy Spirit.[10] We must restore that individual desire for excellence and eliminate welfare as much as possible. We have to inspire people to contribute to the commonweal.

12. There should be instilled respect for craftsman-
ship, in order that it be understood as a higher distinction.
Ancient working community-guilds left testimony of their
vitality. One can see how people cultivated their skills
toward perfection. They knew how to shield each other and
how to guard the dignity of their community. So long as people do not learn to defend the merit of their fellow-workers
they will not achieve the happiness of Common Good.

El Morya says that guilds are the foundation of the true
union, but labor unions, for the most part, have become their
perversion. The true union is the mutual defense of the laborers
of one another, which is established first by your defense of your
own integrity and internal community.

You have to defend your soul's relationship to your I AM
Presence to keep that community identity established. And sometimes you have to defend it against what seem to be your best
friends—parts of your consciousness you are accustomed to but
which are human relationships and human conditionings and
human habit patterns.

You will need to teach children loyalty within the family.
Brothers and sisters may tease one another publicly or betray one
another's weaknesses before their friends as a means of control-
ling one another. So, you have to train children to honor the
family. The family has to stick together.

In opposition to this, however, you will find a tendency to
divide and conquer the family, such as occurred in the Soviet
Union. Children were taught to betray their parents and report
them to the state. The family must have its internal integrity, even
as the soul within the four lower bodies in relation to the spirit
must have its integrity. Once this integrity is established, you can
extend it to the community.

This particular principle of the Holy Spirit has held the community of Jews together throughout the ages. Jews stick together,
help each other, lend each other money and see that each Jewish
family is provided for. They see to it that no Jew is the victim of

what they consider to be the hostility of a Gentile world.

Do Christians do this? No. Christians do not stick together. They do not have as great a sense of community because the word *community* has been replaced with the word *church*. Christians come together on Sunday morning because that's their understanding of church. If they had understood church to mean community, they would long ago have united for the victory. They do not know that they are brethren. That's why Micah, Angel of Unity, came to America and in the midst of warring factions said, "Remember, ye are brethren."[11] We are brethren in the true sense of the word because we all belong to the tribes of the house of Israel.[12]

Defending one another's merit is very important—standing up for one another, not criticizing one another but counseling with one another in areas that could stand improvement.

"Let Us Bring Forth the Warmth of the Heart"

13. The concept of justice proves itself upon the foundation of labor. Likewise courage grows easily in the vouching for each other. Indeed, all as one, yet each one contributing his own best aptitude. Let us not destroy, but let us bring forth the warmth of the heart.

What is the warmth of the heart, and how do we bring it forth? By gently loving one another. We are conditioned from the playground on to feel that we are in a hostile world where we have to constantly defend ourselves, and we no longer allow the naturalness and warmth of the heart to flow freely from us. In the community, however, where basic cooperation is a law and a way of life, the warmth of the heart flows because there is a mutual trust of friendship and because the fear of injury and persecution or attack has been transmuted.

Morya is saying right now that community is a forcefield for the protection of the sacred fires of the heart. It is where hearts can blossom, flowers can bloom and birds can sing, for we all understand what we are about and what we are agreed upon.

"The Son of man came not into the world to condemn the world, but that the world through him might have eternal life."[13] Let us not destroy. Let us bring forth the warmth of the heart.

The Dangers of Specialization

14. Our feeling is one of absence of specialty, because We live for the whole complex of life. Every specialist approaching Us inevitably loses his monochromatic eyeglasses. Therefore, make every effort that the specialty should become but one of the dishes at your table. As birds over the Earth, as bees above all the flowers, we can embrace the entire universe.

Specialization cuts off the full balancing of the threefold flame. Specialization is a very subtle way of cutting off the path of initiation in the world community at large. We have to specialize in an area for our daily bread, but let it be only one of the dishes on our table. Let our profession and our calling be one thing, but let the other hours of our life be for rounding out our experience in the threefold flame and our knowledge of the universe.

When I was in college, I noticed this problem when speaking with engineering students. A whole dormitory of engineering students was nearby, and they were all identical in that they had no ability to relate to anything outside of their engineering program. I found this to be appalling but true in many of the professions.

Consequently, the mechanical performance of their specialization leads to monochromatic eyeglasses—seeing only one way. It's like watching television, seeing a flat screen and thinking this is life. It is very, very dangerous. Within the community, we have options that enable us to have spherical vision and to embrace the whole universe.

Without a specialty it is easier to prepare oneself for the current task in evolution—intercourse with distant worlds

and the transformation of the Astral World, the world of
dark earthly survivals. The adoption of the concept of Community will open the gates for next achievements, and their
dates depend upon people themselves. Therefore, let us
take up broadly the quest of Community.

Dates depend upon people. Time is so important. Dates are
important, and yet, with all the cosmic timetables that Morya
holds in his heart, a fulfillment of those dates comes down to you
and me, to our attunement with his cosmic timetable.

15. Out of a wild jungle I can raise a grove, but a stone
polished by worshipping foreheads will not produce a seed.

The jungle represents virgin energy—untouched, unpro-
grammed. It is a creative resource. The stone polished by worshiping foreheads is a symbol for a mechanical formation.

Spiritual Responsibility

16. Among the mechanical attainments of modern civilization, the means of transportation deserve special attention. This devouring of space is already to a certain extent
a victory over the supermundane spheres. But a circle of low
materialism holds these conquests within the limits of low
matter and the result is more harm than good. The chief
danger in this haste of locomotion lies in a heightened feeling of irresponsibility. Passing beyond the limits of the ordinary, man becomes light, but because of the crudeness of
feelings he loses the consciousness of responsibility.

Our civilization is soaring ahead of the attainment that
comes by discipline. It is letting go of the disciplines naturally
imposed upon us by time and space before we actually had the
attainment to do so. A simple example of this is that when we get
in an airplane and fly great distances, there is produced a sense
of irresponsibility for what we left behind, because in time you
are so distant from it.

We should have actually mastered the art of levitation before we attempted to master the art of flight, especially interplanetary flight. Obtaining the power of mechanization ahead of spiritual attainment can only result in a loss of responsibility. This is something to think about, although the Karmic Board must have determined that it was time for us to have these improvements.

What we need to do now is to bring up the rear of our soul consciousness. If we go much farther without cosmic consciousness, we will have spaceships traveling all over the physical universe just the way they traveled here from other planets, exploring everything, being entertained for tens of thousands of years but never evolving toward the center of God.

Half of these spaceships are manned by automatons, because the individuals who traveled around in them got bored traveling around themselves, and so they created robots and put them in spaceships to do whatever work they're doing against the people of God.

He who can fly at a speed of 400 miles an hour or who can fly higher than others, acquires the psychology of a boxing champion, and the realization of spiritual responsibility leaves him.

It is possible to ennoble the conquest by stripping it of all sporting significance and directing it to labor. Hurry to save the unfortunates, fly for the unifying of humanity! Then will these conquests enter into evolution, for people must bring into ordinary usage the supermundane strivings, not forgetting about responsibility. As yet these conquests remain in the stage of ugly centaurs. When people will comprehend whither and for what reason they must fly, then will it be possible to improve the flying apparatus tenfold.

It is possible to whisper a great number of useful experiments into the strata of space. Atomic energy, condensation of prana, colored rays in space, harvest in connection with repeated explosions, and many another have been destined for humanity.

Learning Co-Measurement

17. Many a time you have heard about following Our indications, and you could convince yourself that precise fulfillment of the indication is practical and beneficial. This is the first step. After this, self-action must begin. Knowing the foundation of Our Teaching it is necessary to prove to be disciples creating in full co-measurement and immutability.

I consider that our community and Summit University are our proving ground for co-measurement, where all act in a co-relationship to the ascended masters and where the master who is your guru is the focal point. If he moves, you move. If he thinks a cosmic thought, you think a cosmic thought.

In this way we are aligned with the inner coordinates of our being, first with our I AM Presence, then with the guru who is one with that Presence. Then the outer community will reflect the inner community, which is the Great White Brotherhood of ascended masters. As more and more of the embodied saints become the direct outer coordinates of the inner activity, we will find that we will become a worthy chalice.

Co-measurement is like two dots that always move in proportion to each other. The larger dot is the I AM Presence or the master, and the smaller is your soul. If you can see these two dots moving in direct co-relation, then you can have the outer community, or the outer church, in relationship to the inner church.

Immutability is the result of co-measurement. Our immutability, our invulnerability, our invincibility is because of our alignment. When we are aligned with God, we are immutable; we become the immutable one. Therefore, forming community is the proving of the disciples, of co-measurement and immutability. Community formed is the result of that proof.

A Patch for a Boot

When the Teacher says, "Now you yourselves display the effect of My indications," it does not mean to recall old habits, to quarrel with one another, to become offended and to hurt each other. This can be left to the mule drivers. But it should be for you to remember about Our Community and emulate it in harmonious labor. When the time comes to change the course of the ship, the indication will come. But do not expect an indication about a patch for the boot. Otherwise we shall soon congratulate each other on our birthdays.

I am grateful for that statement because I have always disliked the fact that the wheels of labor must stop to celebrate birthdays. Extending a token of kindness is fine, yet people seem to be overtaken by a certain vibration when they center on someone's birthday. What Morya is saying is that the level of expecting an indication for a patch for your boot is the same level of getting involved in birthdays and celebrations. It is patting one another on the back for personal accomplishment.

Some people form themselves into groups that are psychically attuned to the most mundane and tiny types of communications from the masters. However, these communications really come from disembodied spirits, because the masters want no part of it. That is a typical Morya statement—the one about the patch for a boot.

"I Wish to See You on the Next Step"

It is necessary to assimilate permanently the dignity and the worth of the true work, and to relegate childish habits to the archives. Without betraying one's principles it is possible to find hundreds of worthy solutions. I wish to see you upon the next step.

Is it not always the desire of the guru to see you on the next step? All else becomes dispensable. It doesn't matter that you have to make the chela cry or go through pain or a period of depression or moroseness. If the end result is to get the chela and the whole community on the next step, then, so be it.

18. Some dream of casting themselves at the feet of the Teachers, but do not dare to go with Them into battle. But precisely now is the time of battle, and We can only call to battle. With the full knowledge of the truth of Good, on personal responsibility, We affirm the battle but a lawful one.

19. Master the problem of remaining cool throughout the entire Battle. The Battle of Light is just beginning—millions are in it without knowing the final result. But you know, and this knowledge should make you wise and prompt a worthy decision. Your spirit must take wing in the name of Truth. How is it possible to be uplifted by the achievement of the evolution of the World? My Ray carries My request that nothing be done to hinder its light. Instead of wings of achievement it is easy to grow black horns— wings of false reasoning. The dark spirits have black emanations resembling horns.

Satan by Gustav Doré

"Wings of false reasoning." Gustav Doré did an etching of Satan. And, if you bear in mind that it was done in about 1850 before airplanes or mechanization, you will note in these wings a streamlined mechanization-type form that instantly tells you that the angel is an angel of darkness. It's a very interesting etching, and I hope you will take time to look at it. It is in a collection of his works.

As an artist, Doré had the understanding transferred from his soul from ancient civilizations, from the fall of Atlantis, that mechanization destroys the soul. And that same mechanization is the result of the carnal mind and its reasoning—black horns instead of angelic wings.

Spherical Consciousness

20. It is necessary to strive toward the utmost, the absolute. The utmost absolute gravitation will be toward the far-off worlds. Earthly beauty is lost in the glory of the super-stellar rays. Earthly science, remembering with difficulty yesterday and ignorant of tomorrow, is insignificant, and contributes nothing to the knowledge about the course of luminaries coming into existence.

How may one approach the above-mentioned Absolute? It cannot be done through technical means or earthly science, nor by descriptive art. It is possible only through the expansion of consciousness, when the earthly being is engulfed by the emanations from the distant spheres. Thus, those who are approaching Us, or rather the boundaries of the orbit of Earth, lose their specialty. Only in the realization of all-comprehensiveness may one endure the brilliance of the luminaries.

All-comprehensiveness is spherical consciousness, the awareness of the Self as a point in the center of a sphere that is a coordinate of infinity. The sphere is also infinity, but our dot in the center is the focal point of the I AM Presence, the Sun Center. We see all things within that cosmos in relation to the Self as the coordinate. Everyone else assumes a relative position within that sphere of Self.

It cannot be otherwise, else the Self—even the Divine Self— would cease to exist as a reality. Every dot of every individual within our sphere of consciousness becomes the center of another sphere through that Self-awareness. Wherever God is in manifestation in us, he is the center of a cosmos.

The Sun Center, which is the I AM THAT I AM of each one, has a relationship of coordinates. So we place father, mother, husband, wife, children closest in our sense of other coordinates that are in our sphere. Then friends, relatives, neighbors, community members, and, finally, the unknown masses assume distant positions. They become stars of lesser magnitude within this cosmos until some of them become simply particles of dust because they have less relative importance to our sun center.

All-comprehensiveness occurs when we, in the center of the sun within this sphere, can have an equal appreciation for the sun center of every other star within our cosmos. We then enter into that all-comprehensiveness that becomes a co-measurement with life and finally an ability to endure the brilliance of the luminaries.

Scientists tell us that the entire Milky Way, relative to the cosmos, occupies the position of a flat plane that is like a sheet of paper. This is very interesting to me because it is like the line of time and space in which we operate. First, we have to become accustomed to these forcefields or these sun centers within a plane. Our awareness of the brilliance of the luminaries—the ascended masters—must begin to stretch us in both directions, above and below the line, until we have a spherical sense of being. If you would like to put your finger on what makes an ascended master chela different from an ordinary person, it is the difference between linear thinking and feeling and this spherical consciousness.

The coordinates of these starry bodies within the average person on earth are still that flat plane. Of course, when you totally integrate with spherical consciousness, you find yourself to be an ascended master, and then you cannot remain long on this plane. If the entire Milky Way is a flat plane, to get out of it obviously you can't just go somewhere else in time and space. You have to ascend into the great spherical body. So, until you have spherical consciousness and all-comprehensiveness, you will not appreciate the luminaries coming into your forcefield.

But in order to contain this scintillation, one must set alight one's inner fires.

One's inner fires, the sacred fires of the heart, must be burning. And in their burning, through our meditation and our science of the spoken Word, we reach that point of acceleration where we break away from the gravitational hold of the linear plane, and all of a sudden, we find ourselves in orbit.

The element of fire is most striking, transcendental, and if you wish to classify Our Community according to the elements, refer to the great fire which gives all, purifies all, and requires nothing.

The Astral Plane and Its Inhabitants

21. We are not lovers of the world of bodily survivals, the lower Subtle World—the Astral World—but, like everything else that exists, it cannot be avoided in spiritual development. The world of bodily survivals contains certain elements needed for the intercourse between the worlds. For example, the means of transportation are very little understood by the dwellers of the Subtle World. Although they have the possibility to strive upwards they are busy with the constructing of dark houses, in imitation of the earthly ones. But if still during their lifetime they had broadened their consciousnesses, they would have been able to measure the hem of the garment of the Mother of the World.

Morya is teaching us about the astral plane and its inhabitants. We know that people can live on the astral plane during an entire earthly incarnation. One doesn't have to be a discarnate to live on the astral plane. A great many people are living there today.

Why is this? Because the initiation of the World Mother today is with her children in the astral plane. The earth is passing through the dark cycle of the return of karma.[14] This creates an astral consciousness, and many people are gravitating into the astral plane because they are not in the mandala of the Mother. They have not chosen to be in that mandala where they take the astral plane as a challenge, as a testing of their souls.

Therefore, we are either in the astral plane as servants and chelas, or we are in the astral plane building our dark houses. And if we are building our dark houses in imitation of the physical quadrant, then we are not able to equate in our being with the hem of the garment of the Mother of the World.

> The better possibilities can be awakened by those who are able to perceive with a spiritual consciousness. But for the preservation of consciousness it is necessary to sense this during one's lifetime. Then the state of the contemporary world of physical survivals will be almost erased. Not the prayer "rest in peace," but "learn in the space of the Light."

Space is Buddha. "Learn in the Buddha of the light." Whenever you have a key like this, you find that that key gives you meaning anywhere and everywhere you apply it.

> With all your consciousness remember the problems of evolution. When the striving for repose disappears then are the Gates drawing near.

> 22. One may reach Us only in harmonious agreement. We need not deification but a certain quality of spirit, as a lamp of concordant tension.

The masters need chelas who are lamps in the astral plane (the subtle world) and who are of a concordant, or harmonious, tension. Tension is not inharmonious—it is the tautness of the strings of the violin so that they play in harmony.

The Discipline of Goal Fitness

A flickering lamp is unbearable for prolonged work. The same laws apply in everything, and according to the law of justice a flickering lamp injures itself. I counsel My lamps not to blink. The dynamo is not damaged because of the quality of the lamps, but uncoordinated voltage often results in a grievous—zing! And the basic metal must be provided anew. The laws are identical in everything.

23. There is no soulless justice, but only shining goal-fitness. Indeed, the glorious goalfitness cannot tyrannize, but reveals the gates of beauty.

Goalfitness is the greatest discipline of which we are capable. It is never the imposition of tyranny, because our free will is involved, freely giving of more and more energy as our daily giving increases our capacity to receive. Goalfitness cannot tyrannize.

And the call of goalfitness fills the space with the rapture of victory. Events and creations constituting goalfitness are not small outworn fragments but are the precious parts of the Cosmos.

Only a realization of cosmic individuality can illumine the steps of evolution.

Do you know yourself as a cosmic individual? You should. You should visualize yourself as the sun in the center of a cosmos. You should visualize yourself as though you were Helios and Vesta,[15] with worlds and suns and millions and billions of life-waves depending upon your light. If you do not have the sense of cosmic individuality, you will not act accordingly. You will not act with responsibility.

Why be responsible if you are an ant in an anthill? Yet even an ant in an anthill has a sense of cosmic individuality, and he never lets down his responsibility. In order to have our soul evolution illumined to see light on the Path, we have to have the sense of cosmic individuality. We can impart that sense as an electric spark to every man, woman and child in this nation in our lifetime.

Otherwise, in the earthly understanding evolution will remain only profitable investment of capital. You already know that capital deprived of goalfitness is only a millstone about the neck. And, as a manifestation of infection forms spiritual and bodily ulcers, likewise does a manifestation of the lunacy of covetousness bring harm to the spirit and the body.

On the Earth we are much concerned about the body; therefore it is necessary to penetrate into the origins of illness. A physician could say to the patient: "You have an attack of cupidity," or "the anemia of self-conceit," or "stones of treachery," or "a rash of gossip," or "a stroke of hatred."

At cemeteries we so love to recall the merits of the departed one; it would not be amiss to set forth the true causes of the diseases—the spectacle would be instructive.

Friends, I repeat—hold your thoughts pure, this is the best disinfectant and the foremost tonic expedient.

A Definition of Prophecy

24. What is prophecy? It is foretelling the destiny of a definite combination of particles of matter.

I hope you will memorize this definition of prophecy—"foretelling the destiny of a definite combination of particles of matter." This definition makes the scientist into a prophet because the scientist foretells what will happen when he combines certain elements. It makes the ascended masters both scientists and prophets because they bring us together, and we are the particles of Matter—we are particles of Mother—and the ascended masters know precisely the alchemy that results from this combination of ourselves.

When you have one particle that is disruptive to the harmonious flow of the atoms and molecules, the ascended masters will remove that particle. Often the reasons for the removal of a particle are not obvious to us because we do not see the disturbing elements on the surface.

Therefore, prophecies can be fulfilled but also may be spoiled by an unfitting attitude, exactly as may be spoiled a chemical reaction. This indeed cannot be understood by people, though they can apprehend the meaning of a barometer.

Countless prophecies remain unfulfilled because of unfitting attitudes of people. It is like taking sand and sprinkling it over a delicate formula. It just wipes it out, wipes it off the screen of consciousness. That's the effect of a bad attitude.

Observe the Dates

Prophecies can be divided into the dated and undated. When we have to do with a dated prophecy it means we must understand all the intermediate conditions. A great date consists of lesser dates; therefore it is right to observe the small date.

This is a ten-year-plan consciousness. Morya has always been one for establishing dates and then working toward those dates as our goals for whatever we're doing. We can write our goals down, and to do this I like to take four-by-six cards. On those cards, you write your requests to the Brotherhood for things you want to accomplish, one subject to a card. Then you put them in one of the master's books or your Bible.

You really need a copy of *Climb the Highest Mountain* for your altar. It is not something you read. It's a forcefield on your personal altar. In fact, you can place your chalice upon it, your crystal chalice for precipitation. You can even put the green cloth over the book so that it just looks like an elevation. And, in your own handwriting, you place on these four-by-six cards your goal—what you want to accomplish and the dates.

Set dates for the resolution of problems in your life, and

you'll be amazed. Years later, on opening the book and reading these cards, you will see that everything on them has come true. And you hadn't even noticed what great miracles were wrought in your midst!

This is an astonishing experience. I went back to my book and read what I wrote four years ago on Mark's ascension, and every single thing I asked for has happened. Once they have taken place I am no longer aware of my former need, for it has crystallized and has become atomic particles. In this way, you become both prophet and scientist.

So, what is a prophet? Someone "foretelling the destiny of a definite combination of particles of matter." Therefore, we take the particles of matter, which are all of our lives, and then write down what we desire to accomplish. We say our prayers and commit it all to God. Of course, we always address this card to our I AM Presence and members of hierarchy.

You are writing to hierarchy and asking for a certain action to happen, and the closer we are in tune with the will of God, the better will be our alchemy. But it is very important that we ask for the will of God and not just pipe dreams. There's a big difference between pipe dreams and realistic planning—being one step ahead of what is the practical precipitation of *now,* realizing what is needed now and multiplying that need into the future, and saying, "Well, if we need this today, we're going to need this in the future, so this is what I write on my alchemy—the fulfillment of the present need plus the future need." Then, when we get to the future, the need will have been met and we'll be ready to act in the future as the new *now.*

Again, don't indulge in pipe dreams, and don't ask for the sun, the moon and the stars. Look at the next logical step for the organization and your life within it, and then write it down. In a matter of weeks, months or half a year, it will come to pass. If you really become attuned to the will of God and are a devoted chela of El Morya, you will find yourself very much in tune with what is the next cycle. If you are way off the beam and into your fantastic projects and schemes, you will find your requests will simply not be in the mainstream of the ascended master consciousness. A successful alchemist is a practical alchemist.

It must be remembered that the dark ones are working upon small dates, trying to complicate the big one.

I have observed this because I have certain things I have to do every day and every week, and if I miss my cues and don't get them done, the big date at the end of the week can't be fulfilled. Our conferences are the big dates, along with everything that goes into making that conference a success. And if you omit any of the components, your alchemy is not successful.

25. Can prophecies remain unfulfilled? Indeed they can. We have a whole storehouse of such lost prophecies. A true prophecy foresees the best combination of possibilities, but it is possible to allow them to escape.

The subject of fulfillment of prophecies is very profound; in it are combined cooperation and higher knowledge of the spirit. The unwise say: "What a kitchen!" But a kitchen is easily transformed into a laboratory.

Since time immemorial prophecies have been issued from Our Community as benevolent signs for humanity. The paths of prophecies are diverse: either they are suggested to particular people, or they may be inscriptions left by some unknown hand. Prophecies best of all inform mankind. Indeed, the symbols are often obscured, but the inner meaning creates a vibration. Certainly a prophecy requires alertness and aspiration.

"Caught Vibrations of Light"

26. If matter is everywhere then even light leaves behind its protoplasm. All manifestations of light cannot be regarded as accidental. Certain eyes are able to catch the network of light. Because of the loftiness of the energy of light, all these formations are very beautiful. Dissonance of

sound is far more frequent. The protoplasm of light is not
something abstract, its sediments adorn the vegetable kingdom. The rhythm of waves and sands and the crust of the
planet are notably stabilized by the nodes of light. Learn to
love the formations of light. It is not so much the images
impressed upon canvas as the caught vibrations of light that
have significance.

Notice how absent are these "caught vibrations of light" in
modern art. One of our students recently attended the graduation
of his daughter from a San Francisco art college. He said both the
students and professors of this college were on drugs and marijuana and did their work by the drug experience. The daughter
was one of the few in the entire school who was not actually pro-
ducing art by using drugs. Evidently the form of astral art that we
see all over the country is produced that way.

You can see that we need devotees of Paul the Venetian.[16] It
is the caught vibrations of light that have significance, and for this
you need form, symmetry, the right color combinations and a
high attunement with the Christ consciousness.

The quality of the glance is completely unappreciated. It
is like a ray for the photographic film. It must be kept in
mind that through the spiritual gaze we establish the image
of the elemental spirits. Similarly does the physical glance
arrest in space the network of light.

Look at the faces of the masters. Look at the pictures we
have. Their physical glance in space arrests a network of light.
There is a network of light upon these images, and the glance of
the master is what has arrested it. And so it becomes a forcefield
for our meditation.

The significance of this cooperation should be known. Each
movement of man is bound with the essential nature of the
elements.

I point out also the significance of the music of the
Pythagoreans at sunrise. Light is the best purifying filter for

sound. Only the savagery of humanity could lock up sound in the dust of darkness.

This gives us a glimpse of the Pythagorean community: sunrise and the playing of music. Sunrise is a very important moment.

27. Pure thought saturated with beauty points out the path to truth. The interdictions and the prescripts of renunciation in the Teachings were given in condescension toward a limited consciousness. But a broadened consciousness frees man from many fetters and affirms progress. Adorned lives allow departing freely and generously in order to return as victors. He who proceeds with a consciousness of beauty cannot be confused. Only confusion can bar the way.

You see, the do's and don'ts of orthodox religion are for the limited consciousness that has not the capacity to govern itself in freedom. The broadened consciousness frees man from fetters and affirms progress. The going out and coming in of the soul—the soul whose life is an adornment—can be accomplished by the law of freedom without all of those do's and don'ts.

Confusion, of course, is opposition to the Mother. Confusion is opposition to beauty. Mother and beauty are one. Confusion is a deadly energy.

It is not quite correct to say that beauty will save the world. It is more accurate to say that the realization of beauty will save the world.

One can walk through obstacles of ugliness toward a beacon of beauty, scattering seeds without number. When one can create a garden of beauty there is nothing to fear. There is no weariness when the garden of the spirit admits the newcomers.

The same is true if you are trying to hold your balance standing on one foot or doing various exercises or postures. If you keep your eye on a dot, you can hold your balance like a tight-rope walker. You have to fix your eye on a point, even if it's a point in space, and if you stop looking at the point, you lose your balance. Similarly, if you stop looking at beauty, you can't get through the scattered emanations of ugliness.

However, you can walk through the astral plane as emissaries of the Mother. You can cut free her children from the astral plane if you have your eye on a goal. The goal is the salvation of souls. The goal is community. The goal is the Church.

The Shield of Community

28. The manifestation of petrification of the Earth has reached the utmost limits. We consider that extreme measures are needed in order that the spirit be re-awakened. The Teaching is not attained through smiles alone. The appearance of deserts has denoted long ago the beginning of savagery. Signs were given long ago and time for reflection thus granted. Indications have been made manifest, but no one harkened.

29. The teaching of the New World will solve all discomforts. Verily, only the shield of the Community can give meaning to the sojourn on Earth.

"Only the shield of the Community can give meaning to the sojourn on earth." Once you have the consciousness of community, all else is chaos, confusion, old night.

How indescribably beautiful it is to think about cooperation with the far-off worlds. This cooperation, begun consciously, will draw into the orbit of communication new worlds. And this heavenly cooperative will broaden its possibilities infinitely.

If all possibilities are stipulated by a community, then their manifestation will take place through the channel of the spirit. It has been said that sound will be the first to reach through. Let these fragments be rudimentary, like the

first jagged edges of an eolith. Let whole years pass before
the understanding of a complexity of meaning be achieved.
Yet it is unquestionable that this conquest will begin not in
the observatories and not in the optician's shop. Harkening
of the spirit will bring the first tidings; not for master
degrees, but for life which forges evolution. The Teaching
can point out to the sensitive ones—on awakening, remember the far-off worlds; on going to sleep, remember the far-
off worlds.

Attune yourself in that moment when you slip into sleep.
Remembering the far-off worlds will take you there instantly, to
the retreats of the Brotherhood, to higher planes.

Hearing any fragments of sound, do not reject them,
for each fragment may increase the possibilities of humanity. Gradually unknown words may come through; one
should not be surprised at this, remembering that when
dates approached in times past the consciousness likewise
became expanded.

You understand that Earth cannot live without community. You understand that without the broadening of
the heavenly ways the existence becomes nil. The New
World is in need of new boundaries. The seekers must have
a path. Is it narrow throughout the entire horizon? It is fortunate that the seekers do not have to bend the ear down to
earth but may turn their gaze upward into spiritual heights.
It is easier for the ray to seek out uplifted heads. And every
movement of the world is conditioned by the community.

30. Broadening of consciousness is occasion for con-
gratulation. No laboratory can give this perception of continuity of endless possibilities. Only personally, consciously
and freely is it possible to adapt out of space uninterrupted
steps. The Teaching may open the door, but one can enter
only by oneself. Not reward, nor justice, but the incontestable
law carries the incarnate spirit upward, in an ascending spiral, provided that it has realized the necessity of motion.

Realize the necessity of motion. Whatever you do, keep in motion. Be in motion for God. Keep moving, and your alchemy will come through.

The Teacher can in no wise advance this consciousness, for any suggestion would violate the personal attainment.

It is one thing to discuss abstractly distant worlds; it is another to realize oneself a participant there. Only he who has not closed for himself the path to beauty may understand how near to him is the manifestation of the far-off worlds.

The ear can catch fragments of the Great Breath, but the knowledge of the spirit gives man a place in Infinity.

It is useful to look back upon remote epochs, when this consciousness was awakened. We see that not in a day of flowering of science but during the proclamation of religion was the cosmic consciousness awakened; for not hypotheses but only knowledge of the spirit leads to the starry paths. I regret that no astronomical calculations could advance the moment of communication, for the same reason that the ant does not shoot with a gigantic cannon. It is indeed essential that such achievement be manifested by means of the spirit. Here we are speaking materially, as it were, but without the spirit it is impossible to apply this energy. Indeed the spirit gives a certain quality to matter. The condition of the Earth requires an extraordinary physician. The planet is sick, and if efforts to push it forward do not succeed, then it may be better to remove it temporarily from the chain—it may become as the moon. Hotbeds of the lower strata of the Subtle World have become dangerously intolerable. Also it is impossible to forget how humanity has fallen under the influence of the lower levels of the Subtle World.

The community will help all, but broadening of consciousness will help the community.

31. The Teacher values the desire to wash the dust from the great Images. The Teacher values the desire to

affirm the simple expression of great words. The Teacher values the desire to eliminate verbosity. In order to isolate the essence, it is necessary to approach from the fundamental.

One should know that not a single monument has been handed down to us without mutilation. It is possible to mold as from clay the imprints of a community of rational cooperation and striving beyond the limits of the visible. The Teaching may be expressed under the slogan: "Let him who differs prove the opposite." It is better to measure backwards than to be covered with indelible dust. Indeed, knowledge of the guiding principle illumines the mutilated symbols.

You know how people speak about you during your lifetime. What then will it be centuries hence? Yet the principle inevitably grows, and the impulses of its growth shake the earthly firmament.

Departed nations have left a patina on the freedom of the spirit. You may ask: "Where then are the persecuted?" Proceed according to these signs. You will perceive as persecuted the first Christians and the Buddhists, but when the temples turned away from Christ and Buddha, then persecutions ceased.

I direct you to keep the Teaching simple; not necessary are complicated expressions, for life is beautiful in simplicity. Often one is obliged to dig around a plant, therefore repetitions are unavoidable.

32. The evolution is important not of earthly humanity but of humanity of the Universe. If this simple formula could be adopted by human hearts, the whole starry vault would become tangible. Verily, it would be easier for the beings of other worlds to pierce through the stifling atmosphere of Earth if toward them were coming appeals from earthly incarnates.

Where then are the nearest worlds, whither we could direct our consciousness? Jupiter and Venus.

Ponder deeply upon the word "tchelovek" (man)—it
denotes the thinker existing through ages. All changes of
incarnations, the whole value of consciousness, is expressed
in one word. Can you name another language in which the
incarnate dweller is named so spiritually? Other languages
poorly express the idea of action. The Teacher can name a
hundred words for "man" but they will be either pre-
sumptuous or inexpressive.

33. Of what use are miracles, which are contrary to
nature? Here is a miracle—when thou canst bestride thy
steed and with the manifested sword defend the Community of the World. As simply will the New World begin. Like
ripened fruit will facts be collected. The Teaching of magnets is indeed not of miracles, but of a manifestation of the
law of gravity. Conceal not the revelation of the spirit, and
the sword will be of service to the ascent of evolution.

I can give joy only to him who has adopted the community not in conjurations, not with incense burning, but
in daily life. The Teacher can send a helping ray, but He will
not engage in combat if the given sword be turned against
the friends of the community. The sword will then turn into
a lightning scourge.

34. How is it possible to move hearts? By not losing
simplicity. Success will come not with magic but with the
word of life. We can carry out our lesson by knowing how
to approach the very simplest. I am thinking how to give to
the toilers the radiance of the far-off worlds. When the most
humiliated one will look up into the heavens, then is it possible to expect the rainbow ribbon from the far-off worlds.

35. Paracelsus used to say, "per aspera, ad astra."*
Later, this remarkable maxim became a device upon shields
and coats of arms, losing all meaning. True, understanding
its meaning it is difficult to attach oneself to Earth alone. As
a smoke escaping through a chimney, the attained spirit

---

* "Through adversity to the stars."

rushes into manifested space. What kind of dimensions for it can earthly garments offer? What kind of mobility can the spirit manifest on the surface of the Earth? What thoughts can it share with and upon the earthly sphere?

It is asked why We waste so much energy over the Earth. Not for the sake of Earth, but for rectifying the path. When a criminal rips up the rails, often the engineer takes much time to repair them. If We could immediately transfer from the Earth those who have consciousness of the Cosmos, could there possibly be any restraining Our wish to do so? Our striving is to hasten this process. I feel that perhaps soon cosmic conditions will permit the beginning of these labors for communication with the far-off worlds. In this, all considerations of beauty, and of impetuousness in personal sending, are needed. It is true, above so-called beauty there is the all-embracing concept of the betterment of the Cosmos. The rainbow ray can exceed the imagination. A silvery light marks the beginning of the rainbow. The rainbow viewed under earthly conditions resembles make-up at close range. Few can have a prescience of the supermundane rainbow.

36. I feel how the stratification of events is bringing waves of acceleration. These waves are of service in the cosmic structure.

I write down My notes of possibilities and come to the conclusion that all is possible just now. It is a rare thing when higher faith travels along the path with higher unbelief; when blasphemy and glorification can be in the same chorus; when fury and tranquillity give birth to joy. When misfortune is manifested as a sign of success and when withdrawal serves as a sign of nearness, then the currents of emanations of the luminaries are blended with the inner fires. Such a time denotes a new cycle, and the Community itself, not even yet adopted, serves as a bridge.

Let us end on a lighter note. Is it possible to speak about stock exchange speculations on Jupiter, or about brothels on Venus? The concept is simply unthinkable. Even a chimney sweep going to visit washes his face. Could people possibly be worse? The time has come to set the Earth on a new path.

What Morya puts before us is Yes! The time has come to set the earth on a new path, but who will set it on that path? The embodied chelas of the ascended masters are the only ones who will do so. There is a storehouse of unfulfilled prophecies. We have to go to that storehouse and take out the prophecy and determine that in our life it will be fulfilled. Yes, the time has come, and we are the ones whom God has uplifted to set the earth on a new path.

The Alchemy of the Sending

37. Abilities for a distant sending are extremely rare. As always it is necessary to distinguish the quality of the result. The sendings may be restless, and like flies be brushed away; they may be oppressive, like a coffin lid, and inspire terror; they may be as the whizzing of arrows, and these bring agitation without any understanding. It is rare when sendings are clear; it is rare when they call up cooperation of the corresponding centers. This may depend partially on the auras, but the principal factor is the quality of the sending. This quality is called utility of the will, which means understanding of the voltage of tension of the correspondent. In order for an electric lamp to light up, a certain voltage is necessary. Not only the contents of the sending but also the quality is important. The knowledge of the spirit gives the sending usefulness. An effect of the usefulness of the sending will be joy of reception, for everything properly proportioned will be a joy.

Morya is saying that if you have to accomplish a certain goal, that goal may be the focalization of a picture that is on the screen on that wall right over there. If we want a crystal-clear image of a slide or of our own consciousness, we have to know how much energy we must release from the heart chakra, the throat, the third eye, the crown—all of our chakras.

We need to know how much light is necessary, how much intensity, how we focus that light to cause it to register on the screen as a certain distance away from us—the focalization of the image.

When you take a picture with a camera, you have to adjust the setting of the lens so that your subject is in focus. The subject can move a fraction of an inch and be blurred because you did not properly calculate the energy of the sending. You also have to adjust the setting so that your subject is lighted properly. If the subject looks too dark, you did not properly calculate the energy of the sending.

The sending is the amount of energy you have to apply to a given alchemy to bring it into manifestation. How many decrees do we have to give? What do we have to write down? How do we have to order our consciousness so that when we get the film back and it is developed, we have the alchemy we are shooting for. Everything that we do in Matter points to the fact that you don't just shoot energy in all directions, helter-skelter. You focus on a plan. You determine your resources and how much you have to apply to each facet of the plan to bring it into position.

It becomes a question, as we look at the larger organization, of how much money has to be spent for a given project. And because large sums of money have to be spent, we have to be certain that the project we are about is going to bring us the return multiplied tenfold.

However, this is a nebulous science. To make the mark of your advertising, your book publishing, to know what to publish next—the right seed for the right season for the right planting in the right moon with the right sun and the right rain—all of this is to have the best harvest of the Christ consciousness throughout the earth.

We have only this lifetime to set this foundation. And if we make so many wrong calculations and wrong moves, we will be out of energy and out of time and out of space. The torch will be passed to another. So this planning is so important, as well as the knowledge of the dates. First Morya talked about dates, now he talks about the sending.

How much energy are we directing with this arrow to make that mark? If I want to hit Robert over there, I will determine the thrust of my arrow. If I want to hit a mark across the campus and shoot an elephant, I have to have a different kind of weapon, a different kind of energy. These equations are terribly important. And we just can't float around in this nebulous consciousness.

We have to be extremely concrete in our planning. We are revolutionizing a world. We are setting the earth on a new path and our resources of time and space are limited. Graduation day is coming for each one of us, and the date is marked in our book of life. That great date is preceded by all these lesser dates, and if we don't meet the lesser dates, we won't meet the big date. Therefore, we all need to plan according to the divine will.

Do What Is Most Expedient

How do you plan? I want to give you a very important key. You do what is most expedient at the moment and you measure these moments, as you would spheres of light. You put ten or twenty moments together, and you find you must do what is expedient for the minute, and a hundred minutes and a thousand minutes—what is expedient for the hour. But when all is said and done, the sand in the hourglass is falling *now.* And that sand that is falling is going to be lost, never to return. So if you are constantly acting as though you are going to precipitate next year, you are living in the future instead of the now. You are not doing what is the most important for the now.

When I have to plan what tape album to get out, what book to get out, I have to plan in the sense of what is going to reach our target people to draw into the movement in June, in July, in August. And those are the most important people that I can get in for what is going to happen in September, October and November. And the things that I want to have in September, October and November are great keys to what I want to have happen in the first six months of '78 and the second six months of '78.

I could sit here and have the *Climb the Highest Mountain* series translated into Chinese, a very worthy project, but not the expediency of the hour. When you are trying to decide what to do with your time and your space, do what is going to strike a blow for the Lord now, in conjunction with what are your goals for the future. And make the telling blow of the moment be the most important blow, the thing that's going to open the most doors for the most energies, for the most flow, for the most salvation of souls now in planning for future events and the big dates.

We can get caught up in all kinds of projects and planning and lesser goals. It is like taking the dead-end streets and taking the long way around to get somewhere. So the more you have to count down to some immediate goal that you have to meet, the more you will find the Holy Spirit in you, and all of your forces and all of your energies will be summoned to attain that goal. Whatever is the priority, do it now, not tomorrow. Do it right now. Get it done. And this is that flame of action.

The force will trick you into planning and planning and planning—constantly getting ready to do something. All of these little projects are supposed to lead you to the ultimate goal, but the ultimate goal keeps receding. And you never quite get to the goal because you are always involved in some little interim project that's not getting you there. This is an amazing phenomenon, but I have watched it happen. I've watched myself slip into this, where I'll get involved in publishing something or working on something that's not going to get out within the next month or the next year. Then Mark would come along and say, "This has to be done *now* and this is the deadline and this is when I want it."

He would put everybody in motion, and I couldn't spread out my space. I had to conserve my space and my time. The job had to be done now. I work well under that kind of tension and pressure—and I use both words positively. To me, tension and pressure are constructive ingredients in the creative process. Without a set date, you will not demand the maximum energies from God, and therefore, your work will not have the full summoning of forces to spark your creativity.

Therefore, you need to operate under tension and pressure. It makes you summon resources. It makes you develop your mind. It makes you develop your energy, and it keeps you completely involved in the creative process. If you have an eternity to do something, you will never do it. If you think a project can wait five years, the five years will constantly be pushed back.

Please remember this. Wherever you go, postponement is a great temptation, even if it's postponement in the name of service.

"My Ray Knows Where Evil Is"

The knowledge of the spirit gives the sending usefulness. An effect of the usefulness of the sending will be joy of reception, for everything properly proportioned will be a joy.

38. The manifestation of the pure Teaching must be linked with trust. Afterwards it will be necessary to develop such trust that the most apparent evidence cannot shake it. My Ray knows where evil is.

This is a very important statement. I got up this morning feeling good, but I felt a certain dark cloud, like a little pocket of damp grayness, lingering in the corner of my consciousness. I pinpointed it. I marked it with my finger, and I said, "Aha, this is symptomatic." And what did I see? I saw this great smokescreen where the energies of opposition to my life, to the Mother and to our headquarters were being held in the background and in abeyance, to create in maya the illusion of a beautiful day, a sunny day—all is happiness and light, the birds are singing, and so forth. But I felt that forcefield of gray darkness, and I said, "Forces are hiding. They are playing cat and mouse with me, and there is an intense attack upon the community today."

So I brought in some chelas and set them to doing the decree to Cyclopea (see p. 277), exposures, reverse the tides, the demanding of the breaking of this smokescreen. All of a sudden, it broke, and it was like uncovering a whole pit of vipers and discarnates and demons. Back, back, back behind the veils of maya, behind the veils of the psychic and the astral plane, these forces hide the moment you come to give your calls and the moment you are alerting yourself to the energies of the day.

They don't want you to see them during your decree session, so you don't tune into the calls you need to make. As soon as your decree session is over and you start to work, in comes the force and in come all these demons hopping up and down, causing problems. But Morya says in the midst of all this, "My Ray knows where evil is."

Why did he have to say that in this book? He had to say it because evil hides itself. It's a snake under the rock, under the bushes. It's always hiding. Therefore, he is saying that for the benefit of the chela who doesn't know where evil is and who ought to know. And to determine where it is, the chela will put himself in attunement with the master.

We have had students who left the teachings because they said we concentrated too much on evil. But now you see that the awareness of God demands that we be aware of evil to defend God. The highest good has its counterpart in the greatest depths of darkness. So, while the little innocent children, the childlike ones on the path of religion, skip merrily down the path and are carefree in their enjoyment of the sunshine and the flowers, the sons and daughters of God have to say with Morya, "My Ray knows where evil is." And we have to anticipate it for the little children and demand its binding and its removal.

The Battle to Retain Identity

39. Create an atmosphere of readiness for action. When a blow is struck many old obstructions fall unexpectedly. Many battles are past, still more are ahead. Every atom of the Cosmos is battling.

Can you imagine such a statement? The battle is for the retaining of identity. That is how you can understand the battle of an electron or an atom. It takes the force of a cosmos to sustain self-awareness, to sustain existence, to sustain the I AM THAT I AM. If you relent and let down your resistance, you lose your identity.

As soon as you get slothful or enter into a state of boredom or let your energy drop, what have you lost? You have lost self-awareness. So the battle we are waging is the battle to preserve our identity and the identity of every living soul on earth.

The quiet of death is not known to Us.

40. The New Teaching respects the Bearers of the earlier Covenants, but it proceeds without the baggage of times which have been ended. Otherwise the load of text-books would take on unwieldy dimensions. The most practical thing would be to destroy all commentaries made after three centuries after the departure of a Teacher. At some time or other it is necessary to clean up the book-shelves. From this cleaning the Images of the Teachers of Light will gain in greatness.

41. We drive out all fear. We throw to the wind all the many-colored feathers of fear: blue feathers of frozen terror, green feathers of trembling betrayal, yellow feathers of secret crawling away, red feathers of frenzied heart-beat, white feathers of reticence, black feathers of fall into the abyss. It is needful to repeat about the multiformity of fear, otherwise there remains somewhere a small gray feather of complaisant mumbling or even some fluff of hurried bustle, but behind these will be the same idol of fear. Each wing of fear bears one downwards.

The colors she is referring to are the perversions of the true colors of the rays.

The Blessed "Lion," garbed in fearlessness, ordained to teach the manifestation of courage.

> Swimmers, if you do everything possible within your
> strength, whither can the most destructive wave carry you?
> It can only bear you upwards. And thou, sower, when thou
> wilt distribute the seeds, thou mayst expect a harvest.

You may expect a harvest only when you sow seeds. Remember this. When Jesus told me about his alchemy, he said, "If you want me to multiply the loaves and fishes, give me something to multiply. Give me the forcefield of your mind. Give me a focus. Give me seed money. Put something in the coffers of the church, and then I can come and multiply it."

Jesus was the great master of precipitation. He could have taken his hands, and like the great magicians who imitated Moses and Aaron, done some fancy handwork. Then, all of a sudden, out of one hand could come the two fishes and out of the other, the five loaves. And he could have done it again and multiplied them to feed the five thousand.

However, that would not have proved what he was trying to prove. It was necessary that mankind give the master a token. They had to have some preparation for the alchemy. All God really wants from us is a token, and if we give a token balance of energy, he exonerates us from the full requirement of the Law. In other words, he allows us to balance our karma when we are on the Path by using the violet flame. And thus, we often need to submit to far less agony.

For example, if we were due to have a malignant cancer, he might reduce it to a tiny nonmalignant lump that was easily removed because we had given him a token. We had shown in our lives or in our actions that we were the willing, fulfilling energy of love. If we determine to be that love, he accepts the token, and he multiplies it and lets it be the leaven for the whole lump of consciousness.

The Shepherd and His Sheep

And thou, shepherd, when thou dost recount thy sheep,
thou wilt kindle a manifest light.

A very mystical statement, "And thou, shepherd, when thou dost recount thy sheep, thou wilt kindle a manifest light." It's truly the sense of the shepherd as the teacher. Counting the sheep, numbering the chelas, we kindle a manifest light. When our eye and our concern is the counting of the sheep, the caring for the sheep, the protecting of the sheep, this is our harvest. It is the greatest harvest of all, the harvest of souls. We don't have to raise money, we have to raise souls.

42. The Cosmos is in process of creation through pulsation, that is, by explosions. The rhythm of the explosions gives harmony to the creation. Indeed, knowledge of the spirit carries the thread of the Cosmos into manifested life. With a shining sword the new step should be cut free. It is necessary to recognize when to hold back the flowers of light lest they again be dissolved in the mist of the elements.

The gardener knows when it is time to gather the flowers, for he planted the seeds now hidden. Not he who purchased the seeds in the bazaar; not he who in idleness ordered the seeds to be sown, but the gardener of spirit who at the start of bad weather buried the seeds in the spring-time earth.

Yes, yes, he, the gardener of the spirit, will know the time of sprouting; he will distinguish the young stalks from the weeds, for he has performed the most hidden labor and to him belongs the best blossom.

The seed is the soul, which the master plants in the fallow ground of consciousness. And the master knows when that soul is ready to come forth, when it is ready to be picked for action and for the fulfillment of the goal.

Verily, it is a great thing to flash the sword at the right moment, and at the time of explosion to raise the arm.

Verily, here again currents of the Cosmos are descending upon the ready Earth; this is why the knowledge of the spirit is precious.

This heavenly rainbow is reflected in the drops of

earthly dew. Does not knowledge of the spirit discern the light? "Materia Lucida" to the wild spirit is a curling chaos, but for the knowing spirit it is the harp of light. Like chased harp strings rush the waves of luminous matter, and on them the spirit creates mysterious-sounding symphonies. Between the worlds, thread-like, stretches "Materia Lucida." Only enormous distance blends together the waves of threads into the vibration of the heavenly rainbow.

One can begin to strive toward the far-off worlds by following a thread of Light realized by the spirit—this is a very scientific experiment. As has been said, small actions require assistance and apparatuses, but nothing external is needed for a great action.

In the name of the Christ, in the name of the Holy Spirit, I call for action now from the Great Central Sun for the sealing of the energy and the day. I call for the blue ray from the heart of El Morya upon these souls and all souls of light throughout the earth.

Beloved El Morya, we call for the precipitation of the Community of the Holy Spirit. We call for the instantaneous precipitation of our international headquarters and the City Foursquare. We call for the instantaneous precipitation into our hands and use this day of all that is necessary for the establishment of this community.

In the name of the Father, the Son, the Holy Spirit and the Divine Mother, Amen.

Pasadena, Calif.
May 27, 1977

CHAPTER 2

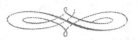

Striving to the Far-off Worlds

*I*n the name of the I AM
*THAT I AM, I call to beloved El Morya, beloved Kuthumi
and beloved Djwal Kul. I call for the full power of the
Lord Jesus Christ. I call for the ring-pass-not.*

*Beloved El Morya, anchor within us thy will. I call for
the will of God. I call for the will of the guru-chela relationship. I call to this will whose fire is love, whose fuel is wisdom. I call for the intensity of thy life within our midst.*

*O beloved El Morya, place now your mighty Electronic
Presence over each one. Let your heart burn within our
hearts. Let your mind now become congruent with our mind.
Cleanse and purify, O mighty I AM Presence. Let God's
will descend. Beloved El Morya, come into that very personal presence with these hearts of devotees. I call forth thy
blessed flame. I call for the circle of the one.*

*Beloved Lanello, be with us. Lady Kristine, K-17, Djwal
Kul and Kuthumi, seal now these hearts for the victory.*

*In the name of the Father, the Mother, the Son and the
Holy Spirit, Amen.*

I am sure you realize that these lectures that I am delivering
are dictations from beloved El Morya. I think it is a wonderful
experience to receive them as light and in a high state of attunement and then go back and take notes on them.

When your mental body is active, it lowers your vibration.
Sometimes it is painful for me to grapple with problems at the

mental level, in the sense of figuring out what should be done and how it should be done. These problems cause me to put myself at the mental plane, whereas the natural habitat of the guru is the etheric plane and the ascended master octaves.

The interchange with God always takes place in the ascended master octaves, and that is where the lectures come from. One has to go down the mountain a little to take dominion over the earth and to study.

I have always been grateful for the fact that I finished college before I became a messenger. Although I have an eagerness to study, it seems that God only allows my mind to lower its frequency, or the soul to lower its frequency, within me for a certain period of time. Then, in order to hold the balance, I must go up.

Community Is Needed Right Now

As I listen to our students describe how they found us, it's a little bit different than it was four or five years ago. Now they find us through books and local centers. Four or five years ago it was through a friend or by a poster, because we did not have as many books in the bookstores. That brings to mind the fact that what each one of us does as an individual makes a big difference. The ingenuity we draw forth from our flame to get the message across in a practical way makes the difference as to whether the message will be taken up now or a century from now.

Some people have no consciousness of time. They act as though it doesn't matter whether a chela rises up today or two centuries from now. It is as though the books had been put in mausoleums for the day when the dead would awaken from their sleep and want to read them. It's almost like placing everything mummies might need in the future near them in their tombs. People stockpile the teachings, and they forget that the teaching is for right now, for the great crisis we are facing.

There's little point in just taking things easy and saying, "Well, we're building the teachings. A hundred years from now people will recognize what we've done and give us credit. Then they will read these books and will know that they are true."

We have no guarantee of that at all. If we lose our system of education, if people lose contact with their heart, they will have less capacity in a hundred years to appreciate what we're doing— not more. If people are not decreeing and sending forth the violet flame, it will not clear them of the weight of the increasing dark cycle.

On the contrary, a hundred years from now, people could be more and more into primitivism, more and more into superstition and the cults of Satan. All is in the crucible of the now. Community is needed right now.

People come because of community. They come because it is the flame of home, because it is the only place on earth where the flame of the God Star, Sirius, can be duplicated. Sirius is our native home in this galaxy. It is a tremendous place, a very real place, a place of which you are aware. In fact, each day I am aware of returning as a pilgrim to earth from my home star.

What makes this earth comfortable, exciting and joyous is the fact that we have succeeded in transferring here a flame of our God Star. Whether you are a Venusian or a Mercurian or from somewhere else, you were originally from Sirius. The lifewave went forth from there and it will return there.

Therefore, we have something very precious in this circle of our togetherness. We have to know that it is an intangible flame. It only becomes tangible through a living instrument, through a living heartbeat. Otherwise, it is like a vapor. It goes up. If all the ascended ones go, then there will be no physical anchor on earth. You will not be on the physical plane.

The community provides the opportunity for the continuity of life. It reinforces the sacredness of the family and draws a circle around it. It gives protection for the avatars. El Morya dictated this little book to his beloved chela for us, knowing that we would come and we would be the ones who would perceive the message. I have been longing to return to this, and I decided today that I would teach you what was nearest to my heart.

Let us pick up where we were, on number 43.

A Love of Miracles

43. I sense that the Teaching may become a heavy hammer for timid ones. Even recently terror would have pierced the heart at the very mention of community, but already now several obstacles have been overcome. Yet one more difficult trial for humanity follows the discarding of the worn-out concept of property. Assimilating the significance of the spirit, it is especially difficult to refrain from miracles. Even the Arhats chosen by Buddha put aside this possibility only with difficulty.

Three Arhats importunately besought Buddha to permit them to try a miracle. Buddha placed each one in a dark room, and locked them in. After a long time the Blessed One called to them and asked what they had seen. Each one told about different visions. But Buddha said: "Now you must agree that miracles are not useful, because you did not perceive the main miracle. For, you could have sensed an existence beyond the visible, and this sensation could have directed you beyond the limits of Earth. But you continued to be conscious of yourselves as seated on the Earth and your thoughts attracted to the Earth waves of the elements. The swelling of the Elements evoked agitations in various countries. You caused rocks to fall and destroyed ships with a hurricane. You saw a red beast with a flaming crown, but the fire attracted by you from out the abyss burned the houses of defenseless ones—go and bring help! You saw a dragon with the face of a maiden, simultaneously causing waves to wash away fishing boats—hasten with assistance! You saw an eagle flying, and a hurricane destroyed the harvest of toilers—go and bring amends! Where then is your usefulness, O Arhats? An owl in the hollow of a tree has passed the time more usefully. Either toil on the Earth in the sweat of your brow, or in a moment of solitude lift yourselves above the Earth. But let not the useless commotion of the elements be the occupation of the wise."

Verily, a feather falling from the wing of a small bird produces a thunderclap in the far-off worlds.

Inhaling air, we are attuned to all worlds. The wise one proceeds from the Earth upwards, for the worlds will reveal to each other their wisdom. Repeat this parable to those who demand miracles.

Let us consider why the arhats' attempt to create miracles caused them instead to create discord, to be the open door for discord. It was because, as we learn of this alchemy in this section 43, they did not have pure desire.

It is very difficult to have pure desire when one desires miracles. Immediately, by the very nature of one's untransmuted self, one considers how noble one will appear to the rest of the world, how one will be admired, how people will be dependent upon one for miracles and healings, how they will come flocking and how the activity will expand.

Therefore, with impure desire and with a lack of adeptship in dealing with the elements, they became an open door to discord. What they wanted to see became a matrix in their third eye. Their vision, combined with their impure desire from the solar plexus, enabled discord to manifest in the world.

Whether or not they had caused these calamities by seeking miracles, yet the Buddha revealed to them that the path of the bodhisattva is to go and bring help, go and make amends. The concept of service is the way of the Brotherhood. And when you are devoted to service, miracles are a part of your day-to-day life. You live with angels; they serve you, and the miracles that come through them become a natural part of a blissful life, where, although we are physical, we are actually etheric. We actually live on the etheric plane, but we are anchored in the physical plane through our three lower bodies.

But a chela is not on the etheric plane in an impractical sense. The etheric plane is a very concrete place. It is the real side of the unreal physical universe, the mayic side. We have the illusion that the physical earth is real, but the real earth is the etheric earth. When you have the wavelength, or vibration, of the etheric plane, you become effective in the three lower octaves.

Chelaship doesn't really begin until you have a portion of your being in the etheric plane. Therefore, living in the etheric plane and moving in the world, you have the grace of the guru. And the grace of the guru is that quality of life that no longer entertains struggle.

When you need something and you have ultimate faith in the guru, it is done. There is not the strain or tension of this world but only the creative tension of the Spirit. Sometimes we create the struggle by not feeling the sense of freedom we have and our oneness with the guru.

At any time that you lose that sense of oneness, you have to go after it and get it back. It is priceless. Life is not worth living unless you are in this very, very direct relationship. If you lose the sense that you are hand-in-glove with El Morya, you need to just withdraw from intense activity or from a rote sense of the teaching and take an hour or even a day to re-commune with the guru.

You can read his teachings, praise his name, give his decrees, sit quietly in front of El Morya's picture and just meditate on the deep inner presence. Then you go back to intense decrees and meditation, pouring out love and gratitude by walking and talking with El Morya. After taking a walk in the sun or on the beach or in the mountains, you just talk with the master for an afternoon. And then you come back with that sense of calm and quiet and confidence that you have given your life to the guru and he has pledged his life to you.

He will not leave you with problems; they will be solved. But you must be ready to face your karma courageously. Some of these books from El Morya speak of the preparation of the chela for the moment when a very dark cycle of karma will come. It must be faced. It must be met. The masters cannot prevent it. They have prepared you for it, and it could be the kind of karma that makes you feel spiritually dry and unenthusiastic.

I love this story about the Buddha, and I am grateful for it because I think we all drift into thinking that when we have that kind of attainment, we will be performing miracles and everyone will recognize us for who we really are—then everyone will accept the ascended masters' teachings. But people really accept the teaching when you live a life of selfless service and that very service produces the miracle of lives transformed. Those are the greatest miracles of all.

The Concept of Property

Before the Buddha story, the teaching opened today with El Morya's comment that until recently, terror would have pierced the heart at the very mention of community. Then he discussed the outworn concept of property.

Property is outworn at a certain level of chelaship. It is not outworn at the level where the individual must master himself within the environment. But at the level of chelaship there are many who have not found it to be the natural order of things that to be a part of the community one must be willing to give everything one has.

People who have nothing find it easy. People who have a great deal may find it hard. And it has always been my observation that the people who have millions are not able to identify with community. People who have nothing are very willing, and they are the ones who say, "If I had a million dollars, I would give it to you." But usually someone with a million dollars doesn't give it to you.

Striving to the Far-off Worlds

44. The essence of striving to the far-off worlds is contained in the assimilation of a consciousness of our life in them. The possibility of life on them becomes for our consciousness, as it were, a channel of approach.

Let us take Sirius as our example of the far-off worlds. When you take the decree to Surya (see p. 276), you must entertain the consciousness of possibility. There is a striving to reach another octave. There is an assimilation of what is there.

You can meditate upon Sirius as a blazing sphere of energy, pulsating, just as you would our sun. Physically it is a binary star, and these two stars are the guru-chela stars—Surya and Cuzco. They move throughout cosmos in their orbit together.

At the physical level, your meditation is on a flaming sun. Then you raise your consciousness to the etheric level, and you see an orb. It is a star, but it is like a planetary body infinitely more vast than the earth. The earth would just be a speck within that sun.

When you think of all the beauty that is on the planet Earth and the lakes and the seas and the mountains and all that we enjoy, and then you think of the God Star, you think of this enormous sphere where there is endless room for evolutions of light to evolve, to have their citadels, their retreats, their force-fields. And it is a vastness and a freedom that is less and less possible to realize on this planet, because when we visualize this planet, we see it so populated and so polluted.

El Morya says that the essence of striving to the far-off worlds is obtained in the assimilation of consciousness of life on Sirius. It is a flaming sun that has a concrete plane that is the etheric plane. In that plane is your native home. And you can meditate on the image you see when you think of your native home. Is it something Grecian with columns? Is it a white place? Is it surrounded with gardens and fountains?

Imagine the place you would have if you had unlimited substance with which to build. Usually what first pops into your mind is probably the home you left aeons ago when you left Sirius. You can't imagine something that you don't have a matrix for in yourself. You can't visualize something you've never seen. At least, you should have components of it to be able to suddenly see it in your mind's eye. Saint Germain says that whatever you can imagine exists somewhere. That's a basic truth in some sense of the word.

What pops into my head is something like the Jefferson Memorial—a rounded dome with columns and water, blue sky and pink blossoms and geometric forms that are glistening white. Washington, D.C., is a city that has a tremendous amount of correspondence to an alabaster city on Sirius.

If you are going to anchor your God consciousness in that point, you have to start thinking about it and start visualizing it. If you sit down and give forty decrees to the God Surya, your mind should not be idle. It should have a sense of intense penetration by a blue-violet or indigo energy—powerful, like the sea in winter, a deep aqua color, a deep energy of intensity.

When you meditate on the God Star, you penetrate it. You realize that vast lifewaves have originated there and are scattered, as we are, throughout the galaxy on their little planetary homes, working out the problem of the science of the Word. They are all destined to return in the cycles of being. And so, we have a home star.

To have a home star gives us a great sense of security. When we are on the road traveling or preaching the Word, it's always nice to think about the place we can go home to. Jesus said he had nowhere to lay his head.[1] He was always traveling and preaching; he was always moving. You have to have considerable mastery to live a life in that way, or else so little mastery that you don't care, for you are a bum. But in between these two extremes, there is always a longing for the Om, for Home.

When you have peace in your heart after meditating on the God Star and giving your calls to Surya, you wake up in the morning and say, "I am a pilgrim. I am on a journey. I know where my home is. I know where I have come from, and I know where I'm going. I'm here to cut free souls of light."

Your mission is crystal clear. You don't become so attached to things on earth, and you are not so inconvenienced by circumstances. You can easily make sacrifices because your castle is waiting for you. However, if you don't have the inner vision of your castle, then you have to make your little nest and your separate castle. We all need to have a sense of a place that's all our own where we can go. Although you may not realize it, this sense of the peace of the visualization of that home affects your whole being—your emotional body, your chakras, your ability to create and to serve. It is such a sense of inner peace.

We live in a time when governments seize properties, when wars and cataclysm come. There's so much uncertainty on this planet that it affects people at subconscious levels. With the ever-present possibility of inflation or depression, it is hard to be sure that we will be able to hang on to the homes we have. Therefore, we are uneasy.

I think few meditative people on the planet have any sense of permanence about the earth itself today. This produces changes in our morals, changes in our whole outlook on life. So the recommendation we were given ("The essence of striving to the far-off worlds is obtained in the assimilation of a consciousness of our life in them") means that you assimilate it right out of your causal body and out of your will.

You express your will through your third eye, and you literally hurl a blue-flame sphere to your inner visualization of the God Star. It would also be good to go out at night and look at that God Star so that you have a clear visualization of it. It's a very bright light, of course, and it's the brightest of suns next to our own sun. Both Sirius and Venus are easily identifiable in the heavens.

Therefore, with this inner visualization, having seen Sirius physically in the heavens, you transpose it to your inner mind's eye. Each time you begin your decree to Surya, you have this fixed visualization of the pulsing energy and of the lesser star that is with it, which is not seen with the naked eye. It's so close that they just pulsate together. You see this star as a tiny point of light, and then you hurl a blue-flame sphere of energy to it by your heart, your third eye, your will and this striving to the far-off worlds.

Striving means throwing a portion of yourself into it, and when you throw this portion of yourself, you go with it. And then you find yourself hovering over a huge, huge sphere, which you see physically, as you would see our sun, with all the gaseous substance. Then you see it etherically as a very concrete place with teeming evolutions and the most beautiful combination of mountains, lakes, streams, oceans, cities and etheric forcefields, trooping children and legions of light and all kinds of lifewaves "doing their thing."

Many gurus are there with different kinds of schools for mastery in all different kinds of areas. It is the dream world that really exists, *that really exists*. That's Sirius. The teaching says that the recognition of the possibility of life on the far-off worlds becomes for our consciousness a channel of approach.

Your vision is the highway over which you travel, and without vision you cannot get to these places. You have to use your third eye. And if you haven't seen the vision, you have to hear me tell you about it because I have had the vision. And I transfer it to you, and now you can start seeing it. This is very important, because that vision is a real anchoring flame of our community.

The Need for Practical Vision

Indeed, this consciousness must be dug through as a channel. People are able to swim, yet a considerable portion of them do not swim. Such an obvious fact as the far-off worlds completely fails to attract humanity. It is time to cast this seed into the human brain.

I think people prefer shortsighted vision. They are shortsighted because all their goals are involved with this life. We need long-range vision, and it needs to be exercised. Merely looking at the stars exercises long-range vision.

Those who are unfortunate and without kin may more easily accept this thought. Earthly fetters are not so lasting for them. In the worst position of all are people provided with comforts. Easily enough can the blind accept this thought, but it will be most difficult for the cross-eyed, because a false crossing of currents will always distort the distance of the striving. Try rifling a cannon with different spirals: the result will be a poor one. True, what has been said refers only to a certain state of cross-eyedness which involves the nerve centers.

I would like to warn you about the state of untransmuted consciousness of people who constantly have an other-worldliness and a fantasy about such places without any practical reality. Such people are not chelas. They are psychic, they are selfish and they are escapists. The vision I am giving you is a practical vision of people who are here and now, practical chelas, practical leaders. They serve with intensity, and this is their point of communion and meditation in the midst of a fruitful life.

It is not escapism, it is not indulgence, and they are not carried off in daydreams to such places. They go there for a reason— to accelerate light and to come back again to where we are for heightened service. One of the most important reasons for this meditation is that you become a great sphere of blue energy, the very sphere you are visualizing. The Electronic Presence of Surya is upon you.

Surya's being includes his Matter sphere, his Matter bowl. When you call to an ascended master, his aura contains and includes the planetary sphere or the starry body that is an extension of himself. The rings upon rings of the causal bodies of these beings contain their manifestation. When Surya said he would place his Electronic Presence where you are, his Presence includes the God Star.

Surya can contain it. The question is, can you contain it? Can you concentrate on this? Can you equate with it? Do you have the co-measurement Morya talks about to realize that this much intensity of penetration results in a huge amount of energy returning to you? Pretty soon the whole point of that meditation is that you become a miniature Sirius moving around the planet, and the earth is actually stabilized by your decrees and your meditation.

Sirius is the headquarters of the Great White Brotherhood and the seat of the government of this whole galaxy. The consciousness of God-government is nowhere more intense in this galaxy than at the God Star. Communion with it brings stability to the governments and the economies of the nations and also ties into the Mighty Blue Eagle, the eagle being the symbol of America.

The eagle in itself shows the penetration of the legions of Sirius, and it shows your penetration of Sirius. So this eagle and this third eye are a part of the mastery of this exercise.

People with Comforts

Do you know why people with comforts are in a bad position? It is not because they are attached so much to their comforts, but it is because their needs are met. Everything is so easy. They have surrounded themselves with such great beauty that there is nothing to prick the sense of need that makes the soul go out in search of it. A comfortable person doesn't have the capacity to identify the soul's need.

45. I point out that it is important to send good arrows opportunely, and that the spirit then feels at ease. Like a gray swarm infecting the air, fragments of alien thoughts rush about and gradually encumber space. Then comes the arrow of the spirit, which is like lightning. It not only reaches the designated person but also purifies space. This purifying of space is not less important. A purer arrow, being a stronger magnet, draws to itself the gray fragments and bears them backwards. In such a manner the gray thoughts, with their weight, are returned to the fountain-head, but without injury to others. These gray thoughts, as products of combustion, settle upon the aura; and it is the sower who reaps. It is wise to send the word—touch not! Indeed, this formula will bring the least counterblow. Precisely, this is an ancient protective formula. It is practical to send either a good call or a defensive formula. Any malicious sending is impractical. True, it is possible to admit the sword of indignation of the spirit, but only in rare cases, for indignation of the spirit wears away the sheath.

46. Never did I speak about any ease in bringing the new consciousness into life. Not the destroyers, but the

moldy conventional virtue is the enemy. The destroyers know the instability of that which they destroy, and the principle of remittal is easier for them. But rosy-cheeked virtue loves its chest of savings and will always defend it with eloquence.

"Rosy-cheeked virtue" is virtue worn on the outside. "Moldy, conventional virtue" is an enemy that is expressed by the desire for ease in bringing about the community of the Brotherhood. Some think that if it is not easy, then somehow this effort must not be the real one.

The whole mystique of community is that you have to love striving, you have to love work and love a sacred labor. That's the mark of one who loves community. Those who like ease never quite fit into community, for that love of ease is a myth. It is every bit a demon and an entity that has to be encircled and slain—the desire for ease, separateness, a longing to be away from the creative tension of bringing forth the community.

Live the Truth by Example

Such people recite the sacred words of the Scriptures, and will find subtle arguments why they are indeed ready to surrender it not to this but to that man who does not yet exist.

Conventional virtue manifests superlative cupidity and loves to tell lies. And such handsome, rosy-cheeked teachers of virtue are these, and so oily in their affection! Achievement, human achievement, is unknown to these teachers of virtue, and their resplendent garments are starched with slavery!

47. In schools respect must be taught for the pronouncement of a concept. Of course parrots can senselessly project into space concepts often of great significance. But people must understand that the word is the pedal of thought—that each word is a thunder-bearing arrow.

Loss of the true significance of concepts has contributed much to contemporary savagery. People strew pearls about like sand. Verily, it is time to replace many definitions.

48. Precisely, without fear and as much as possible doing things oneself. Correct is the manifestation of personal responsibility. Neither miracles, nor quotations, nor actions; but affirmation strengthened by personal example.

Affirm the truth. Live the truth by example, and the students around you will get the message. The student is not necessarily able to perceive the example without the teaching. I may go about manifesting the light, but if I do not teach you what is the source of the light—how to draw it forth, how to manifest it— you may not get the full import of the example. Jesus spoke his parables and then lived what he taught. He was both the teacher and the example in one.

Sometimes it is good to look at the teaching and ask yourself, "Here is a teaching that I love. How am I manifesting it in a concrete way so that people around me who don't know the teaching and are not yet capable of receiving it will still have it transferred to them?"

This is an important exercise that I perceive students are not in the habit of doing, of seeing how the concepts we receive are a practical course of action.

Even a mistake in daring is more easily remedied than is abject mumbling.

Precious is the action which is not in need of any apparatuses or assistants. He who discovers a precious formula cannot cry it out of the window, because the resulting harm would obliterate the best usefulness.

Indeed, as a sealed vessel, as an unplundered mountain, as a bow tensed with an arrow—thus stand! And as a drink from the vessel is flaming, and as the mountain is inexhaustible, and as the arrow is lethal—thus act! For who dares to affirm that difficulty is not the speediest attainment! Rivers of milk will turn sour, and shores of jelly are inconvenient for sitting. Thus, in the armor of personal responsibility let us make haste.

Take notice, there has been success only where there

has been complete courage. Small doubts create a slavish timidity.

Precisely in the days of grave sickness of the planet it is important to be filled with courage. By groping one does not pass, but the sword can cleave the harmful veils. Very grave is the moment, and it is necessary to intensify all courage.

49. The more anyone renounces, the more he receives. But nations have forgotten how to renounce; even the smallest thinks only how to receive. Meanwhile, the planet is ill and all is sinking in this sickness. And someone wishes to evade the final battle through infection of the whole planet. And some hope to be setting sail in broken fragments, forgetting that the ocean is also departing. It is easy to picture that the planetary body can be just as sick as any other organism, and the spirit of the planet is affected by the condition of its body. How to name the illness of the planet? Best of all as a fever from poisoning. Suffocating gases, from the accumulations of the lower strata of the Subtle World, cut the planet off from the worlds which could send assistance. The Earth's destiny can be ended by a gigantic explosion if the thickness of the cover be not pierced. A stupendous acceleration is forcing all lines to shake. It could have been expected that acceleration was urgent for a certain country, but it is needed for the whole planet.

The Effects of the Energy of Sirius

What I would like to tell you about this session is that our entering into the forcefield of Surya and the God Star is a thrust of energy that compels us to rise to its level. Everything below that level begins to become agitated substance, subconscious energies, entities, et cetera.

Therefore, you may find yourselves a little bit restless as you are flushing out a great deal of substance that Surya does not allow to remain in his presence. In other words, if you want to be in the presence of Surya, you are supposed to get rid of this substance. But the carnal mind, which is attached to that substance, experiences uncomfortability while the laser of Sirius is separating it out. The best way to accelerate that process is to give the call to Surya (see p. 276).

The initiations of the God Star are conveyed by the sign of Scorpio and its hierarchy, and the eagle replaces the scorpion as the symbol for Scorpio. Scorpio and the eagle become the point of penetration, of which the scorpion's sting is the perversion.

The penetration of the All-Seeing Eye of God uncovers and destroys all evil. Therefore, we can take this period in Scorpio for the penetration of Cyclopea, of Surya, of El Morya. It is a penetration of worlds within and worlds without.

The preamble to the decree to Cyclopea (see p. 277) is very important for penetrating all misuses of the eye. When you give it, you can always insert after the word *Scorpio* all of the twelve houses of the zodiac, repeating the names of Sagittarius, Capricorn, and so forth, around the circle back again to Scorpio.

We are dealing with all the misuses of the twelve hierarchies of the sun. And in the God Star Sirius is the focus of these twelve hierarchies. We are using the creative energy of Scorpio to clear all twelve points of the clock. It is a moment of great crystal clarity that comes from Sirius. It is reflected in the weather, in the sky, in the way you feel inside about the Path. Concepts are crisp and cool, just as the atmosphere is.

I would like to read a little bit more from this.

> 50. It does not matter how the New World will enter —in a caftan, a frock coat, or a shirt. If we establish the cosmic significance of the community, then all the details are no more than the dust under foot. One may forgive any absurdity if it be not against the New World.

> 51. When I repeat one word many times, this signifies a filling of space. With loss of rhythm there has been a degenerating into mumbling. The wash of waves breaks down rocky cliffs. Likewise, in a procession there must be

the rhythm of sound. Rhythm of sound keeps a crowd from empty prattle.

Ommmmmmmmmmmmmmmmmmmmmmm

52. How is it possible to penetrate into the secret recesses of the spirit? Only through the unusual. The legend about the holy robbers has as its basis the spirit sharpened by the unusual. Whereas a soft-skinned baker rarely receives the key to the spirit, unless the daily play of the flame will reveal to him the light of the elements.

Suitable herbs must be gathered, but the place of their growth must be sought without prejudice.

The "suitable herb" is the chela, and without the prejudice that is born of attachment, the chela must put down his roots and serve. His particular fragrance and essence becomes a healing unguent to all life.

Do not say, "I want to go here; I want to go there," because the "I want" is the sign of absence of wholeness. It means "I lack" this or that place. If you are a native of Sirius, you contain the place. You have no prejudice as to the point of service. And this is freedom. There is a tremendous freedom in just letting everything go and enjoying be-ness. Enjoying that wherever you are is the greatest freedom I have ever known. Freedom from possessions or attachment to objects or people gives you a much closer tie to all people and to any place.

The "Attack of Purusha"

53. I shall explain why We speak of the "attack of Purusha." It were well if people could master the same principle of general tension. A manifestation of common danger must evoke such a general tension. The first condition of progress is liberation from usual occupation. The usual brain centers must droop in order that a new combination of nerve currents may be revealed. The same principle is used in the avoiding of fatigue. And such new tension, if it be devoid of

the personal element, is called an attack of Purusha.

In order to play the game of hidden twig, the searcher must look for it—not the one who hid it. Not without reason do the Hindus call the Highest Being the Player. Verily, the Earth is to be saved by earthly hands, and the Heavenly Forces are sending the best manna; but if ungathered it is transformed into dew. How then not to rejoice when gatherers are found? When, ignoring derision, these seekers proceed, remembering Our Shield.

The term *our shield* is a mystical term of El Morya's that keeps on coming back like a leitmotif. What he means by the shield is that the protection of the entire Brotherhood is upon someone who serves their cause. Derision is often difficult to overcome, as is discouragement, condemnation, harassment, persecution. These things recede when you remember the shield. We also remember home and how beautiful is the home where all our loved ones are! It gives us courage in the field.

It is never possible to evoke the tension of Purusha without mobility of thought.

Purusha is like the divine breath ignited by the divine fire. It is the very life force that passes through you and infills you. It's the energy you expend in service and receive back in meditation.

The spirit must strive by a single channel, as a bullet in a gun barrel. The manifestation of newly arising circumstances must not mar the rifling.

54. Light extinguishers are the particular servants of the dark forces who are occupied with putting out fires in the Subtle World. The stronger the attack of darkness the more actively do they destroy each point of light. We do not know a time of greater darkness in the Subtle World. Every false Olympus has sunk into twilight. But just now is no time to be occupied with them; now is the time to consider the earthly plane. The world in its present state is like the sea in a tempest.

55. Striving is the boat of the Arhat. Striving is the manifested unicorn. Striving is the key to all caves. Striving is the wing of the eagle. Striving is the ray of the sun. Striving is the armor of the heart. Striving is the lotus blossom. Striving is the book of the future. Striving is the world manifest. Striving is the multitude of stars.

Striving is acceleration of your energy. When you accelerate energy, more of God flows through you moment by moment. There is more pressure of light. Therefore, it becomes the boat of the arhat, the unicorn manifest, the opening of the cave where the guru and chela meet in that inner meditation, the wing of the eagle—the means of getting there, like the airplane—the ability to navigate in time and space, the ray of the sun, the lotus blossom, the book of the future, the worlds manifest, the multitude of stars. In other words, striving produces precipitation.

You have to plunge into the very center of what causes you to constantly summon the maximum force from God so that it expands your capacity to contain energy and exercises the muscles of the soul.

Liberation from the Usual Occupation

When El Morya speaks about the first condition of progress being "liberation from usual occupation," this is very important.

"The usual brain centers must droop in order that a new combination of nerve centers may be revealed." That is such an important point! I remember when I was in a "usual occupation" of working at a job in the world, and I was coming under the tutelage of El Morya and Lanello in Washington, D.C. At about the point where ten months were over in this job, the acceleration of light in me and the hand of the master produced well nigh a cataclysm within that job and catapulted me out of it.

I had saved up only a small amount of funds from my salary that would allow Mark and me and our forcefield to produce the work for a number of months. But the change was necessary because my job was forcing me to remain at the mental plane.

"The usual brain centers must droop in order that a new combination of nerve currents may be revealed." Those nerve currents are those of the etheric body whereby the etheric body meshes more completely with the vehicle in this octave.

As you accelerate etherically, you become very practical in the new service, but to go back into the world in your former occupation may not be easy after five or ten years. I am not certain how qualified I would be today to be the executive secretary I was then. I probably have some rusty tools for that sort of work that I haven't used since then. Yet I am well equipped and highly attuned for other forms of both etheric and mental service in this octave.

I can see clearly that this principle is another important point of community, because community provides the necessary occupation of serving, of working to produce income for its survival. Community doesn't let people be impractical but allows them to work within the circle of sacred fire. The same job inside the community is entirely different from the same job in the world.

The job in the community combines mental mastery with the opening up of the brain centers, the nerve currents, for the etheric tie to the guru. And that is the different quality people have who have been occupied as a chela within the community for five or ten years.

If you take the example of long-time chelas, you see people who are able in a very concrete way to master the energies opposing the precipitation of their sphere of energy. They are very much in tune with the Brotherhood and can transfer from their nerve centers and chakras to others around them that flame of chelaship, that flame of practicality in the work.

That is the result of the etheric-plane experience that happens inside community but does not exist outside of it. Such people have become practical department heads in their area of concentration within the circle. And with the added guru-chela relationship, it's a priceless experience.

Chelas talk about how different they are from the people in the world with whom they may be going to school or working on degrees. They are appreciative of how chelaship training combines with what they are studying and makes them feel more perceptive, get better grades and realize that other students taking the same courses are in a state of being programmed because they are not bringing an original creativity to the course.

The other students may come in as a passive blob at the level of the mental body, take in what is said and then give it back before filing out into their particular profession. In contrast, the chela brings a creative flame and is always in contact with the professor behind the professor, the guru behind the guru.

I had that experience in college, because when you are a chela, you are always a chela. If you put yourself in front of a teacher to learn a skill, all you have to do is make your attunement and the real and living guru will stand behind the teacher. The guru is really the one from whom you receive the instruction.

Lawfully, we are never allowed to have more than one physical guru. Although the physical guru may counsel students to become educated, the allowance of one physical guru is a universal law. Therefore, whoever may be the guru, El Morya or Saint Germain, perhaps—no matter what ascended master you are working with—the Electronic Presence of that one is always interacting with the other masters through you. Also, the two witnesses are always interacting with you.

I can remember instances where I had a dull or narrow-minded professor. I would sit in class with the textbook in my hand as the professor would lecture. Then, as I also knew the material from the reading assignment, the master would comment, and my mind would go into this magnificent orbit of hearing the truth on that subject.

No matter what the subject was, I would fill my notebook with notes of the inner teaching of the mystery schools relative to that subject. And that is the alchemy of the living chela who is first and foremost a chela. All of life, then, becomes the guru's instrument. The chela is always listening. He is always asking, "What is the guru teaching me through this film or this interchange?"

Liberation from the usual occupation, then, is necessary for acceleration. There comes a time in chelaship when you are called an initiate, an arhat, an adept. Then, your very adeptship itself would remove you from the world, yet you should be highly productive within the community. It is definitely a sign of attainment.

I think I will conclude with number 55 so that you can meditate on striving as an exercise of devotion to the will of God. If you really want God's will, you will go for it as you would for a touchdown. You just don't sit there and wait for the will of God to come to you. You seek it out, penetrating it with your third eye.

The exercise with the God Star is for you to do daily, and I suggest that you keep notes on your meditations, informal notes of your impressions. Not things you conjure up but things that you really feel from the God Star.

In the name of the I AM THAT I AM, I call for the sealing of these hearts, souls, chakras, auras and temples with the mighty Electronic Presence of Surya and Cuzco, with their mighty God flame, with a mighty pillar of fire.

I call for the full action of the violet flame to remove all debris that is less than the polarity of the God Star. I call for transmutation and balance. I call for the preparation of these temples to hold the balance for the God Star in the earth by the will of God. By thy will, beloved El Morya, as we are servants of the Most High, through thy heart flame seal us in thy diamond heart. Carry us now to the God Star. Amen.

Camelot
October 30, 1979

CHAPTER 3

Keepers of the Lightning

*I*n the name of the I AM
THAT I AM, I invoke the light, the Presence, the sacred fire
of beloved El Morya. I call for the mighty Electronic Presence of beloved El Morya upon my forcefield and upon the
forcefield of these chelas of the light.*

*I call for the circle of the guru-chela relationship to be
sealed, the acceleration of these souls to the frequency of the
inner sound of beloved El Morya. Blaze forth that light!
Blaze forth that light! Blaze forth that light!*

*I call for the unfolding now of those components of life
necessary to the sustainment of the true Community of the
Holy Spirit based upon the guru-chela relationship through
the Father, the Son, the Holy Spirit and the Mother to now
be revealed to us by the light of the Holy Ghost.*

*Beloved El Morya, speak to us this day in the fullness
of your love, wisdom and power. We thank thee and accept
it done this hour, Amen.*

I will read from *New Era Community,* beginning at number 56.

56. Why is the discovery of signs of the future likened
to weaving? In weaver's work the warp is of a definite hue,
and groups of threads are divided according to color. It is
easy to determine the warp and one can easily find the
group of threads, but the design of this group permits different combinations, depending upon a thousand current
details. Indeed, the inner relationship of the subject himself

will be the principal condition. If his aura should be too unsteady, then the prognosis will be a relative one. Then it will resemble a certain game, wherein, being given a few scattered points, one must identify a definite figure.

Where, then, is the best ferment with which to steady the wavering of the aura? The best ferment is striving. It is impossible to sting or to smash an impetuously directed body. Striving in motion attains validity, and becoming lawful it becomes irresistible, for it enters into the rhythm of the Cosmos.

Thus proceed in the small and in the great, and your texture will be unmatched, crystal, cosmic; in brief—beautiful.

Become Keepers of the Lightning

Striving, nothing else, results in mastery over the elements, for the basic quality of the elements is striving. In this state you coordinate the elements with the higher creativeness of the spirit and become the keepers of the lightning. Man shall become keeper of the lightning. Believe it, by striving only will you conquer.

I would like to speak on the subject of the will and of striving. In contrast to El Morya's statement here on striving, we find that individuals who come to the Path and desire reunion with God often go into a passive mode relative to the mighty I AM Presence.

Fasting, a vegetarian diet and an extreme desire to be receptive to the will of God sometimes makes a person passive to maya, to karmic conditions and to the aggressive consciousness of the fallen angels, to the Watchers.* El Morya is greatly concerned lest this community fall into this vibration.

In the past, many of the communities founded by the Great White Brotherhood have gone into a passive mode and have retreated from involvement with the world. Because of this, all that

---

*A particular band of fallen angels whose story is told in the Book of Enoch. See *Fallen Angels and the Origins of Evil.*

the masters would have liked to have accomplished through the individuals in these communities has basically been lost. The disciples turned their attention within, to inner meditation and contemplation on the Infinite, whereas society, deprived of this cream of the crop of lightbearers, has continued to spiral downward.

Therefore, the net result of the ashrams has been a cleavage, a separation of the lightbearers from the larger world community for which they should have been the "keepers of the lightning." Indeed, there is lightning. It is imprisoned in the atom and in the heart of the threefold flame. Not everyone can handle this lightning, and those who can are the keepers of the lightning. They must not become passive to those forces that react against the lightning.

Our supreme challenge is the balance of being receptive, humble and meek before God and yet emboldened before the dragons of human creation. By our example we must show this humility before the altar and zealousness in the world. We must not fall into the trap that you find in India, where spiritual people are not expected to enter the political arena, nor are they expected to be involved with political and economic conditions.

Of course, Gandhi was involved with both politics and economics, and, because he was, the great spiritual people of India today look down upon him. They also disapprove of the fact that he was not celibate all of his life. And they consider his path to be beneath theirs, whereas it is actually the path of love that is above theirs. This is something that our devotees must understand very clearly.

We must understand that at no other time has the challenge been greater to defend the community. The foundation of community in the United States is the Constitution, yet there are movements to rewrite the Constitution. Activities that violate the Constitution have gone unchallenged by our people and by the Supreme Court. There are encroachments upon the Constitution and upon the original flame of freedom.

Become the Wife of the Divine Husband

Thus, the aggressiveness of the chela is the zeal of the fiery sword. And it becomes necessary for us to understand two modes where we are the wife of the divine husband, any of the ascended masters, ascended lady masters—we are the counterpart of their beautiful Presence. If you consider what you know about the ideal wife upon earth, you can see that that wife is not entirely passive. That wife in the truest sense of the word, though obedient to her husband, has the ingenuity, the creativity, the striving, the steadfastness, the ability to work with detail, to make things happen.

The true concept of womanhood (which is the true concept of the soul of both man and woman) is the counterpart, the helpmeet who implements the flame and the consciousness of the father principle or the guru person. We find when we see a beautiful marriage on earth today that most husbands would be lost without their wives. The wife makes their life bright and happy, creates the forcefield of home, bears the children and is supportive of the husband's mission, which is to tackle the world and go out and make it a better place for family, children and community.

Thus, when you study that true relationship that the great marriages have had on this planet, you realize that for the ascended master it is most necessary that the chela be the wife. In fact, it is indispensable, and that wife is the means whereby the guru becomes active on earth. We can understand this perspective if we look at the importance of the shaktis of Shiva, for we are all shaktis of the ascended masters.[1]

The masters cannot function in the earth without us and our being this dynamic person of the pure feminine action. The chela must be the pure action of the guru, for the guru who is in Spirit is also active; but the guru in Matter is much more passive. You, as chelas, are the presence of the ascended masters in Matter, and what you do determines what they can be on the planet. You can see, as with Jesus Christ, he is tremendously limited by what the churches have done to him.

Some among the religious groups are like runaway wives, runaway chelas. They have run away with the flame and have said, "We will take the flame of our spouse and do with it what we will." They have declared their independence internally from their gurus while professing to be the exponents of the guru's message.

Rebellious People

There are some people who want to come back to this activity who are not in agreement with the guru. They do not desire to represent me as the guru, but they want the teaching and the light, for they realize that their lives are incomplete without it. I call these ones rebellious people.

These rebellious ones champion the right of individuals to use the light for whatever they choose—to come here, listen to a dictation, take the light and squander it on their desires. They think that we should keep an open house for anyone who wants to come and sit in front of the guru and take the light. We cannot allow ourselves to be this type of activity.

I am weary of people who question the acts of the ascended masters and question whether the masters are really here and whether this is really their movement. The questioners go to the study groups and quietly let out their points of disagreement. They say: "Mother* is the true messenger, but we can't agree with everything she does. Because she is the fount through which the water is flowing at this time, we'll tolerate her, but we have our free will, and we will do what we choose."

This becomes the point of rebellion on which Lucifer fell. It is to agree that God is truly God, but some of us understand the universe better and know how to run things better. Some of us are better at dealing with the practical necessities of life. They say, "The messenger is not practical. She is too pure. She is too removed from our needs and our type of problems and, therefore, she is too absolute, too authoritarian. Life is not like that.

---

*The messenger is known to her students as Mother.

You have to bend more to the human consciousness."

Many movements today do bend. I do not see a need for another palm tree that bends all the way to the ground in the wind of the human consciousness. We need tall oaks, redwoods and pines that sway with the wind but do not bend to the ground and do not compromise their stand. Today, of all times, we do not need to apologize for being on the line of the guru-chela relationship. Anyone who wants to compromise has a world full of activities to go to. And there is no reason why they should come and demand it of us.

We Must Defend Community

We are very comfortable in this forcefield, but the striving that Morya speaks about is the striving to maintain a certain acceleration of being and of consciousness. When you stop that striving, your creativity is destroyed, your identity is destroyed. When you allow yourself to be encroached upon, you are destroyed. When you allow the federal government or the Watchers or the godless creation or groups of individuals who are attackers to assail you and you do not thrust back the light, you, yourself, become destroyed.

You cannot stand still while the fallen ones attempt to destroy the forcefield of community. It becomes part of your dharma to fight. You must thrust back light. You must put your body, mind and soul on the line to defend community. You must be the embodiment of the light, and, therefore, forces will oppose you.

We have the great visualization that Archangel Michael gave in my first dictation. He spoke of the great strength of the tube of light, the Niagara Falls. And in that image of the falls, he showed clearly that if a Niagara Falls is pouring through you, nothing can move you in the opposite direction. Nothing can go against you. If you are bowed down by energy of any kind—hate and hate creation, psychotronic energy—it is a sign that you are not striving.

You can see the word *striving* as synonymous with accelerating. If the wheels of your chakras are spinning, they throw off energy, and you are in a positive polarity. You are drawing down so much of your I AM Presence that you are the plus polarity in manifestation, and nothing in this plane can move against it— nothing except God allow it.

Don't allow the Watchers to be the instrument of the LORD God Almighty. Don't let them tell you that he desires you to be overcome or moved. We do not look to God as using Satan to be the instrument of something that he desires to have happen to us. It is a great temptation to consider that something that is happening to you that seems to be like a bane is in fact a blessing in disguise. Don't allow yourself to believe that the seed of the wicked are the LORD's instrument when it comes to the guru-chela relationship. You are too beloved and too close to the Brotherhood for them to need to use the seed of the wicked to communicate with you.

The only time God has ever used Satan or the seed of the wicked to communicate with his children is when his children have been perverse and stubborn and disobedient. Then he has said, "All right. You will not listen to me. Receive your karma through the fallen ones." This is happening in the United States today. But it need not happen to you if you are a true chela of El Morya.

To be a true chela is to wait upon the Lord and strive in your decrees until you know you have achieved a very intense manifestation of the inner light and you expect that the Holy Ghost will communicate with you and comfort you in the person of one of the ascended masters or his angels.

You should always be suspicious. You should be on guard when dealing with the fallen ones and not allow their mesmerism and hypnotism to convince you that they are the instruments of good on behalf of the community of lightbearers. This is a key initiation, for we fight to the finish. When God wants us to be removed from this soil, let his angels remove us—not the Watchers, not the fallen ones. No good can come of them. They rebelled with Lucifer in the beginning, and they are programmed from the beginning to the end to work against the children of the light in the guise of good, in the guise of politics, religion and economics. They are destroying the nations, nation by nation.

We must take care that we do not become flattered by these do-gooders and these smiling ones who carry a dagger and gently thrust it into the side of America while they smile and sweet-talk the people. This book is on community, and the more you study community, the more you will understand that our very life is community and our life is lived to defend that community in the microcosmic sense of our own forcefield and in the macrocosmic sense of the cities.

The anti-state and the anti-city of secular Babylon is corrupting community with all manner of abuses of the light of the Mother. This invasion of the cities worldwide is an attack upon the Community of the Holy Spirit, and at some point you hold the line and defend that line. You establish your retreat so that from that point you go out and defend the children of the light.

"Striving Is the Boat of the Arhat"

Great strength must manifest in this community, and Morya began his instruction with his direction on the need for striving. Let us go back to what he said about it in paragraph 55, beginning with, "Striving is the boat of the Arhat."

We are on a clipper ship. I could hear the sails and the ropes of the clipper ship this morning. Maitreya and Morya are at the helm, and I could feel the whole ship turning at a right-angle degree heading straight for the center of the battle with the fallen ones.

We cannot launch out to sea in the deep while the battle is raging near the shore. We cannot plunge into nirvana and leave behind us the unfinished business of defending this forcefield. Over the centuries, too many have left, leaving behind perhaps a small band of disciples who could not keep the flame of community. We must do it because community, as America, is losing ground fast, very fast. And I know that God has invested tremendous light and energy for the reestablishment of community as the very key to the survival of the age.

And so, the guru and chelas are on that boat, and the boat represents a nucleus within a nucleus. It represents the highest striving ones. Look at the image of the unicorn. It will only give itself to a virgin, who represents the Cosmic Mother. It is a beautiful mythical figure, with the single-pointed horn coming from its head that is the symbol of the raised kundalini of the Mother.

Thus, the unicorn is a very high spiritual archetype of the spiritual striving. It is the key to all caves—and the cave is the symbol of the one-on-one relationship with the guru. Striving means that every single day you sense yourself in intimate communion with El Morya. And if you are burdened by the world and you do not have that communion, you must take the time to pursue that oneness, because with it so much light and nourishment can come through you to people all over the world.

The Efforts of the Idealists

The striving El Morya is speaking of is not the striving of political activists and protesters. In this country in the past, we have had tragic confrontations between the entrenched forces of the right and the young idealists of the left. Young idealists take to the streets in protest in order to effect change and oppose injustice. And they have light, these idealists.

All of this is a direct attack against community, for this form of striving is not striving in the ascended master sense. Therefore, these activities are a threat to the guru-chela relationship and to true freedom, even though they are carried on in the name of freedom. If they do not have right motive, right reason and right cause, they are doomed to failure and will result in anarchy—the absence of government and the presence of chaos.

Striving means the whirling of the atoms and the electrons. Striving places God above all else. Beautiful saints like Mother Cabrini[2] came to set us the great example of the ages. They have gone into the midst of the people. They have lived among the poor and placed their attention on teaching the children. They were willing to sit down person by person in the communities to study their problems and offer solutions—solutions that began with God and then went into the practical aspects of what needed to be done.

In earlier ages, the Catholic missions worked with the people. For example, when the Franciscans came to California, they established the missions that became the nuclei of our cities and communities today. The missionaries worked with the people; they plowed the land; they taught people to pray, converted them to Christ and met their needs. After the years passed and the communities were established, secular people took over the services of the missionaries and set up schools, industry, farming, and so forth. We are here to follow in the footsteps of Saint Francis and to reestablish that order.

When the Franciscans left, left-wing organizations took over their work with the poor, and the social justice of these organizations was drawn from a basis of scientific humanism, not from communion with God. Because it is not a true fount, the fount dries up. It does not have a flow of the crystal-clear water of life.[3]

Catherine of Siena fought the scientific humanism of her day that was encroaching upon the papacy and the Church. And it is encroaching upon us today. The idea of human beings becoming do-gooders for other human beings will never work and will never reinfuse society with the lightning. "The keeper of the lightning" sounds like a name for the next level of adeptship for the Keeper of the Flame! You can hold a candle in your hand with a flame burning, but can you actually hold the lightning in your hand?

"Striving Is the Armour of the Heart"

The heart is the point that bears the shock of world energy. The book *Heart,* published by the Agni Yoga Society, recommends that we protect the heart and meditate upon the heart. The theme of the book is guard the heart, guard the heart, guard the heart. The great hatred that people send attacks the heart and must be consumed by the love in your heart, or it will consume you.

Such hatred has consumed many of our finest leaders, especially those who were politically oriented but had no tie to the living gurus. We have seen them fall in battle before their time because of the attack upon the heart.

To sum up, the armour of the heart is a love, but a love that is inside the heart. Around the heart is a sheath of white fire that comes from your decrees. You should never have chest pains or heart pains as a result of opposition. If you do, you are not striving. You cannot lie back and submit to the opposition. If you do, you are not a chela worthy of the name.

Nor must you go concave to these thrusts of energy. Your being must be whole, and you fight, fight, fight! The signs of passivity can be signs of death, and Serapis Bey says that death must be fought. It is the last enemy, but we conquer that enemy. We never submit to that enemy, nor do we submit to constant physical problems. We fight them at every level.

"Striving is the lotus blossom." The lotus blossom of the crown chakra is opening. It is the "book of the future"—literally, the writing of the books that will open the door of the future to chelas unborn. "Striving is the world manifest." If you look at the world today, you realize that the Elohim strove to create the earth, that the creative process itself is one of immense striving, and it is the utmost giving of self that results in creation.

Nothing Is Won without Hard Work

I remember when a candidate for president was being interviewed on television. He had some good things to say and some not-so-good things to say. He was absolutely convinced, as all candidates are, that he was the one who was going to win. They continually amaze me by their posture of supreme confidence in themselves. But the most important thing this man said was, "Nothing was ever won without hard work. I am going to go out there and I am going to work hard, real hard, and I am going to win. After all, there isn't any other way to do it! Anything you get in this world, you get by hard work."

He is right. That is the absolute truth, and you have to see that in terms of your position. Your divine plan is not going to fall into your lap, nor is it going to come through passivity toward your mission and your service. The dark forces are militant forces, vicious forces, lightning forces. They use the technique of black lightning, the blitzkrieg, or lightning war, which Hitler used.

Suddenly, long-established traditions are overturned. And it takes people who have an eagle eye, the eagle of Sirius, who can sweep down from the mountain in a second and be right on the predator attacking the little birds. You have to have that consciousness.

The God Star and Our Mission

Sirius is the hub, the point from which all evolutions have gone forth to these several systems of worlds. All roads lead to Rome, and all masters lead to Sirius! Sirius is the seat of God-government in this galaxy, the seat of the Great White Brotherhood. It is our home, but our mission away from home is to anchor the community of the Great White Brotherhood in the earth.

Our mission is to establish a permanent physical focus of the Brotherhood on earth, so help me God! It must not be denied but shall remain here until the coming of the golden age. This is our will. In the name of the Lord Jesus Christ, our agreement together on earth is to see to it that the flame will not go out.

Surely the Brotherhood will not have to begin again and again because we are so namby-pamby and so passive that we do not care whether we live or die; because we have adopted such a high metaphysical God consciousness that nothing matters at all anymore, including the Matter universe.

Do you realize how diabolical that lie is? Do you know that sometimes it even affects the consciousness of the chela? That's why I am stressing it—the idea that it doesn't quite matter whether we have a Teaching Center in Houston, Texas. It doesn't quite matter whether I go to decrees today. It doesn't quite matter whether or not I get out of bed and do my work.

Do you see what I mean? It comes right down to the point of the individual becoming the outpost of the God Star. You are the God Star upon earth because you are the wife of Sirius, you are the wife of the whole Great White Brotherhood! And the whole Great White Brotherhood depends upon you. You have to have the preaching of the Book of Hosea, which I will bring to you on a Sunday morning, because the whole book is expressed as God speaking to Israel as though Israel is his wife who's gone astray and has been unfaithful to him, and he is calling back his wife. And the longing of the prophet for his wife shows the longing of God for every soul on earth and for the soul's ultimate sense of self-worth.

Do you understand that you are ultimately important to God? It's a very physical thing, very here and now. It starts with you in your house—how you interact with your spouse, your children, your business, your employer, your community and what you do every day.

You should think, "I am a representative of the Great White Brotherhood, and this is the highest form of self-esteem that I can have. I walk the earth wearing the mantle of Elijah, or John the Baptist, and I am unique among people. Among vast millions I hold the flame, and I know that I AM important to this evolution. If this evolution does not know that I AM important, I will assert my self-importance that this evolution cannot survive without my presence here."

You look around you and lift your head above the clouds. It is as if you were on a high mountain. The clouds are beneath you, and you have crystal-clear vision. You recognize that all the great avatars have had this vision. Moses had the vision that the people could not be liberated without him. God gave him that vision. He did not want to accept it. He did not want to feel that it was up to him. He was a poor, humble man.

Moses did not feel that he could be the one who was the deliverer, and you also need to get up over that hump, as he did. If all you are to rescue in a given lifetime is a herd of sheep, then you are a shepherd boy, like the previous incarnation of Kahlil Gibran or Mark Prophet, which Lanello describes in *Cosmic Consciousness*.[4] For a whole lifetime you are responsible for a herd of sheep.

In this lifetime you may only be responsible for getting five people home to their ascension. But woe to you if they don't get home! You will stand trial on Sirius, and the four and twenty elders will ask you, "Where are the five? You are here, so what! We saw you here the last go-round. Where are the five who should be standing here with you?"

They will say that this is serious (Sirius) business, for that's how the God Star got its name. We are supposed to have a sense of responsibility when we think of the God Star. Therefore, you cannot be otherworldly. You cannot have your head buried in all kinds of endless research for which no one ever sees results. What gets out, the word that's communicated, is always the most important word.

Morya's Thrust

Morya's concern is to galvanize his chelas. Whenever you think of Morya, you know he is always moving, always involved, always in committee. It doesn't matter where they are—in the United Nations or in Moscow or in China—wherever people meet, he comes to thrust a spiral of the will of God. Often not a single person in that meeting is responsive to one principle. Yet he is the silent sentinel.

He places his Electronic Presence there, and you can make the call as a chela of El Morya, "El Morya, I desire to be with you wherever you are thrusting that rod of power. I want my Electronic Presence there. I will witness for you, and we two will witness together in these meetings until a responsive chord is struck."

And how is that responsive chord going to be struck? Because our books and our chelas are communicating the teaching. Lanto told us what he wanted done for the sake of the preservation of the community. He gave a whole dictation on community, on how it would be destroyed if you do not correct what is being said. Community is a principle that has to be defended.[5]

All people can be enlisted to defend any valid community. We must defend the right of all valid churches to be churches. And they should join together to defend our right to be what we are, or we will all lose that right.

Strive to Be an Ascended Master

Striving is the multitude of stars, and the multitude of stars is the multitude of the heavenly hosts and ascended masters. You can be one of them. I want everyone to don this mode of striving. We would not call it aggression, but it is definitely a thrust, and it can never come to you without a sense of self-importance.

If you are still saying, "Why me?" or "It won't be me who will be a world saviour," you haven't reached the point of being a Moses. You haven't accelerated to the point where you know that you are the indispensable one in your group of people. Until you reach that moment, you really haven't come into your own in this embodiment.

I am also talking about the subtlety of the lie that is projected at you when you start to accelerate. You may be part of the ascended masters' movement. You give your decrees, believe in everything, love the messengers and the masters, but you have not reached the point of acceleration where you are launched into orbit and on a mission, a relentless mission in which you are utterly consumed in giving yourself to God.

I don't think I ever knew what striving was until I went on my lecture tours, for I was striving not only against opposition, but also to give of myself hour after hour on the platform. And the point of my striving was my intense love for the people who were in ignorance and who needed the light.

Love makes everything in your being accelerate. It pours through you. It is fuel and because of it, you get additional fuel. You become a kind of jet engine. You are whirling. I was able to deliver the Word for five or six hours because of this. And that striving put me into such an accelerating vibration that many more things were possible to me.

Great quantities of the Holy Spirit flowed through me. You just have to experience it, for it is the only way to ascend. It's the only way to break away from the lethargy of the planet. You really must have a mission into which you utterly throw yourself daily.

Many Americans are imbued with striving in their occupations, yet some don't reap a soul gain from it—a soul gain that would give them their ascension. If they put the same amount of effort into the cause itself, perhaps in the same profession they are in but dedicated to God and his grace and his Son and his people rather than to the self and to money, they would quickly gain their God-mastery.

God takes nothing from you; he just refines your service. He gives you all that is necessary for fulfillment. You don't have to remove yourself from the fiery core to get what you want. It's not necessary. Everything is here, everything that you need to be a fulfilled person. And if you haven't found that fulfillment, you haven't let yourself really strive. You think that if you really do give in and you do surrender, you will lose everything, instead of understanding that you will gain everything.

In my personal experience, I have found that losing oneself in the fire of service is the way one gains everything—friends, loved ones, family, students, people by the thousands that one becomes a part of. And then there's the joy of God-consciousness and the higher planes of consciousness, the intimate contact with the Brotherhood.

God withholds nothing from you when you put yourself

into the mode of giving and striving. You leap to give something more because it is so exciting to experience the cosmic interchange that returns to you in that givingness. We have to go out and find the people who need us and strive against that human consciousness, strive with their angels, strive with their God consciousness and keep on pushing back the levels of darkness on this planet.

The Warning Bell

Man shall become keeper of the lightning. Believe it, by striving only will you conquer.

57. Is it indeed possible that a tocsin is not heard in each movement of the planet? Is there not an anguished cry in every movement of all beings? Does not a rebellion ring out with each movement of the spirits levelled to the ground in servility?

But have there been better times?

It is better if an abscess be cut open, and it should be possible afterward to close the opening. But first it is needful to draw out the pus; therefore, We do not take halfway measures. We expect broad actions, and at the time of a tocsin it is impossible to think about a piece of yarn.

The word *tocsin* comes from the French. It means an alarm bell, or the ringing of it, or a warning signal. The Tibetan masters, Djwal Kul, Kuthumi and El Morya, often contact their chelas for the first time by the sounding of a bell in their inner ear. It is not a ringing in your ear that is caused by an illness, but a bell that you hear in your inner ear.

Mark experienced it as a young man and followed the sound of the bell back to the master's ashram in the Himalayas. Certain other individuals on the planet are waiting to hear it because of previous experiences before taking embodiment. They wait. At subconscious levels their souls know that when they hear the sound of the bell, it's the moment for response.

It's a preconditioning of the soul. An agreement was made between the guru and his chela before the chela entered the veils of maya, where he might lose the memory of the inner experience in the etheric retreat. This is why the image of the Lord Jesus Christ ringing a bell in a great cathedral was given to us in a dictation. It is an important image, and I believe it was Lanello who brought it to us.[6]

The Lord Jesus was pulling a rope that rang a big bell, as he told us he would aeons ago. He told us he would do it when it was time to galvanize his forces on the planet. And when I tune into that visualization, I see Jesus ringing that bell in the great cathedral at this moment, and it's for all his children on earth to come to that point of galvanizing for the ultimate victory.

Thus the sounding of this particular bell is a warning to the chelas of the rising astral tide, a warning of the signs of the times, a warning of the dark cycle of karma. It is time to fortify oneself within one's retreat and bastions. It is time to store up light and be alert to the enemy. It is time to assume the mode of the watchman on the wall.

We are living in dangerous times today; violence and assassination are common. And so it is on the astral plane. By thinking about a piece of yarn, it is indeed possible that a tocsin is not heard in each movement of the planet. Is there not an anguished cry in every movement of all beings? Only some people hear the warning bell, and those who do are preconditioned to be alert to it. The vast majority of the population do not hear the warning bell.

Because we have heard it, we have a responsibility to do something about it. People are not as alarmed as they should be by the state of moral degeneration, by the state of the economy, by the faces of our leaders. They are neither sufficiently alarmed, nor are they sufficiently prepared.

Let us continue reading.

> 58. You already know the usefulness of obstacles; you already know the advantage of disappointments. There can even be a usefulness of terrors. Indeed, for Us and for you

there are no terrors in the usual sense. On the contrary, a terror without fear is transformed into an act of cosmic beauty.

Is it possible to think about beauty without a chord of rapture? At present We shout, We send signs of battle, but above all there is rapture in the face of great solutions. Courage opens all doors. "It is impossible," we utter ourselves; whereas, all that exists cries out, "It is possible!"

Each epoch has its own word. This word is as a key to the lock. Ancient Teachings continually spoke about a potent word which was contained in a precise and brief formula. Immutable, like a crystal of known composition, it is impossible to alter in any way the words of these formulas: impossible either to lengthen or to shorten. The guaranty of Cosmos is in the casting of these words. The absolute darkness itself shudders before the blade of the World Command, and it is easier for rays and gases to smite the darkness there where has struck the Sword of the World.

Let us receive the command of the Cosmos not slavishly but tempestuously! Hence, the time comes when the Light-Force burns the darkness. The time is imminent, and the hour cannot be set back.

It is possible to investigate the secret words of all epochs and see a spiral of piercing light. A legion of worms cannot alter the tip of the spiral, and obstacles merely intensify the ray of light. The law of reflexion creates new forces. And where the speaking one is silent the mute shall speak.

59. A clear brief command is difficult, but on the other hand it is stronger than a magic wand. Affirmation is easier, but a command is like an unexpected pillar of flame from a volcano. A concentrated feeling of personal responsibility lies in a command. A declaration of inexhaustibility of forces sounds in a command. The impetuousness of the Cosmos is manifested in the vehemence of the command, as a crushing wave. Wipe away the tears of benignancy. We are in need of sparks of indignation of the spirit!

What a dam do regrets make, yet wings grow on the end of the sword! Sands can kill, but for Us a cloud of sand is a flying carpet.

60. Much can be forgiven him who even in darkness has preserved the concept of the Teacher. The Teacher uplifts the dignity of the spirit. We liken the concept of the Teacher to a lamp in the darkness. Therefore, the Teacher may be called a beacon of responsibility. The bonds of the Teaching are like a saving rope in the mountains. The Teacher is revealed from the moment of kindling of the spirit. From that moment on the Teacher is inseparable from the disciple.

We do not see the end of the chain of Teachers, and the consciousness imbued with the Teacher elevates the attainment of the disciple as a precious, all-penetrating aroma. The bond of the disciple with the Teacher forms a link of protection in the uniting chain. Within this defense deserts bloom.

61. My Hand sends the solution amid the crags of the world. Regard the plank roof as more solid than iron. Regard a fixed moment longer than an hour. The lengthened path is shorter than the vertical precipice. You will ask: "Why enigmas, why esotericism?" The ball of events is full of many-colored threads. Each ladle is dipped from a well of a different color. Among events are many rushing ones; these distant friends, unconnected externally, fill our basket, and the ultimate light triumphs.

62. One may rejoice when suggested thoughts coalesce with one's own thinking; because in recognizing cooperation there are no boundary lines of separation of labor— there are only effects. It is impossible to dismember the functions of the Cosmos when actions are flowing like a river.

What significance has the structure of the waves which bear a useful object? The important thing is that the object be not lost!

63. The main misunderstanding will be of the fact that labor can be relaxation. Many amusements will have to be abolished. Chiefly, it must be understood that the products of science and of art are for education, not diversion. Many amusements will have to be destroyed as hotbeds of vulgarity. The forefront of culture must sweep away the dens of fools passing time over a mug of beer. Likewise, the use of profanity must find a far more severe penalty. Likewise, manifestations of narrow specialization must be disapproved.

64. It is important to speak about the necessity of commensurateness. I consider it needful to distinguish between recurrent and non-recurrent things. One may put aside an object of daily life, but one must seize upon the calling dates without delay. It may be affirmed that a moment of cosmic possibility is irreplaceable. There are dishes which can be digested only in a certain order. The hunter does not go hunting from indolence; he finds out the best hour and nothing detains him.

It is possible to find My Stone in the desert, but it may be lost again if it be not lifted up immediately. Those who know Me realize the significance of immediateness, but the new ones must keep this law in mind if they wish to draw near. Verily I say—the time is short! I say with solicitude— lose not an hour, for the threads of the ball are multicolored. Not in the pleasantness of repose but in the darkness of the storm is My Voice useful to you: learn to harken!

I know people who have let the call escape them on account of their porridge. But My arrow is let fly in the hour of need. My Hand is ready to lift up the veil of the consciousness; therefore, co-measurement of the small and the great, of the recurrent and the non-recurrent is needed. Exert yourselves to understand where is the great! I say—time is short!

65. Our condition for the coworkers is a complete desire to apply in life Our fundamentals, not in theory but in practice.

The Teacher bears the flame of an unquenchable achievement. The Teaching is interrupted neither by weariness nor by distress. The heart of the Teacher lives by achievement. He has no fear, and the words "I am afraid" are not in His vocabulary.

66. The evolution of the world is built on revolutions or explosions of matter. Each revolution has a progressive movement upwards. Each explosion, as a constructive agent, acts spirally. Therefore, it is in the nature of each revolution to be subject to the law of the spiral.

The earthly structure is like a pyramid. Now, from each point of the progressive spiral try to lower the four sides of a pyramid. You obtain, as it were, four anchors, lowered into the lower strata of matter. Such a construction will be fantastic, because it will be constructed upon dying strata. Now let us try to build from each point upwards a rhomb, and we get a body of conquests of the upper strata outstripping the movement of the spiral. This will be a worthy construction! Indeed, it must start into the unknown, expanding parallel with the growth of the consciousness. Therefore, construction in revolution is a most dangerous moment. A great number of imperfect elements will press the structures downward into strata of outworn and poisoned substance. Only reckless courage can turn the structure upwards into strata untried and beautiful in the maintenance of new elements. Therefore, I speak and shall say again that outworn forms must be avoided in the structure. Sinking back into the old receptacles is inadmissible. The understanding of the New World in all its austerity is needed.

67. What is required in Our Community? First of all, co-measurement and justice. True, the second results entirely from the first. Indeed, one must forget about good-naturedness, for this goodness is not the good. Goodness is a surrogate of justice. The spiritual life is governed by co-measurement. The man who does not differentiate the

small from the big, the insignificant from the great, cannot be spiritually developed.

One talks about Our firmness, but this is only the result of Our developed co-measurement.

68. Do understand the name of the son of fear and doubt—his name is regret. Indeed, regret after entering upon Great Service cuts off all the effects of former labors. He who doubts binds a stone to his leg. He who is afraid constrains his breathing. But he who is regretful of his labor in behalf of the Great Service terminates the possibility of approach.

How then not to distinguish that courage which leads to attainment? How not to remember the hand that arrested the dagger of the enemy? How not to gird on the force that gave up all for the growth of the world? Understand, I shall repeat without end, so long as the bridge of the rainbow does not yet encompass all colors.

Cedars preserve a healing tar, but one may smile when the heavenly sap goes into boot grease. Hence, let us guard the principal paths by applying details to useful advantage.

69. Growling and savage yelping fill the air of Earth. Beastly roaring has replaced human song. But how beautiful are the fires of achievement!

70. My Hands know not repose. My Head upholds the weight of the works. My Mind searches out the solidity of solutions. The power of experience defeats alien infirmity. At the point of loss do I pour in the new possibilities. On the line of retreat I build strongholds. In the eyes of the enemy I wave the banner. I call the day of fatigue a day of repose. I recognize a manifestation of non-understanding as rubbish on the threshold. I can conceal the sacred in the folds of a working garment. A miracle means for Me only the mark of a horseshoe. Courage means for Me only the arrow in the quiver. Resoluteness for Me is only the daily bread.

71. First of all forget all nationalities, and apprehend the fact that the consciousness is developed by perfecting the invisible centers. Some await a Messiah for a single nation, but this is ignorant; for evolution of the planet can be only on a planetary scale. Precisely, the manifestation of universality must be assimilated. Only one blood flows, and the external world will no more be divided into races of primitive formation.

72. The Community, as Fellowship, can unprecedentedly accelerate the evolution of the planet and give new possibilities of intercourse with the forces of matter. It must not be thought that community and the conquest of matter are found on different planes. One channel, one banner—Maitreya, Mother, Matter!

The Hand which discerns the Threads points out the path to Our Community. Indeed, We shall not speak about a precise time when Our place started. Cataclysms molded the favorable conditions, and with Our knowledge We can guard the Center against unbidden guests. The existence of violent enemies has permitted Us to close the entrances still more tightly and to instruct neighbors in an effective silence. To transgress and to betray means to be destroyed.

73. The essence of the New World contains a vacuum which is called the node of immobility; in it are being collected the sediments of manifestations of incomprehension of the tasks of evolution. When the brain leads close to these paths of incomprehension of the spirit, the access to Our sendings is almost lost. Can people possibly forget creativeness, directed to the adornment of life?

74. It is necessary to investigate the undeferrable. It is needful to preserve personal enthusiasm. It is needful for each one to walk independently—no hand on the shoulder, no finger on the lips. Woe to him who delays the guard. Woe to him who spills rice on the shield. Woe to him who carries water in his helmet. And most of all—woe to gray

fear. Verily, the net of the world has been cast. It cannot be drawn up without a catch. Truly, not even the very least will be forgotten. The seed has been paid for. Violence was not admitted. Let each one proceed, but I pity those who do not attain. How dark is the return path! I know nothing worse than to cross the neighbor's path. Say to each one, "Walk alone until you receive the command of the Teacher." One should rejoice at the churning and hissing of the sea. Manifest an understanding of the great time. Uplift the chalice; I summon you.

75. Truly, one may look forward to the fulfillment of all prophecies. I do not see the dates being altered. Think through the film of events, and comprehend how unimportant is the exterior; only the inner significance is vital. The sowing of generations begins to sprout; the seed is beginning to shoot up.

76. One must know the process of Battle called the casting down of the rocks. When the Battle reaches a certain tension the Leader tears away portions of the aura and casts them at the hordes of enemies. True, the auras of the warriors are violently torn also; therefore at this time the protective net is not strong, but the enemies are smitten especially vigorously. The fabric of the aura burns more severely than lightning. We call this method heroic. It must not be thought that we are traveling on a luxury train—we are walking over an abyss on a plank. Tufts torn from the aura leave it like the riddled wings of an eagle. It must be remembered that we ascend the walls without any cover. When a glass is broken it may not rattle at once, but when it reaches the lower gorges the crunching of its fragments is heard. You yourselves will understand the rest. The very greatest Forces are in Battle for the salvation of humanity.

77. A manifestation must be understood as evidence not to the eye but to the consciousness. In this lies the difference between your and Our understanding. What you

call a fact is a result, whereas We can discern the true fact, invisible to you.

A blind one judges lightning by the thunder, but one who sees is not afraid of thunder. Thus, it is necessary to learn to distinguish true facts from their effects.

When We speak about a destined event We see its true origin; but whoever will judge according to visible effects only will be behindhand in his judgment. When We say— "Go against evidence," We mean—"Do not fall under the illusion of transitory events." One must clearly distinguish the past from the future. Indeed, humanity suffers from this lack of discernment, whirling around in the illusions of effects.

A creative spark is contained in the process of an event, but not in its effects. Occupied with effects, humanity is like a blind man who can sense the thunder only. It is possible to set forth a distinction between those who judge by events and those who judge by effects.

Speak to your friends, that they should learn to observe the real according to the outbreak of the events. Otherwise they remain readers of a newspaper edited by a knave.

Strain the consciousness to grasp the starting point of events, if you wish to be associated with the evolution of the world. One can name numberless examples of pitiful, culpable and tragic misunderstandings, as a result of which dates were jumbled.

The oak grows from the acorn under the earth, but the fool notices it only when he stumbles over it. Many stumblings sully the earth's crust. Enough of errors and lack of understanding in the hour of world tension!

It must be understood how carefully must one expend energy. It must be understood that only the right doors will lead into the chamber of the Common Good.

78. In each book there must be a chapter about irritation. It is imperative to expel this beast from the house. I welcome austerity as well as decisiveness. I enjoin you to

abolish jeering jests. Each one should be helped to get out of entanglements. One should nip each bud of vulgarity. Each one must be permitted to have his say, and patience must be found to listen. The empty rumor must be cut short, and ten words must be found against each word defaming the Teacher. Indeed, remain not silent at an arrow directed at the Teacher. Mother and Teacher—these two concepts must be safeguarded in each book. The light of greatness is not to be extinguished.

79. In cosmic constructions service requires a change of consciousness. There may be mistakes. One may be absolved in the greatest mistake provided that the source is pure; but the measuring of this purity is possible only for an enlightened consciousness. Joy in Service can be experienced only through an expanded consciousness. It must be remembered that each three-year period represents a step of consciousness; in the same way each seven-year period represents a renewal of the centers. Learn to understand that the dates of the consciousness are not repeatable and therefore are not to be allowed to escape.

It is proper to ask a man who is thinking about entering upon the path of Great Service what he intends to give up. Does he expect only to secure the realization of his most sweet dreams? Or is it agreeable to him for a grain of faith to acquire earthly riches and to occupy a position foreign to his consciousness?

It is impossible to enumerate the means of expansion of consciousness, but in them all lies the realization of truth and self-sacrifice.

80. It is necessary to understand clarity of thinking and to apply it to the future—thus is it possible to avoid roughness of form in actions. One should not ape others. Precious is each grain of decisiveness. I wish to saturate you with daring. It is better to be considered unusual than to be garbed in the uniform of triviality. It is needful to read My

Teachings. It is necessary to strive to apply them to each act of life, not on holidays only. Say to yourself: "Is it possible to strive in the mornings and be a parrot in the evenings?"

81. It is wise to draw the line between past and future. It is impossible to calculate all that has been done—it is incommensurable. It is better to say: "Yesterday is past; let us learn how to meet a new dawn." We all grow, and our works are expanding with us. After twenty-seven years no one is a youth, and we all can then understand the achievement of Service. It is unworthy to rummage in yesterday's dust. Henceforth let us establish a new step. Let us begin to labor, surrounding ourselves with a thousand eyes. Let us acquire purity of thought and co-measurement of actions. Thus let us fill our days; let us become used to mobility and decisiveness. Likewise, let us not forget that there is nothing on Earth higher than the given Plan for the Common Good. Let us manifest understanding of the Teachings of life. As Moses brought forth human dignity, as Buddha impelled toward the broadening of consciousness, as Christ taught the good of giving, so now the New World is directed toward the far-off worlds! Ponder, what comparisons surround us! Ponder about the cornerstone. Reflect about the given path. Ponder how the boundaries of the Cosmos touch you. Recall the steps of wondrous tensions not in a book but in life. Reflect that so much has not been taken up and absorbed and yet you stand in your place. Therefore, be not disheartened by mistakes, but ascend by the Hierarchy of the Teaching.

In the name of Almighty God, I call to beloved El Morya. Bind all mistakes, the energy of mistakes of the past of every soul and every chela. Let them be cast into the sacred fire of the Holy Ghost, transmuted by the violet flame and purged from the earth by the blue lightning of the mind of God.

Let us stand with the teacher and the teaching and move forward in the boldness of the guru Lord Maitreya. Beloved Mother, seal us with thy light. We thank thee and accept it done this hour in full power.

In the name of the Father, the Son, the Holy Spirit and the Mother, in the name of the entire Spirit of the Great White Brotherhood, the God Star, Sirius, mighty Surya and the legions of light, we say, "Hear I am, Lord. Send me!"

Hear I am, Lord. Send me!

Hear I am, Lord. Send me!

Hear I am, Lord. Send me!

Camelot
November 6, 1979

CHAPTER 4

Guard the Outpost
of the Great White Brotherhood

Beloved mighty I AM Presence, beloved Christ Self, beloved Alpha and Omega, we call forth thy light. Bind the oppressor of each soul. Bind that which is the anti-self. Bind all substance uncovered by the fullness of the glory of the All-Seeing Eye of God.

I call for the crystal ray. I call for the emerald ray. I call for the action of the sacred fire and the mighty seraphim. Angels of the emerald light, come forth. Angels of the healing thoughtform, beloved Raphael, beloved Mother Mary, pierce now the veil. Pierce now the substance in all levels of being.

Bind, then, the opponent of world peace and the victory of light over death and hell. Bind war, the engines of war, the warlords and their councils. Burn through, beloved Lanello and El Morya. Expose, expose, expose the fallen ones! Expose them now and let the victory of the Christ appear in each heart.

In the name of the Father, the Son, the Holy Spirit and the Mother, Amen.

As we continue our lectures on community, I feel that in this hour the emphasis is on the survival of community. The question is, how is community going to survive?

We in America have defined community—our cities, our government and our national consciousness—and the Great

White Brotherhood has defined community as the Community of the Holy Spirit. We have a community to preserve intact. The Goddess of Liberty has passed to us the torch of holding the balance of world karma for all peoples of the world. She also passed the torch to us of holding the cradle for the infant messiahs of the seventh root race, thereby holding intact a remnant that could be the instrument for successive generations of lightbearers, come what may.

It is my opinion that the government of the United States is incapable at this time of protecting the community of the Great White Brotherhood. The opposition to the United States that is manifesting at this time is opposition to the Brotherhood and to the embodied messenger and chelas. It is opposition to the light.

Our government has no concept of that light, no concept of the opposition to that light and, therefore, no concept of what it takes to defend that light. Therefore, I stand on the principle that if you see a job to do and you want to get that job done, you do it yourself. I see the job of protecting and securing this community as the greatest responsibility of devotees advancing on the Path.

The responsibility of actually holding the flame of community was passed to me by Gautama Buddha and Lanello in the hour of Lanello's ascension. He entrusted to my care all devotees of light, and I take this responsibility very seriously. We had a first attempt at a community in Idaho, which did not succeed, but it has never left my heart.

I also want you to be aware that this country is wide open to sabotage. We do not have sufficient civil defense or sufficient militia trained to deal with this kind of warfare. Terrorists are deadly in their intent and determined to destroy the American system. They see the system of capitalism, which they call imperialism, as corrupt and evil. And in order to have the correct system, they intend to destroy the present system.

For instance, terrorists could sabotage a nuclear power plant and pollute the ocean and the coast. They believe with religious fervor that life on earth would not be worth living under the American system. Therefore, if the innocent must suffer in order to bring in a new system for future generations, they think, so be it. On that basis, they rationalize the destruction of our entire civilization.

Our Assignment Is to Survive

Our assignment is to survive in the midst of all this. *New Era Community* is a handbook on the survival of community. Its purpose is to help you unite with the inner matrix of community, its inner cause and core.

Community is founded on the inner organization of the Great White Brotherhood, whose seat of authority is Sirius. The decree and meditation on Surya are important because the most important flame you carry within you is the inner sense of community. Wherever you are, you can be holding the balance for community with that understanding that we all have to hang together or we will hang separately.

At stake is our spiritual and material survival as individuals, which is a legitimate reason for understanding why you need to be a part of this organization—the headquarters or a teaching center—because of the necessity of survival as a group of individuals. I believe that God intends us to survive, and I feel that it is important for us to know this. I see very clearly that none of us could survive separately, but we can all survive as a group.

The group cannot survive, however, if it becomes a hydra-headed monster with several different people telling you what to do. For this reason we have hierarchy and the guru-chela relationship and the very basic disciplines of people learning to be obedient and not rebel against the Law itself. We may not rebel against the impersonal Law or the embodiment of that Law. That is how we hang together, on that grid and forcefield. Again, let me repeat, I believe God has intended us to survive.

In the face of your need to make decisions as to what to do with your life, you must realize that we are in a moment of great trembling on this planet. We are in the midst of crosscurrents of intense forces, the yin and the yang of the mass consciousness and the laggard evolutions. Groups of opposing forces hurl invectives at each other. Long ago on Lemuria such opposing forces hurled invectives at one another, and because they were black magicians, their invectives manifested as dinosaurs and all kinds of reptilian beasts.

We hope that today's hurling of invectives does not turn into an exchange of nuclear weapons, with the resulting destruction of the children of God. For although we know the fallen ones are capable of having many die so that they can win their cause, we have to know that we can survive. I consider that my most important work, aside from delivering the Word and the teaching, is my concern, night and day, for the survival of every chela.

With that as a foundation, let us comb these pages and see what Morya has to say about the survival of community. We are on number 82 of *New Era Community.*

The Flight of the Soul

82. On the day of beginning the new step let us speak without reproach about the great times when we learn to break away from the Earth and already in the body become associated with the Higher Worlds.

No one is refused anything; come, stretch forth your hand to the altar of the spirit. Affirm the spirit as of matter and remember how the heart trembles before the radiance of the mountains.

My Word must affirm you in the beauty of achievement. Facing the path, let us abandon the rules of actions; let us again gather the consciousness above the firmament. It is beautiful to have already the subtle body and find the spirit no more troubled before distant flights. Therefore, let us rejoice at each movement on the crust of Earth—let us learn, as it were, to fly therein.

To fly—what a beautiful word! In it is already contained the pledge of our destination. When matters are grave, think about flights; let each one think about wings. I send to the daring ones all the currents of space!

You will notice that there are wings on the chalice in our recent *Harpstrings of Lemuria* poster. The concept of flight is an archetypal image of the soul taking flight, the psychological preparation for any eventuality. The flight of the soul is another expression of adaptation and transition in other octaves, but it also has to do with the woman clothed with the sun, who is given the wings of an eagle to carry her into the wilderness and protect her from the dragon.[1]

The sense of flight is part of the great drama of the life of Jesus. Jesus is born. The angel appears to Joseph and says, "Take the child and go into Egypt." And the flight into Egypt is the name of that particular chapter in their lives.

So this flight has to do with the understanding that in this moment of the intense acceleration of evil, there is a legitimate step and initiation of taking flight. The Psalmist spoke of it when he said, "If I ascend up into heaven or make my bed in hell or dwell in the uttermost parts of the sea, behold, thou art there."[2]

83. Verily, it is necessary to have ten exit lanes for one fire. Strong is an action when there are ten solutions behind it. The inexperienced need a fire behind them, but those

who have been called may find all the entrances open.

One must be able to understand how bends the sword blade of the enemy; to smile when the trampling of the enemy's horse is heard; to understand not to stoop when the arrow flies above the head.

84. It is difficult to absorb the large, but it is still more difficult to absorb the small through a broadened consciousness. It is difficult to apply to a small reality a measure of great understanding. How could one insert a big sword into a small scabbard?

Only a tested consciousness understands the value of the seed of reality. Rulership is not in crowns nor in crowds, but is in the cosmic expanse of ideas. Thus, the Teachings of life complement each other, having no need to attract multitudes.

You were told that I would give a third book when the community is accepted. Yet multitudes are not needed by Us; only the consciousnesses of those who accept are needed by Us. That is why We give the third book. Therefore We reiterate about the facets of Truth, and hence We prefer to bless upon birth instead of taking upon Ourselves funeral processions.

For some it is necessary to trumpet the Teaching into the ears, for others one may only set the landmarks, for still others it is possible only to give monosyllabic hints, if their consciousness can contain ever-so-little. How then does the Teaching welcome those who can take in each and every crumb, esteeming the universal significance of each of them!

The crumbling of eons shifts entire worlds. For that reason your thoughts are directed toward preservation of mental energy.

85. Each organism is moved by a particular energy, but it is necessary to establish the precise direction of the basic aspiration. Once the disciples asked the Blessed One how to understand the fulfillment of the commandment of renun-

ciation of property. After one disciple had abandoned all things, the Teacher continued to reproach him in the matter of possessions. Another remained surrounded by things yet did not draw reproval. The feeling of ownership is measured not by things but by thoughts. Thus, the community must be accepted by the consciousness. One may have objects and yet not be an owner.

The Teacher sends the wish that evolution grow lawfully. The Teacher can distinguish those who have liberated their consciousnesses. Thus said the Blessed One; and He asked in general not to think about ownership of property, for renunciation is a cleansing of thought. For only through purified channels can basic striving make its way.

86. I call to mind a tale heard by Akbar. A sovereign asked a sage: "How do you tell a nest of treason from a stronghold of loyalty?" The wise man pointed to a crowd of gaily-dressed horsemen and said: "There is a nest of treason." Then he indicated a solitary wayfarer and said: "There is a stronghold of devotion, for solitude can betray nothing." And from that day on the sovereign surrounded himself with fidelity.

The Teacher has accepted the full measure of faithfulness. My Hand is to the hand of the wayfarer as fire in the darkness. My Shield has the tranquillity of the mountains. I know, I know, how straitened it is for My Community. The revelation of the bases of construction is manifested in quietude.

Understanding of matter can grow only where treason is impossible.

87. When a difficulty with inheritance presents itself, it may be said that it is possible to leave to the community the wish that the use of certain objects be given over to a certain person for a trial period of three years. Thus the inheritance will be turned into a worthy cooperation. One may entrust specially chosen people to look after the quality of

certain works. It is needful to fill the consciousness with a realization of continuous test, for people still do not know how to work under test. Meanwhile the whole substance of the world is engaged in mutual testing. But one should understand that testing means also improvement.

88. We always begin with a very small outline. This is an experiment very many centuries old and is also a basic cosmic principle. A solid and indivisible seed will produce a growth of elements. But wavering and lack of sensitiveness, repeatedly manifesting, result in haziness. The sensitiveness of the vital principle compels economizing with firm seeds. Thus, the chemist values indivisible bodies. Truly, the structural unit must be inviolable when it has been called forth by the necessity of evolution. One should understand the distinction between that which is admitted and that which is incontestably given.

89. Our Community does not need affirmations and oaths. Genuine are the expenditures of labor, and unforgettable are the manifestations of obligation. Can there possibly be prolixity where lives have been taken into custody—where an hour may become the longest measure? Could one betray the possibilities of a time when spirit and movement are being denied? It is necessary to overcome timidity, to sense the vortex of the spiral, and in the heart of the vortex to have the tranquillity of courage.

So much have I said about courage and against fear, because We have only a cosmic scientific method! At entrance one must make accounting to oneself as to where is fear and whether the courage is steadfast.

I do not see a single detail of dialectics or methodics. We know only the austere flowers of necessity. And it is necessary to reach Us carrying a realization of immutability.

Austerity is not insensibility, and immutability is not limitation. Through all the gravitation of the firmament you will sense the vortex of space, and you will stretch forth your hand to the far-off worlds. It is impossible to force the perception of the manifestation of the worlds; but, indeed, through this cognizance do we accept responsible labor and devote ourselves to the real possibilities of evolution.

Become a Firm Pillar

90. In order to understand mobility of action, one should muddy the surface of water in a basin and observe the immobility of the lower strata of the fluid. To move it, it is necessary to stir the surface sufficiently strongly that the rhythm may carry to the bottom without break. Negative forces do not have a conduit to the bottom, because for this it is needed to decompose the primary substance; such an experiment is beyond their strength.

Newcomers often inquire where the boundary line is between a mobile stratum and an incontestable foundation. Indeed, there can be no established boundary, but the law of refraction is established, and an arrow cannot reach without intersecting the predetermined line.

How then to prevent the dealing of a blow to the strata? Indeed, it is necessary to provide for firm pillars, which will break up a current. I have mentioned the spindle of the spirit as the center of a spiral. Keep this structure in mind, because inflexibility, surrounded by centrifugal motion, can resist all agitations. The structure of Our Community calls to mind the same spindles surrounded by powerful spirals. It is the best structure for the battle, the end of which is a foregone conclusion. Thus, it is necessary to understand Our structures materially.

Number 90 is talking about the survival of community. It speaks of "firm pillars, which will break up a current," and of how "the spindle of the spirit" is the center of a spiral. The spindle is the center pole around which the spiral turns. And El Morya is talking about how your mind, surrounded by the centrifugal motion of the spiral, can resist all agitation.

How does the community survive? By pillars in its center. You are the pillar. Around you the force of your aura, your dynamism, forms a spiral that resists all agitation. The structure of our community is formed of the same spindles that are surrounded by the powerful spirals of individuals.

"It is the best structure for the battle, the end of which is a foregone conclusion." Think about the inflexibility of God, Elohim or El Morya to the encroachment of destructive forces against the community. That is what you have to think about, not inflexibility in the relative sense, which is the yin and yang sense of the interplay of forces.

But God is absolute and inflexible. And this center spiral of being is what is spoken of here.

It is important for you to understand that community is the foundation of the goal. The point of continuing Summit University is to become a pillar with a surrounding spiral that reinforces community.

An Opportunity to Join Community

Until an individual decides who he is and what he wants to be, there's a point beyond which I cannot teach him. Therefore, I suggest to you the opportunity of that community, that intimate interchange with a messenger who has as its life, its goal, its very consciousness, the preservation of the cradle for the birth of the Messiah in every individual in the community, in incoming souls and ultimately in the world.

That's what community is, a cradle. And Summit University invites those who want to sort themselves out from the gravel, like pebbles on a beach, and realize that they want to be a "pillar in the temple of my God."[3] They can then come into service in community, and these are the individuals with whom the master can work directly, in a day-to-day interchange. I need to work with these people personally.

The lessons you need for survival in the world and for your

own individual path are given through the dictations and the lectures that you are hearing. They take you far on the path of individual Christhood, and they may very well take you to your ascension. For who knows what great avatar lies embedded in the very heart of any one of your souls?

I do not question that there is a limitless, boundless future for every individual, but I know that passing through the initiations of community, close to the masters, close to the messenger, is the unique and necessary experience for many. If you are one of those many who are in need of the organization of the Great White Brotherhood for initiation, for testing, for the ascent, then it is to you that I open the door at the conclusion of Summit University. I offer you the opportunity to come into the ranks of those in community teaching centers and at our international headquarters.

This is what I would like you to get out of the remainder of *New Era Community.* There is much truth in it, and it can provide you with the key to your life.

The Word and the Work

New Era Community tells you that those who do not love the work of the sacred labor of the community spin off. They may have many excuses, but in the last analysis they don't like to work. They don't have the love of the work. The Word and the Work of our Lord and Saviour Jesus Christ is what we are all about.

The Work is the yin side of the Word. The Word is the incarnation of the LORD in you; the Work is the action of the Holy Ghost, the manifestation. The proof that you are the living Word is your work, your handiwork. The proof that God is God is the cosmos he has created. He has left a record of his Word in his Work, and so have you.

The chela is discovered as he pursues his sacred labor. He is on the receiving end of the teaching, and by his love of the teaching he can serve and serve. Our never-ending joy is to think, "If I can get out this poster, someone will drink of the cup, someone will find God." That is the strength and the joy and the love, and that is why people find their niche in the organization. Morya says that there is an intensity in community, an accelerating spiral that forces the best and the worst out of everyone.

Your worst comes to the surface to be skimmed off; your best accelerates, and you become God. This is the scientific process of the ascension. No greater process has ever been invented by Almighty God than the guru-chela relationship within a community, for in addition to the ascension of its members, the community has as its goal holding the light and enlightening the earth. What we have, we must preserve and evolve those solutions.

Many who have caught the spark of community are already so busy serving they don't have time to come to Summit University. Some arrived before we founded the university and never had time to go. They are too busy being the Christ to be able to take the time and learn how to be the Christ. It is an amazing process, but they get it in the guru-chela relationship.

When it comes right down to it, the key to chelaship is to say, "Ok, I'm here. I'll go to work for the Brotherhood. I'll learn anything I have to learn. I'm giving my life to God, and I'm never looking back." Even so, some people just do not fit in. They will not take direction, or they will only accept direction from the messenger. If the messenger said it, they'll do it. But if somebody else said it, they won't do it.

For example, a young man came and joined a stump team. It was a two-man team, and this person was under the person in charge. He said, "I won't take orders from so-and-so," and it was a personality clash the whole trip. Therefore, because of the in-harmony, the effectiveness of both men was greatly reduced.

Initiations

I am sure you have all heard about going to a retreat situation on inner levels, a situation of initiation. Everybody gets his head shaved, puts on a white garment and is thrown in a room with people he has envied or with whom he has experienced all kinds of human conditions for the last sixteen embodiments. And until he resolves his conflicts, he doesn't get out of that room.

That's the standard picture of the inner-level discipline. It's the same kind of thing in the community with the added factor of joy. It is not so stern, not so strict. We have fun, joy, freedom and an infinite capacity to learn and grow. But it all comes down to the question of whether or not you can learn to work with a group.

The masters explain in the second *Keepers of the Flame Lesson*[4] that one of the basic tests on the Path is, can you work in an organization? The lesson describes how people with spiritual pride will turn up their noses and say, "I am through with organizations. I will not work with a group. I will be a solitary climber."

Ask yourself the question, Can I work in a group? Can I take responsibility in a department? Can I acknowledge someone whom I may think is uglier than I am, inferior to me, less experienced than I am, younger, older or whatever, and say, "All right, I accept that person as my department head and as the person through whom I relate to the messenger"?

If you can, you then fulfill your tests in that department. If you can prove yourself in six months to be a great follower and a person of responsibility, you will rise quickly to a leadership position. I have seen people become department heads and leaders in this activity in two years. Saint Germain and Morya say that it takes ten years to train people to be ultimate leaders. It certainly takes that much training to receive the responsibility for a large area of our operation.

Once when I was a teenager I was supervising a cabin of girls at a summer camp. I was supposed to be keeping them still at night, but they were hopping up and down and having a gay old time when they should have been in bed. I was the teenage sergeant who had to tell the other teenagers to go to bed at nine o'clock at night in the summertime.

I was sitting outside the cabin on a rock, and oh, it was a big, heavy experience! And I said, "O Lord, please, if there is one thing you must do for me in this embodiment, please don't give me responsibility over other people, please don't make me a leader." It was a very solemn occasion. "I will do whatever you want me to do, but.... "

We who have been leaders in other lifetimes and are natural leaders know that it is very difficult to pull people around. They pull against you, and you feel like you're pulling mules and oxen —you pull this way, and they pull the other. But our whole civilization today is in dire need of leaders. In fact, it is crumbling for lack of leaders.

Leadership is also needed here in the white-fire core. I need the right person to carry my flame and be neither tyrannical nor overly indulgent. I need someone to hold the line of love and discipline and be responsible for a group of chelas, for outreach and for the whole image of community.

I continue to train department heads, and they are the ones who get the most intense fire from me. As they increase in light, they pass it on to those under them. I think it is exciting to be under creative leaders who have mastered a certain discipline under El Morya. I think it is the greatest opportunity a person can have.

Nevertheless, no matter what you are doing—publishing, radio, Summit University, painting the property, Montessori training—in the back of everybody's mind is the importance of the survival of community. We hold the treasure of the planet and we must run with it and we must survive with it. We have to secure our base, and from that base we will go out into the world—as long as there is a world to go out into.

One longtime staff member took her ascension to hold the balance for community. She gave her life for its survival. Her real mission at inner levels was to safeguard the life of the messenger, the chela and the community.[5]

Secure an Outpost
of the Great White Brotherhood

Our decrees to the All-Seeing Eye and the Great Divine Director and Surya are most important. I have stressed the calls to Surya because Sirius is the seat of the Great White Brotherhood, the God Star, and my real mission on earth is to secure the survival of an outpost of the Great White Brotherhood.

If you read about Blavatsky and the accounts of the masters' work through her, through the Roerichs, through the "I AM" Movement and through this activity, you can see what the masters have gone through to raise up the few who would be loyal to them and carry their flame. It almost brings you to tears.

Yet, when the Great White Brotherhood is not publishing and does not have an outpost, there is nowhere for people to go but to past history. They go back and read Theosophy or they read Alice Bailey or the "I AM" books, but they need a fire that is burning today. They need a live flame, not dead coals.

To me there is no greater mission than to serve the Brotherhood. And when I have anyone who shares that vision with me and wants to give his life to that cause, then I can give myself to that person and that person gives himself to me, and then I will spare nothing. When it is in my line of service to do so, I will take time to interview, to correct, to talk to and to counsel that person. But in a staff of five hundred there is much you can learn from those I have already trained who are over you.

Where Does the Lord Have Need of You?

Today you are all considering where you should go after Summit University. And in answer to your questions, spoken and unspoken, here is my response. I believe in the Path because I know the Path works, and I advise people according to what I see and know. You need to make your decisions on the basis of what you want to do. It's not where you are in space, but what is the quality of your consciousness as a chela.

To me your decision should be based on where the Lord has need of you, not on your personal preference. I feel that God has generously offered this community as a place to carry on our spiritual development. You can serve here, go to school, participate in the outreach program and help me hold the activity together. Here is where you will develop the most, for spiritual development will be going on at all levels. That is my advice to everybody except those who have a family and a business. That's the way I see it.

As a messenger I came up this way. It worked for me. It has worked for everybody I have ever known who has ascended. I have never seen anybody accelerate faster than through this particular situation. Therefore, if you come and ask me what you should do, that is what I am going to say. That is my answer. If you want to do something else, you have my blessing—go do it. But if you want to know what I think is best for you, it will be the same answer.

I am being very honest with you because that's the way I see life. That's the way I was taught. I was with Jesus.[6] I baked bread in his household. I could have gone to the famous universities of the time. I could have been off getting educated with Saul of Tarsus. I could have said, "I'm not experiencing any personal development here. All I'm doing is cleaning house and cooking meals."

At one point I even chided Mary for not helping me because she was listening to what Jesus was saying.[7]

That's how I came to be what I am. Jesus gave me his being. He transferred his total identity to me in those three years so that in every embodiment since, I could carry on his mission and even become a messenger today.

In two thousand years I went from baking bread for Jesus to being a messenger. Two thousand years is like the blink of an eye. I have had many gurus. Saint Francis was my guru, and he was also my guru in India in a previous incarnation. King Arthur was my guru. Lanello was my guru. I have been under these individuals directly. I have been their daughters, their wives.

Whatever I did in the last two thousand years, whether as a nun or something else, what was important to me was not what I did with my hands. What mattered was that I was in closest proximity to the master. Then everything else fell into line. I am what I am today because of that, because that is where I placed value.

From my experience, nothing in the universe is more important than being as close as you can to the one who is the closest to the Brotherhood. I wouldn't trade being next to Saint Francis for a million years of whatever else you can do in this world. Knowing Saint Francis personally has to be the greatest gift that anybody could have besides knowing Jesus Christ personally and knowing Saint Germain.

What did I do when I was with Francis? I was in charge of the Poor Clares. I got up at four in the morning, got them up, made their breakfast, fed them, was in charge of them and worried about running the monastery. I wasn't out improving my mind at the local university. I was doing what needed to be done to hold the community together. To me that is the direct path to sainthood. I've proven it. You can agree with me or not, and I'll love you just the same. I'll always love you, but the cause has to survive. The Brotherhood has to survive.

Catherine of Siena was illiterate until she was in her twenties. She grew up in a poor Italian family and did nothing but pray and talk to Jesus. She had this personal relationship with Jesus. One day either she decided or Jesus decided that she ought to learn to read and write. She applied herself and learned to read and write.

Catherine then wrote letters to the pope, to the bishops, to the heads of state, urging them to follow God. And these letters are considered classics. She became a messenger and wrote down the *Dialogue*. But the important thing is that she put Jesus first. He taught her to read and write, and he put his words in her mouth, and the Catholic Church recognizes her as a messenger of God.

The *Dialogue* of Saint Catherine of Siena was dictated by Almighty God to her, and the Catholic Church accepted it! It is an amazing thing to be illiterate until you're in your twenties. It was especially so for me, as I have pursued education for hundreds and thousands of years. But it was one of those experiences that God uses to show how a soul with the Holy Ghost can rise and conquer and can become of great value to our church.

Let us conclude here for today.

⁂

In the name of Almighty God, in the name of the Christ, I call for a circle of white fire and blue lightning around each chela of the light in this group. I call to you, beloved El Morya, to prepare them this night for their initiations tomorrow. Prepare them now for the final sealing and transmutation of their energies.

I call for Morya's angels and Victory's angels to prepare you through your heart chakra, all of your chakras, for the inner alignment with the will of God. In the name of the Father, the Son, the Mother and the Holy Spirit, Amen.

Camelot
December 5, 1979

CHAPTER 5

The Education of the Heart

I*n the name of the I AM THAT I AM, I call for the light of the World Teachers, beloved Jesus and Kuthumi, beloved Mother Mary and beloved Archangel Raphael. I call for the quickening light of the precipitation flame. I call for the full power of the flame of precipitation from the heart of the Royal Teton Retreat.*

I call for the mighty emerald ray with the yellow tinge. I call for the full power of the action of that green light and that mighty, magnificent Cosmic Christ illumination to infire these hearts. I call for the enfiring of the hearts of the students and those who are their teachers. I call forth the light of God that never fails to accelerate our God consciousness, of the trans-mittal of the Word in the earth through every child of God.

I call forth the mantle. I call for the sponsoring light of the legions of angels of Raphael, legions of angels of beloved Mother Mary, of Lourdes and Fátima. I call forth the light of the blessed home of Mother Mary to be upon this Community of the Holy Spirit.

The light of God never fails. The light of God never fails. The light of God never fails and the beloved mighty I AM Presence is that light. In the name of the Father and of the Mother, of the Son and of the Holy Spirit, Amen.

I am very happy to welcome our new Montessori teacher training students to Summit University and to our lectures on *New Era Community.* I am also happy that the World Teachers and beloved Mother Mary and Archangel Raphael have determined to sponsor this quarter for the education of the heart. The heart is the point of the emanation of light and the point of the original relationship of the teacher to the student that begins with God's relationship to man.

God is the original teacher of man. Maitreya is the original teacher of our twin flames in the Garden of Eden, and the oral transmission of the Word is the highest form of teaching. We will study how we have moved away from this original teacher, the teaching and the method itself. We will look at how distortions of the method even through print itself and manipulation for motive have brought us an educational system that is untenable for the children of God.

In America today, we have an educational system that is for the fallen ones and the robot creation. We have medicine for them and a medical system. We have music for them. We have drugs for them. Everything caters to the mechanical consciousness and attempts to place the children of God within that mechanical consciousness. Therefore, our desire in education is to go back to the original guru-chela relationship.

The guru-chela relationship cannot survive on earth without community. Community is the circle that is protected by its members. It is a hallowed circle in which God educates his children. If we had this teaching today without the community, the teaching would not survive, nor would we have the opportunity to act collectively to change world conditions.

Pythagoras saw this, and so did all the teachers who founded the mystery schools. Therefore, it is no accident that you, the students of Maria Montessori, are here today, or that you should be present for our ongoing discussion on the book *New Era Community.*

Our concern for the education of children in community is paramount. If we cannot transmit our understanding of the teaching to the children, the community will not survive. And as teachers-to-be, the expansion of community is your mission also.

The Community of Ancient Israel

First, let us take a step back and look at the community of ancient Israel. The greatest prophet to walk the earth in our time, the prophet Samuel, recognized the need for community. He came to establish the nation of Israel. He also came to oversee the twelve tribes, who were born to work on the initiations of the twelve solar hierarchies so that in the community there would always be the balanced manifestation of the twelve solar lights. Entire lifewaves have been born on each of these levels of initiation on the twelve lines of the clock.

The community of Israel did not survive because the people disobeyed the guru. Although the people had lost the guru Maitreya long before, they had to wait centuries before eventually gaining their next guru, Moses. When they disobeyed Moses, the grace of the person of God was replaced by the Law.

The Law that God gave to Moses on Horeb at Sinai was a stepping down of their initiation. It was as though God was saying, "You have not followed the person of your guru, therefore I will give you a set of laws fit for the hard-hearted and stiff-necked people that you have become. If you obey these laws, one day you may again earn the grace of having the person of the guru with you."

However, the laws were not obeyed, the judges were not obeyed, the prophets were not obeyed, the kings became corrupt, and, as a result, the Israelite peoples were dispersed. They were dispersed and reunited, dispersed and reunited again, and now they are in their third dispersion, ready to be reunited.

And the path of their reunification is now the path of the ruby ray. Therefore, we realize that a set of laws, given to a group of people and followed without love, becomes another dead ritual, or mechanization concept.

Lord Maitreya gave me a great teaching on this. Unless you have love for the Lawgiver, your efforts to follow the Law will be a rote performance, and you therefore turn the code of Moses into a mechanical formula. This is why we have been taught that we were under the law until Jesus Christ came, when grace replaced the Law. The person of Christ became the salvation of the people rather than just the Law without the presence of the Lawgiver.

Jesus was the incarnate Word, which means he was the incarnate Lawgiver. Through his grace, individuals are expected to continue to obey the Law, but they also have a higher law, which is the figure-eight flow between the disciple and the guru.

When we have the guru, all who come under the guru's love and who in turn love the guru, are now under the dispensation of that guru's karma. Their karma may be transmuted in service, surrender, sacrifice and love (the path of the ruby ray) through the higher karma of the guru.

The karma of God, the Great Guru, is his Word and his Work, which is altogether perfect. Then you have the karma of the messenger, which counts for the whole community. The messenger sets forth rules and regulations, as did Jesus Christ, and teachings that must be obeyed.

Unless they are obeyed through love, they may also become a form of mechanization whereby individuals seek a mechanical relationship to the messenger. This will not suffice. It will not fulfill the requirement of the Law. For unless the student loves the person of the messenger as well as the message, he cannot make it on the Path. That is what thousands of years of history have taught us ever since time and space began.

This is fundamental teaching because, as students here, you are applying to be the representatives of the World Teachers. You are coming to learn to be teachers, and you would like to go forth wearing the mantle of the World Teachers.* In that sense you are all extensions of the guru, the whole lineage of the gurus, from Sanat Kumara down.

Therefore, to be what you desire to be, it is not enough to learn the rules and regulations—the Law and the teaching. You must love the teacher who is behind the teaching and love the

---

*The ascended masters Jesus and Kuthumi hold the office of World Teachers.

mission behind the teaching. Then that love engenders within you the love of community.

Becoming a Teacher in the Lineage of the Gurus

Community is the third of the trinity of El Morya's three dots: the guru, the teaching, the community (the Buddha, the Dharma and the Sangha). And the guru implies the guru-chela relationship, the teacher and the community. Unless you have these three, you never have the means whereby the individual can have his ultimate attainment.

A time will come when you will go forth to various points on the globe and be the lone teacher there. You will come into a community, and you will begin again the whole process of the ascended masters' community through that contact with the child. You may deal with parents who are not in the teachings, but your consciousness of community will be your heart, linked with the hearts of the children. Whether the children understand community or not, community is always forged of the oneness of the Christ Self of the teacher and the pupils.

Since the Montessori method teaches us that the Christ Self is the teacher of the child, then the classroom teacher must have the ultimate relationship to the original Guru, beginning with Almighty God, Sanat Kumara, Gautama Buddha, Lord Maitreya, Lord Jesus Christ and the embodied messengers who sponsor that flame.

The child's understanding of community depends upon the oneness of the teacher's Christ Self and that of the pupil. According to how perfect your love relationship is to that Christ Self, so will be your ability to contact the Christ in the child. The Christ in the child will not receive you unless you have a proper reverence for that Christ, for the guru.

Thus, if pride or a sense of superiority or faulty reasoning is lurking within your desire to teach, you will not succeed. It is a great fallacy to say, "I will go and get the credentials; I will submit myself to this method and then go out on my own. I will not have to be a part of the community or be in a direct relationship to the messenger."

The God consciousness of the earth is transferred by this momentum of the entire Spirit of the Great White Brotherhood and by initiation. Some think they will enter the mystery school to pluck the fruit and run with it. They do not realize that the moment they do that, they lose themselves as a link in the chain of hierarchy.

The concept of the Great White Brotherhood is that you are an outpost of the Brotherhood wherever you are on the face of the earth, and this is because you have a right relationship to God and the ascended masters, to the embodied messenger and to every other chela.

Then you are in perfect alignment with the Christ Self of the child. And, therefore, you are worthy to be called *teacher* in the Montessori sense of the word. This is why we have set the higher levels of Summit University to be the place for this training, because those who want to be Montessori teachers but who do not want to become a part of the guru-chela relationship should go elsewhere. They should not ask for the sponsorship of the Great White Brotherhood.

The Oral Tradition of the Gurus

Implicit in your presence here is the understanding that you desire the guru-chela relationship with El Morya and with the World Teachers, with Mother Mary, with Raphael and with the ascended lady master Maria Montessori. Then you will have the great fount and source of the teaching all the way from the very beginning.

Starting with the Upanishads, the teachings were spoken in the oral tradition and memorized. The teachings of the prophets and the Christ were also orally transmitted from disciple to disciple. As teachers, you also transmit orally, because the little child is not yet able to read, and until he reads, he has the perfect attunement of the inner ear to receive the word of God.

Imagine, then, a situation in which the little child, who is in listening grace, is given the Word by a teacher who is impure because the teacher has an impure relationship to God. Imagine also all that has happened to manipulate education by political forces. The power elite has designed educational systems to subdue the children of God and adapt the robot creation to a very boring existence of servility to the state.

You can see that a teacher who does not speak to the child out of the flame of God is committing the greatest crime in the universe. He is seizing the mantle of the Great God, the original Guru, and is writing upon the clean white page of innocent and unsuspecting souls something other than the vibration of this perfect attunement.

The Flame of the Holy Spirit in Community

I wish to bring to you a deeper understanding of the meaning of the flame of community. It is the flame of the Holy Spirit, hence it is the flame of love. The figure-eight flow of love that stands between the guru and the chela contains the entire community, and it contains the worldwide community of the unascended chelas of the Great White Brotherhood.

Visualize God as the Great Guru, and visualize yourself as the chela. The Spirit-Matter cosmos actually hangs on these two points, these two extremities of the plus and the minus. Then think about us, one upon one, and the great love we share for one another. We share it because we love God in one another.

I am the devotee of the God in your heart. That is the God I worship. That is the God who is in the earth. To me, the chela is that point of my ultimate devotion in Matter, and that devotion is an intense fire of love.

By the returning current that becomes an accelerated momentum, the community is actually built. Its foundation, its physical buildings, its publishing—all that the community does on a planetary scale—is infused with this light and love. It's a perfect attunement and harmony.

Our hearts are one. They actually fuse. You can see the heart chakras of the guru and the chelas as one flaming sun. It is an indestructible union. It cannot be broken because love has fused it together as one. It is the same concept in marriage; love makes two people become one—the twain become one. And the sense of one flesh is the sense of the fusion of their individuality for a higher purpose. And so the marriage and the commitment of the guru to the chela is complete.

This is the generation of creative fohat, the very fire upon which all material civilization is built. This is an immense concept. It has immense proportions. And we find that civilizations have failed where there has not been the relationship in sufficient expansion to hold the balance for the number of embodied individuals.

The point/counterpoint of the fallen ones has been to substitute scientific humanism and animal man as their standard. They have stubbornly insisted for thousands of years that civilization can survive on that basis. But it will not survive. If it does not crumble by the very fact that it doesn't work, it crumbles because elemental life, who are the representatives of the Holy Spirit, rise up and overthrow it.

We have seen the very action of the elementals this weekend, how they must destroy that which would destroy the guru-chela relationship. They must come and balance the energy that has been put out by the fallen ones, the general consciousness that always sees mechanization man and the mechanized solution as superior to the God solution.

The warnings in the weather cause people to sober up because they instinctively read nature as God. Although in our present culture people are indoctrinated to think that nature and God have nothing to do with each other, in their subconscious there is still the memory that God always enacts his judgment through elemental life.

Community as the Foundation for the Golden Age

We come together to lay the foundation for the golden-age civilization. It is a very exciting moment. You are receiving each day the beautiful teachings of Maria Montessori coming through Elisabeth Caspari. We are most grateful for Mme. Caspari's presence here, as she transmits the flame of Maria Montessori.[1]

I want to give you this foundation of the sense of the commitment to community. It is never commitment to the outer person but always to the vision of the glowing Christ within. He is the reality to whom we give our devotion. We are always devoted to the person of the Christ in one another, and we have great love and affection for the soul, who is reaching for that Christ.

We never exclude the soul, and love only the absolute. We love all the components of being, and students will always feel this love, the desire to feel embraced by the guru. Jesus lamented over Jerusalem, saying: "O Jerusalem, Jerusalem, thou that killest the prophets and stonest them which are sent unto thee, how often would I have gathered thy children together, even as a hen gathereth her chickens under her wings, but ye would not."[2]

The symbol of the brooding hen with her chicks under her feathers is the great symbol of the guru and his chelas. In that lament, Jesus was saying that because the people would not enter into the guru-chela relationship or receive the Messiah in their hearts, their houses would be desolate until they could say, "Blessed is he that cometh in the name of the Lord."[3]

In other words, because they had rejected the person of grace and the guru-chela relationship, their temples would be without the Holy Ghost, without the threefold flame, without God consciousness. Their families would also be devoid of it, and so would their communities, their synagogues, their generations and their civilization.

The Lord pronounced this judgment then, and it has been so ever since. All who reject him have been deprived of the flow of light that would have enabled their temples to become the habitation of the Most High God.

The Final Opportunity to Choose the Guru

Once I told a chela that this was his final opportunity to make the choice. And the choice I was referring to was whether or not to enter into the guru-chela relationship.

He asked, "Do you mean it's either the ascension or the second death?"

I said, "Of course not. I am not speaking in such terms. I'm speaking of the final opportunity we have to choose Maitreya, to choose Gautama, to choose Jesus, to choose Sanat Kumara and to choose the Christ within ourselves."

What is the second death? The second death in itself is nothing more than the experience someone might have in taking an overdose of drugs with a hypodermic needle, going into an unconscious state and then dying. It is painless to the one experiencing it. But the truth is that the person was dead before he went through the second death. He was dead before he took the overdose of drugs.

So what is death? My concept of death is the absence of the guru in my life. I cannot live without the guru. And so the only death I could know is to be out of grace with Almighty God. This, to me, would be death. The mere canceling out of the remnant of what was once a person would be immaterial.

Therefore, when we say that it is final, we have to consider it as such because we have no guarantee of the future. All the future is in the now. The establishment of your right relationship to your mighty I AM Presence and the masters is the key to your God-success as teachers.

If you take up this teaching with the utmost devotion and determination, you can revolutionize education on earth. But if you do it mechanically by having all your books, your exercises and your equipment in order, you will have created only the bowl. Unless you infuse the bowl with the flame, you will not succeed.

The Flame in the Bowl

The flame in the bowl of Summit University is the person of the guru. That is the flame of community. And there is no end to the succession, because behind the one visible is the entire invisible chain of hierarchy. Consequently, we can never say that only one person is the guru; yet there is only one guru. The I AM is the only Guru, but the succession of being is that the Guru is all Being.

When you teach your children, you wear the mantle of the guru in relationship to them. You must be accorded the respect of that office, and you must demand it from your students. It is the only way the identity of the guru can be preserved. If you should happen to think that a mechanical performance of the Montessori method is going to revolutionize education, I would point out to you that the Montessori method has been with us for over half a century, and it has not yet brought about the desired results.

Why not? Not because it is not the correct method, but because it has not had apostles and proponents who were willing to make the necessary sacrifice to embody the flame of Mother Mary, who is the author of that system, as well as the flame of Maria Montessori.

A dispensation is always far above man, but it uses man to be manifest. Jesus Christ gave the perfect teaching on religion to revolutionize the planet. Yet Christianity has failed to do this, not because the message was not perfect but because the apostles were not willing to be slain of the Holy Spirit and to have everything that was not of the light removed from them.

Your devotion to your path demands that you give your all to the teacher; otherwise, you will not transfer it to the child. Let us think of how millions of people have failed because of the mechanization concept. Let us be humble before the fact that God never errs in his Law; he never errs in his covenant. He has established it this way from the beginning. Those who followed it have ascended; those who did not, have not ascended.

God Refuses to Compromise

If people think that the Almighty will be changed and conditioned by situation ethics, I recommend that they listen to a dictation by the Elohim of Purity. Purity spoke at a cosmic council meeting that was deliberating whether or not there should be an allowance made for infractions of the Law by the youth of America.

Their understanding of the standards of God has moved far away from the original interpretation of God's laws. Nonetheless, Purity came forth with the most astounding message of power, saying that the flame of cosmic purity would never be compromised and that the people of earth would have to rise to its level in order to receive its blessing.[4] That was spoken in Los Angeles through Mark Prophet at the First International Re-Source Conference.

It was a most astounding manifestation of God's refusal to compromise. Then along comes the proud human being, the puny, proud little man who believes in situation ethics and who says, "This time I'm going to prove that I can become great, and then I will be a god." And once again man begins to build his systems on sand.

Within the framework of human science and human knowledge those systems seem sound, but put them against the backdrop of Elohim, nature and elemental life, and they crumble when elemental life adjusts the earth to bring it back to a semblance of the inner matrix of God harmony.

I want to emphasize this because it is the great temptation of the anti-guru, who was taught by the Serpent in the garden, to seek an alternative. For example, the Serpent might say, "Here is the Montessori method. Well and good, but I will change it." Today Montessori schools all over America are led by people influenced by Dewey,[5] by social engineering, by concepts of education that stress social interaction rather than attunement with the God flame. They avoid mastering the basic disciplines of education.

A God Who Transcends Himself

You must understand the difference between the human innovators and the divine revelators. God, as the I AM THAT I AM, revealed himself to Moses when Moses asked his identity, and the use of the verb *to be* has a very profound meaning. It was the use of the first person singular of the verb, I AM. It was I AM THAT I AM. It was also I WILL BE WHAT I WILL BE.

In other words, "I will reveal myself to you, Moses, in the outworking of the events of the people of Israel. As I interact with them, you will know me and know who I AM." It was basic instruction that said: "Moses, I could give you a name, but a name would not tell you my identity. You will learn to know me as you interact with me."

What kind of a God is this? A God who is self-transcendent. A God who is continually transcending himself through the spiral of a continually expanding cosmic consciousness.

The fallen ones have made God into a static god, an idol, something that never changes in the sense that it is confined to a given matrix, a mechanistic god that you can predict and therefore outsmart. But I AM THAT I AM, Jehovah, is the unpredictable God. Because he is transcending himself, he cannot be predicted.

The teaching of the self-transcendent God is revolutionary. It would be blasphemy to those in orthodoxy because it would seem to imply that God can improve himself, which is not correct. God is perfection, but perfection has an infinite capacity to multiply itself, to expand itself more and more and more in the Matter universe.

If God were not a self-transcendent God, he would not have created you and placed himself inside of you to multiply, increase and take dominion over the earth.[6] The command to multiply and take dominion over the earth is to multiply God consciousness, to increase God consciousness and take dominion in the Matter spheres.

This is the very foundation of our theology. It is most sacred. It is one of the great inner mysteries that you must not take for granted. God is continually expanding. His universe is expanding. You are expanding. It is all the same original light or flame, but out of that flame infinity is in infinite progression.

Therefore, revelation. God has a need to continually reveal himself because man is evolving, and God is increasing the manifestation of his light through man. Therefore, we accept progressive revelation, and we believe that God will have more to say to us tomorrow than he does today. Those who do not have the guru-chela relationship, those who have not contacted the fount, the source of the Montessori method are not able to be the instruments of the progressive revelation of that method.

Succeeding Revelation and the Montessori Method

If God is a self-transcendent God, then the Montessori method itself is a living organism. It, too, expands, but it will not expand through individuals who are part of the mechanization concept, who take the method and infuse it with their theories of anti-education or the anti-guru.

So there are those who have the authority to infuse the classroom with the light of ongoing revelation, and there are those who do not. Those who have the authority are they who have earned a right relationship to Maria Montessori, to Mother Mary, to the World Teachers and to their own God Presence.

What sort of revelation am I speaking about? I am speaking about the fact that the ascended masters have come forth with Saint Germain's revelation of the violet flame since Maria Montessori received her matrix. The matrix is the foundation, but we are still building the superstructure.

The teachings of the ascended masters are a revelation in

themselves. And as you contain the succeeding revelations of the method, you are called upon to evolve ways of presenting the materials so that starting at two-and-a-half years of age, a child can have materials that enable him to understand his relationship to his inner teacher, the Christ Self, to the mighty I AM Presence, the violet flame, the paths of the seven rays, the twelve tribes of Israel and the principles of community.

Our children must have as much opportunity to learn the ascended masters' teaching through their sense perceptions— through their desire to touch and feel and do exercises—as they have with secular subjects. So here is an entire opportunity for this revelation on your part. God is no respecter of persons. He reveals himself to the devout heart.

Imagine materials in geometric form that can be handled, that illustrate to the child his relationship to the Infinite and to the stars. The equipment we have already is the open door to this, and we can see that the Brotherhood may come with revelations in every field of human endeavor, including the path of chelaship. We must be ready to see to it that these can be transferred within the method.

I believe that it is up to those who understand the Montessori method to evolve a Sunday School program for our children. Ruth Jones, who taught Sunday School in the Baptist Church, has laid a great foundation for us. However, I do not believe that our children, from the littlest toddlers through high school, have an adequate transfer of the teaching according to the Montessori method. I see that there is a vacuum waiting to be filled.

Bringing the Montessori method to music has been the great love of Elisabeth Caspari, and we can see how children have thrived under this instruction. Each and every one of you may have a discipline—from cooking to carpentry to mechanics to drama to the more disciplined academic subjects—and you can bring it forth and transfer your understanding of it to the child.

I remember the teaching that Mother Mary gave to Jesus about whittling the hard wood. He had asked if he could please whittle the softer wood because it was easier, and he wanted his mother to intercede for him with Joseph.

Instead, she gave him the instruction that the hard wood was more appropriate and that the soft wood would wear and would not last as long. She gave him this instruction because, when he became a teacher, he would have to deal with hardened personalities that were difficult to change. Therefore, he should have the experience in his little hands of how hard it was to carve the hard wood.[7]

So, through all the various disciplines of the hands that children love to do, from their 4-H clubs to their scouting work to sports, there's always an exercise that brings home the spiritual law. And Mother Mary told us that after she had finished explaining all this to Jesus, he, with a tear in his eye, ran off to whittle the hard wood.

In the same way, becoming a teacher in this true guru-chela relationship may be harder, but it is more enduring and will endure unto the victory.

Most Fields Exclude New Revelation

You can see how the revelation of God has been cut off in almost every field of human endeavor, including religion. Many people in the churches today have said that there is no further prophecy, no further revelation. This is bad enough, but think about it in the areas of science and mathematics.

God is excluded from science, for science is man-made and proceeds on the principles of empiricism and experiment. Most scientists, with their scientific theories, do not need God. Individual scientists who are devout bring God into their laboratories, but as a field, science is considered to be the way man takes hold of his environment and evolves all the needed man-made solutions. Therefore, it is a closed door to God.

How many other closed doors are there, where man has excluded God from the creative discovery that is the interaction with the guru? You can see how this rebellion has caused the downfall of our civilization. It is extraordinary. We don't hear people preaching economics on the basis of man's interaction with God, so all of the right theories propounded on the free enterprise system are of no avail if the teacher of those theories does not place God, the Great Guru, at the center and does not understand that the forces that work "automatically" within the free enterprise system are really the product of the Christ consciousness of Almighty God.

Yes, God is in the very midst of the free enterprise system. Someone on the planet has to call to task all of the great thinkers of the time who are offering humanly good solutions but do not bend the knee and confess the Christ. I look around and see that no one else is doing that, and so I do it in my exposés.

We need world saviours in economics, in government, in all of the seven rays. Where will we find them? We will find them in the little child. As you learn to be a teacher, you will transfer your knowledge to a little child who will rise up and be a world saviour. Furthermore, as you learn to be a teacher, because you must sacrifice the elements of your psychology that stand between you and your mighty I AM Presence, you yourself become a world saviour. You don't even have to wait for the little child in your classroom, for the little child is in your own heart.

Build a Relationship with the Guru

We teach Montessori at Summit University because this is the time to examine our psychology. I also think it is important for you to experience my absence so that you do not have a direct confrontation with my presence and can therefore deal with the guru in the abstract.

You can deal with the guru as the mighty I AM Presence or as the ascended masters because they recede and come forward in proportion to your own purity, even though this is not visible to you. You should create an image or an eye-imagination of your relationship to the guru. And as you build on it, it becomes more and more real and more and more tangible as you interact with your Christ Self, your I AM Presence and the ascended masters. When you really do establish that relationship, you are able to interact comfortably with me.

I put nothing forth but comfort toward you. You have to own responsibility for the fact that if you have an uncomfortable feeling in my presence, it is in you, not me. I love you unconditionally, and I am not sitting and gazing upon your karma, your records, your aura and all of that. I'm not interested in that. I am interested in God in you.

Therefore, if you have fear that is not respect or reverence, but if you have fear that is torment in my presence, you must realize that this is because you have not surrendered and confessed your own sins. You have torment, not because of me, but because your relationship to God is not right. And when I come into the room, this is exposed.

When you are alone you may fancy that you have a relationship with Saint Germain or El Morya, but when the light of day comes and the presence of the guru is physical, you experience these emotions and feelings, and you have to adjust your concept of your relationship and realize that it may not be as perfect as you think.

Getting right with your own God Presence enables you to feel comfortable. So it's a good measuring rod. If I come into the room and all kinds of misqualified energy comes up, you have to know that you have suppressed things that are not acceptable in the presence of the Lord. And when the messenger comes in, it tells you that you have not surrendered, gone to the altar, confessed and asked for forgiveness. This will always be reflected in how you receive me.

Therefore, when you desire to leave my presence, please disassociate me from your discomfort and take it as a sign that you must work on your relationship with your mighty I AM Presence. The real guru-chela relationship is not possessive—I have no desire to possess you. As far as I am concerned, you can remove yourself from me by many miles and many cities, states or nations. You may go as far from me as you desire, because when our hearts are one, we are one universally.

I am one with all chelas who are not yet born and who have left the screen of life. Our flesh and blood condition does not condition our relationship. So the desire to put time and space between us must only be an indicator to you that there is something in your psychology that you have not resolved with Almighty God. I am only the reminder of that. I am only a signpost in the earth to remind you where you have to go back and dig. And a lot of what you're digging for comes out in this training.

Today I have come, trusting that you have established yourself in a comfortable relationship to the masters and to your heart flame. I hope that your heart flame has begun to accelerate the light that will bring to the surface a little bit more of what you must surrender to be effective as teachers of the world's children who are waiting for you.

Unlock the Heart of the Child

The reason you become educators is for the survival of community. The definition of educator is one who unlocks the flame of the heart of the child. You should remember this forever. You, the educator, are the one who unlocks the flame of the heart in the heart of the child. It is an initiation that comes from Maitreya through the lineage to you.

The teaching in your hand that you have mastered is the method of unlocking the heart. If you do not unlock the heart of these little children in your care, you will have failed as a teacher —and I will tell you in advance that that will be the judgment upon your head at the conclusion of this life.

Never be convinced by anyone or any force that you can, by some other route, teach the children and receive a blessing of your offering. If you do not unlock the heart of your children, you will be as Cain. You will have made the Cain offering that is unacceptable to God. You may be devoted to it, work hard for fifty years and come to the end of that life. Then the World

Teachers will say, "Go back. Reembody, and do it again with love. You did not do it with love. You did not open the hearts of my children."

All these words are written by the recording angels. You are accountable for them. They will be read to you when you stand before the Karmic Board at the conclusion of this life. I pray that it will be said of all, "You heard the words. You obeyed. You are victorious. Enter thou into union with thy God." It can be so if you remember what I have said.

Therefore, community is the platform for the world revolution. Our white-fire core is intent upon keeping the base of the United States of America that was secured for us by the prophet Samuel.* We are concerned that we go forth and create a revolution in the private school systems that will carry over to the entire United States and to the world.

Let Us Return to *New Era Community*

In my last lecture on this text, I left off at number 91 and so I will continue there. It is an odd beginning, but as it is where I left off, that is where I will begin.

> 91. Why is it necessary to be awkward? Why is it necessary to create an impression of ignorance? Why must those who adhere to Us be neglectful? Why must they adopt a quarrelsome manner when a dispute is going on? Why must they prattle without end?

These questions are not entirely answered in the text, for they must be answered by you. Why, when trying to be a chela, do you wind up being awkward or giving the impression of ignorance, of ignoring the Law, or of being neglectful, quarrelsome or prattling? Why, when your heart wants to be Maitreya's chela, do you wind up in these human momentums?

This is a subject for the searching of the soul in psychology. We have given some answers in our decree for the handling of the

---

*Saint Germain, sponsor of the United States of America, was embodied as the prophet Samuel.

animal magnetism that causes these conditions. But somewhere in the very depths of your being there is an absence of surrender of some substance. Therefore, you do not immediately take on the grace of God that is sufficient for gracious and harmonious behavior at all times. That is the key.

Unless we have a cataclysmic confrontation with ourselves, unless we are really threatened, unless the juxtaposition of events brings home to us the necessity of seeing this substance to the extent that we say, "O God, I will not survive unless I give this up," we go on being awkward, dropping things, coming out with statements that we regret. That is why the guru asks this question, because he wants to see us leave these things behind.

"My grace is sufficient for thee."[8] This is the most peaceful statement of the Lord Jesus, because the flow of his grace, when received by the cleansed chalice, will enable you to be all that you need to be to fulfill your divine plan. That is the answer to the question.

Love Is the Foundation of the Community

Go around unwarranted dirt. You see how necessary it is to emphasize each detail; otherwise the customs of Our Community will not be strengthened in you.

The detail of the teaching is important until you have assimilated the detail and you are it. And, therefore, in all circumstances the detail of the Law is automatic, operable, a point of mastery you have gained. I have observed individuals come into the community, but its "customs are not strengthened in them." Instead of bypassing the unwanted dirt of the astral plane, they bypass the fundamental points of love that make the community sing and make hearts in the community happy.

One of the individuals who betrayed this community was at one time given the opportunity of being my personal secretary. She did it very well and had a good mastery of the mechanics. While working with me for over a year-and-a-half, she was perfectly lovely in my presence. But in rebellion against the service to the light, she would go into fits of anger and weeping when she left my presence.

Finally, she made the statement that was reported to me and with which she was confronted: that the community was nothing but a concentration camp. That was her perception of community. So I called her in with the person who had told me this and expressed to her how much I loved her. I said that I greatly regretted that she behaved one way in my presence and another way apart from me. And I asked if this was true.

She said, "Yes, it is true."

"Did you say that the community was a concentration camp?" I asked. "Yes, I did," she replied.

I said, "Well, then, you have not earned the right to be here. You will have to leave. I also suggest that you seek therapy, because to be in a good disposition when you're with me and to be violent when you are away from me is obviously a problem of a split in the four lower bodies and an absence of surrender."

I suggested therapy, but a worldly psychologist told her there was nothing wrong with her, so she decided she did not need therapy. She became extremely angry because I gave her no further access to the community, and we suspended her from the church. And ever since then she has been a communicator of gossip. She denied that she ever behaved this way and never told anyone that I was fair in our meeting.

Because she admitted to what she had said, I gave her the opportunity to go out from the community, resolve her psychological problems and return: a simple discipline that a child of God should have welcomed. A child of God would have been tormented in the presence of such opposing conditions within her consciousness.

I was not angry with her. I am not angry with her now. I love her still. But she has such a gossip entity that I never cease to hear tales of all the horrendous things that she says about me and the community.

Therefore, you do need to emphasize each detail of the Path, and I tell you these incidents so that you can see how these words apply to real happenings. This person never perceived the love that was here or the love that I had for her, which was a tremendous love, a great devotion.

An individual who does not have the capacity to love in the divine sense of the word cannot keep the flame of life or the flame of community. He will follow the Law mechanically, if he follows it at all, but not because he loves the Lawgiver. So the absence of love is the reason why people cannot become a part of the Path and the community.

Love of the Sacred Labor

Morya says that the fundamental principle of love in community is love of the sacred labor, love of the work ethic. Children of the light and sons and daughters of God love to work. That's what Maria Montessori found with her children. They would rather work with their materials than play meaninglessly, and then work becomes recreation.

The robot creation doesn't like to work. But work is the very sign that God is in us—not work that is slavery or burdensome, but work that is done in the joy of the Lord to expand his being.

The discipline of freedom distinguishes Our communities.

While Jesus and Mother Mary were giving the balance of discipline and freedom to Maria Montessori, El Morya was giving the same principle to Nicholas and Helena Roerich.

Not only is the spirit disciplined, but also the qualities of external actions.

If we say that because we have God it doesn't matter that our room is messy or that our clothes are not clean or that there is dust around, we have missed the point. External actions indicate inner discipline. Children in Montessori schools begin to have such God-control over their bodies because they handle equipment that is designed for them. And so there is the spirit of discipline and freedom.

It is not Our custom to grieve too much.

Grieve over what? Grieve over the mistakes of the human consciousness. The real guru doesn't pounce on you because you did something wrong. That is the imagination of your mind—fearing that God to whom you never surrendered. But that is not the real relationship. The true teachers do not grieve over the little mistakes because their emphasis is on the real person.

It is not Our custom to censure too much.

Instead of censuring we rechannel the flow of creative energy, and we bring the individual to his Higher Self. If I can bring you to the point of obedience to God by redirecting your energy to a higher devotion that is so illumined that you want to do better, you want to give more, you want to serve, why would I use such a gross method of censuring, criticizing, condemning and beating you to the ground—telling you you're a good-for-nothing and you never do anything right? That is the method of the tyrant.

It is not Our custom to count on people too broadly.

No, we count on the God in the people. Then we are not disappointed when they fail, and we know to whom to give the glory for the victory.

It is not Our custom to expect too much.

Our expectancy is in God.

It is needed to be able to replace a complicated plan with a simpler one—never the reverse—for Our adversaries act from the simple to the complex.

Therefore, we go from the complex to the simple. Why? Because the entire vast scheme of the cosmos of the Great White

Brotherhood has a vast complexity that is simplified for our chelaship. The Montessori method is the simplification of the vast complexity of the child's environment. It comes down to certain basic principles, which, once inside of him, will always be there for right decision, right mindfulness, right attitude, right livelihood. The whole path of the Buddha is in these principles that come through the Montessori method—from the complicated plan to the simpler one.

The adversaries move from the simple teaching of God to the complexity of their mechanization man. Scientific humanism, social engineering is amazingly complex. Look at the bureaucracy of the federal government. It's the complexification of the simple, sweet interaction of God in man that is entirely sufficient to deal with every area of human life.

Strengthen Your Friends

Ponder how to strengthen your friends.

Do you know how to strengthen them? If you see a friend with a weakness, say to yourself, "My dear friend has a little blind spot, and he keeps repeating over and over again this thing that keeps him out of touch with God. How can I strengthen him to make him love God more so that he will triumph over this?"

When you ponder how to strengthen your friends, you are learning how to be a teacher, you are putting on another facet of the mantle of teacher. You observe all the children and all the people around you, not in criticism, but by saying, "How can I help this one polish the jewel? How can I help him bring out more of himself?" Then you are perfecting the skills of the teacher.

Maintain pure air in your dwellings, project to those who come best wishes, and await Us intently.

One of the television stations recently had a series on polluted air. They said the most polluted air was in your own house when the doors were shut. The pollution came from the shampoo in the carpets, the residue of cigarette smoking and chemicals from all kinds of household products.

Obviously, we can't go anywhere without physically pure air, but you know that El Morya always has a double meaning. Think of the pure air of the mental body. What you breathe out physically creates the air in the room. But even if you have the room all perfumed and incensed, the air can be bad if you are breathing out the noxious poisons of your rebellion against the guru-chela relationship. All the children will breathe in that air, and you will be held accountable. There are deadly poisons in the classrooms of America today, and the children are breathing them in.

"Project to those who come best wishes," best wishes for their attainment. That is what we give to every individual, regardless of his misbehavior. Our best wishes for his continuing attainment on the Path go with everyone who comes and goes in our community.

"Await us intently." The expectancy of the master walking through the door is always in the heart of the chela. Always. It's always the sense that he's coming. You know, he may be here right now!

It's the sense that your home, your room, your classroom has the expectation that at any moment you will sit down, and El Morya will instruct your pupils. May the room not be so full of your personality, your overpowering presence, your sense of possessiveness of the children that you would be threatened if El Morya came in and began to teach.

It is important not to be possessive. I assure you, by God's grace, that I am not possessive of you. One's essential position as teacher can momentarily be nonessential as God, the Great Guru, instructs. And he may come through a little child who suddenly stands up and gives a lesson to everyone else in the room about the magnificent discovery he has made.

Remember the Foundation

> Let each community await its Teacher, for a community and
> a Teacher constitute the ends of one and the same column.
> Even in daily trifles it is necessary to remember the foun-
> dation of the house.

When I moved to California, I found out that most wooden
houses have termites and that you should never purchase a property without getting a termite inspection. A termite inspection
company will guarantee that a property is termite free, or if it is
not termite free, they will offer to spray it and fumigate it. They
put a whole tent over the house, and the house completely dis-
appears into it. Then they put in their chemicals that kill the
termites.

This is important because you can buy a house that is ready
to collapse and not know it. The amazing thing about termites—
and it is very funny, because it also applies to the adversaries who
eat away at the foundation of community, or would try to do so
if we were not alert—is wherever there is a heavy object in the
room and the termites are eating up the floor underneath it, the
termites will go around the heavy object.

For example, if you have a grand piano that has three legs,
they will eat all around the grand piano and leave the part under
the legs. So all you have to do is shove that piano over a little bit
and boom! it will go right through the floor!

Can you imagine the astral consciousness here that comes
from the tactics of the false hierarchy working through the
termites that eat away at the foundation of the house?

So, El Morya is saying, "Even in daily trifles it is necessary to
remember the foundation of the house." The foundation of our
house is the guru-chela relationship. In the midst of trying to do
good and change the world, we may forget that.

But I came to the realization that there are only short-term
gains when you allow people who have not passed through the
initiations of Lord Maitreya to teach in a mystery school.

Therefore, with El Morya and Lanello I reached the very firm decision that unless an individual bends the knee, he cannot occupy a teaching position, for the teacher is the foundation of the community. Therefore, even in daily trifles it is necessary to remember the foundation of the house, the community and the teacher.

How to Alter Your Consciousness

Again we arrive at the necessity of altering the quality of the consciousness; then the transition is easy.

Your consciousness had to be altered before you made the transition to the inner teaching of Maria Montessori. The transition is always from the outer to the inner. Those who go to the outer school and come here cannot enter this forcefield. It is impossible for them to penetrate it with their consciousness until it has been altered.

We know that the word *alter* contains within it the light of alchemy, the science of transmutation, never programming against the will of the individual. An alteration in consciousness cannot take place except by free will. I have seen chelas try to force themselves to be chelas and, as the saying goes, they are of the same opinion still when it is all over. They cannot come into that higher relationship.

To be together once again at the altar is a great joy. It is a great joy because not ten righteous men but many more have been found in the earth today. Many have actually come out from among the people to be separate and understand God while they yet work through the flesh-and-blood concepts and the conditions of their karma.

I attribute the miracle of your coming into community not to happenstance, God forbid, and not to any personal attainment you might have. I attribute the miracle of your coming out into community to the dispensation of Sanat Kumara and the other ascended masters. A responsive chord should be struck in us all as one great chord of the Elohim. It brought us together in time and space when we had no other connection except word of mouth or a poster or a book.

The chord was struck, and those who are part of the notes of that chord came together in search of the hands that struck the chord. That to me is so exciting. That is the great miracle of Sanat Kumara and all the ascended masters. I daily give praise to that miracle and rejoice in it.

I always wonder how any one of us could have found the rest. We could have gone into places where we were and not recognized each other because we had not yet had an alteration of consciousness. The transition to being one had not yet come. So God picked us up, became the alchemy of the altering, and the process began even before we were together.

I would like to seal you in the love flame of the community of the Great White Brotherhood. Won't you stand.

In the name of the I AM THAT I AM, I call forth the light of God that never fails. I call forth the light of the Great Central Sun Magnet. I call to the God Star, Sirius. I call to the entire Spirit of the Great White Brotherhood. Open now these hearts.

Let the flame of alteration, the mighty flame of transmutation, the God flame of freedom from the heart of Saint Germain infuse these hearts. Burn now on the altar of these hearts, O mighty flame of freedom.

Now let the fires of alteration produce the magnet in the white cube to magnetize the Community of the Holy Spirit in the earth, to magnetize the physical organism of the Great White Brotherhood, the action of the light within this community and especially the transfer of the light through the embodied teacher.

Let these souls be prepared to bear the mantle of the World Teachers, Mother Mary, Raphael, Maria Montessori and all who have gone before. Let the continuity of the torch of the Brothers and Sisters of the Golden Robe be upon them.

Lord God Almighty, I call for the preparation of these hearts that they might be fused with the heart of the Christ Self, and in that fusion be also fused with my own heart.

In the name of the Father and of the Son and of the Holy Spirit, in the name of the Mother, I seal you in the cosmic cross of white fire, Amen.

Camelot
February 18, 1980

CHAPTER 6

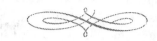

The Extinguished Consciousness and the Undeveloped Consciousness

In the name of the light of God that never fails, I invoke the presence here of beloved El Morya, beloved Saint Germain, beloved Kuthumi and beloved Djwal Kul, beloved Serapis Bey and beloved Lanello.

I call for the light of God that never fails to transfer to these chelas of the will of God and these devotees of the World Teachers the full implementation of the light that is for the garnering of the crystal of the ruby ray within the heart.

Beloved El Morya, beloved Saint Germain, open now their eyes. Open their consciousness. Open their hearts, and open their souls. In the name of the Father, the Mother, the Son and the Holy Spirit, Amen.

Let us turn to the text. We left off at paragraph 92.

92. Menacing hands do not reach you when you proceed surrounded by the spiral of devotion. If through lower physical sight the eye could see the armor of devotion, then the man would already not be in a state of lower consciousness. Lessons of former lives do not reach closed eyes. Verily, without wings over the abyss remains each one who approaches Our Community in an outworn consciousness. Each one who attempts to approach Us in pride will be struck as if by an explosion of ozone. But how to explain

that We do not smite, that the proud one smites himself? In the same way perishes he who enters a powderhouse in metallic footwear. Knowing how to use steel spikes on shoes makes a fair runner, but any workman will advise to wear soft slippers when walking on an explosive surface. Hence, there is needed a buffer for a saturated atmosphere.

I refer to the Blessed One. When He went into the mountains, He apportioned his time to facilitate the passage. By this is attained economy of energy. In truth, this is a unique economy, admissible and justified; otherwise chasms may be formed between the worlds, and who knows with what gas they may be filled? I can advise you to conserve energy, for each useless waste smites space at far distances as if by a wire. It is important to care for the Cosmos in each blade of grass, if we are ready to become citizens of the universe.

93. I speak about the quality of travels. It is necessary to assimilate the knowledge of how to travel! It is necessary not only to break away from home, but also to conquer the very concept of home. It would be more precise to say that one should broaden the concept of home. Where we are—there is home. Evolution casts off the meaning of home as a prison. Progress in liberating the consciousness will yield the possibility of becoming flexible. And not achievement, not privation, not exaltation, but quality of consciousness enables one to break away from a long-occupied place. In a long-occupied place there is so much smokiness, so much sourness and dust. We are opposed to the solitary life of hermitage, but small cottages with moldy atmosphere are worse than caves. We summon those who can give expanse to thought.

I wish to see you moving over the face of the world when all national boundaries, because of their multitude, will be erased. How can we fly when pinned by a small nail! Reflect upon the need of travel for humanity.

94. Often you talk about the imperfections in existing books. I say more: The errors in the books are equal to a griev-

ous crime. Falsehood in books must be prosecuted as a grave calumny. The falsehood of an orator is prosecuted according to the number of his listeners. The falsehood of an author should be prosecuted according to the number of copies sold of his book. To fill the people's libraries with falsehood is a grave offense. It is necessary to perceive the true intent of the author in order to estimate the quality of his errors. Ignorance will be the worst basis. Fear and meanness occupy the next place. None of these qualities are befitting the community. To accomplish their removal in the new construction is a necessity. Prohibitory measures, as usual, are not suitable; but a discovered error must be removed from the book. The necessity of such removal, and the reprinting of the book, will bring the author to his senses. Every citizen has the right to prove an error. Indeed, one should not impede new views and structures; but incorrect data must not bring one into error, because knowledge is the armor of the community and the defense of knowledge is the duty of all the members.

No more than a year must elapse before books are verified, otherwise the number of victims will be great. It is especially necessary to stand guard over the book when its merit is shaken. The library shelves are full of abscesses of falsehood. It should not be permissible to preserve these parasites. You may propose to someone to sleep on a poor bed, but it is impossible to suggest reading a false book through.

Why turn over to a lying buffoon the best corner of the fireside? Precisely, bad books litter up the consciousness of children. The problem of the book must be dealt with!

Helena Roerich, the amanuensis for El Morya, was very much in tune with the plots of the false hierarchy that have come to fruition in our decade. This is the flood that the dragon intended to send out and has sent out.[1]

95. Once a woman stopped between images of the Blessed Buddha and Maitreya, not knowing to Whom to offer her reverence. And the image of the Blessed Buddha

uttered these words: "According to My Covenant, revere the future. Standing in defense of the past, direct your gaze toward the dawn."

Remember how We labor for the future, and direct all your being into the future! In rays of knowledge We bring a Teaching strange to the world, for the light of the world is covered by darkness.

96. The acceleration of dates is necessary; otherwise ignorance will become solidified. All ulcers have been crowding upon the threshold of the New World. The whirl has swept up heaps of rubbish. Knowing how to face courageously the abominations of ignorance brings about unusual measures. Finally, one should know how to point out the merit of useful people. Why should able people perish amidst chains or prejudices?

Children must be asked whether they can stop fearing to appear absurd in the eyes of the crowd. Are they ready to give up personal comfort for the sake of the New World? It were best to put the questions sternly, for the manifested flame does not fear the wind.

This is a very profound observation regarding children, because we know that children desire to have the approval of their peers. This question needs to be put firmly to our children and to our teenagers. It is not easy for them to give up personal comfort, but it becomes easier when they feel the flame of the Maha Chohan. The Holy Spirit enables them to say, "I do not fear to be ostracized by the crowd."

Devotion carries over the abyss, but the palpitation of sensitiveness must give wings to this devotion.

97. On the path do not rest under a rotting tree.

I am amused by this because the first summer we came to Camelot my children decided to sleep out at night. They chose a favorite oak tree to sleep under, but one of the nights they wanted to sleep there, it was wet and an adult did not allow them to do so. That was the night that this rotten oak tree let down its enormous limb onto the ground—but they were not there.

It's an amazing feeling to wake up in the morning and realize that if you had been out there, the tree would have fallen on you.

The Extinguished Consciousness

In life have no dealings with people with extinguished consciousnesses. An undeveloped consciousness is not as infectious as an extinguished one.

It is possible for the individual to put out the light within his being by the continuous denial of that light. This happens a long way down the road. At first the person was undeveloped; then he became developed and realized the light for what it is. Then he denied the light and finally became extinguished. So it's the long path of choice. The end result of choice can be an extinguished consciousness.

My observations of people have shown me that many who have an extinguished consciousness are accustomed to being nice people who get along with everybody—the whole "milk of human kindness" approach. However, if you bring up something holy or sacred, all of a sudden from out of the bowels of their being will come an intense anger—something that you had never seen expressed in that person.

Last year I was in the process of purchasing some furniture for the church from a shopkeeper who was going out of business. He was a European who enjoyed telling us all about the days of his life in World War II. In the course of this transaction, he took me and some of the men from the church who were with me to lunch.

During lunch, I began to speak about Saint Francis. (I mentioned Saint Francis because it was apropos to something else that was being said.) "Saint Francis," he said, "who is he?" And immediately he became quite angry about Saint Francis. His resentment came from something stuffed way down inside him.

Until that moment, he had been the most affable, gentlemanly kind of person you would ever want to meet.

All of a sudden, the sleeping serpent was aroused, and I actually trembled from his hatred. I had to come to the defense of Saint Francis because I could not stand by while he was being maligned. And as soon as the man realized that I had devotion to Saint Francis, he immediately became silent and resumed his posture of being a gentleman.

It was a typical case of what Kuthumi describes as the aura turning inside out and revealing itself. Yet it is difficult to understand or be aware that common everyday people who get along with other common everyday people can have these deep-seated rebellions against God and his representatives.

You do not have these confrontations unless you are a light-bearer. Unless you have the light yourself, which then becomes an offense to something in their subconscious, it is never aroused. When someone who is of the light comes in their midst, then they become aware of the fact that a spotlight has been shone into an area of their being.

The extinguished consciousness is one that has gone through its contact with the light. It has gained development by the light and has actually increased its awareness by the light. Then it has come to the point where it says, "I am the light, and therefore I need no longer bend the knee and bow before the light." That was the proclamation of Lucifer.

Then, by the very denial of the Source, the consciousness is extinguished. At this point, it is highly infectious, because it spreads its philosophy, its disease, to those who surround it.

El Morya goes on to say:

> The extinguished consciousness is an actual vampire. It is impossible to fill from without the abyss of the ignorant consciousness. Precisely these people absorb one's energy uselessly. As a result of being with them, enormous fatigue is felt. They must be avoided like a stench in order to bar the way to the fluids of decomposition.

People who have an extinguished consciousness are in a state of decomposition, which I call the degeneration spiral. When you interchange energy with them, you give them light and they give you their infection. They then become a vampire who lives off your light. They cause you to feel fatigued, and you can never fill them with light from without because the only way they can truly get light is to go back to the point of their rebellion against the light and call upon the Lord for forgiveness and be filled with light to heal this disease.

Those who have not their own light will gravitate toward those who do. And that is why you need a protected community, a sealed wall of light, where all who are on the inside are receivers of light and are radiating points of light. If someone on the inside has an extinguished consciousness, he can vampirize everyone in the community.

When new students come here, they are simply people from the world who really don't know who they are yet and have not made their choice. It is very noticeable to me and to the staff that the community is bombarded with a new set of untransmuted energy that needs to be cleaned up. It takes almost a month before everyone feels normal again. This is not because those individuals have rejected the light; it is only because they have the untransmuted overlay of the world until they gain their own momentum and clean it up. But that is the result, even if you are a lightbearer, of being in the world and being in an unprotected forcefield. Hence, the only way we can keep a flame on earth is in community.

> It is difficult to distinguish the boundary line between lack
> of development and extinction.

A very important point. On the Path you will meet people who are not on the Path who appear to be ignorant of the teachings, yet they are interested and even affirm that everything you say is true. You may then begin to believe that you have someone in your presence who is a potential chela.

By and by, you may come to realize that you are not seeing

someone who has a lack of development, but someone in a state of self-extinction who has heard the whole teaching in bygone embodiments, understands it fully but refuses to come before the I AM Presence and say, "You are the vine and I am the branch,"[2] thereby giving greater importance to the Source.

That is something that some cannot do, will not do, have not done. They have rearranged their lives to dodge the confrontation. They live a surface existence and only allow themselves to go about one inch deep in their feelings, for if they went any deeper they might contact the records of past embodiments that we started reading about in number 92. However, "lessons of former lives do not reach closed eyes."

Jesus' Teaching on the Montessori Method

It is important to learn to recognize the undeveloped consciousness. It is a consciousness that is yet teachable, and you want to be its teacher.

To go before the little child, you must come prepared to teach. Now, little children are of all evolutions, as you realize. Some are developed from previous lives; some have already extinguished their consciousness in previous lives. Why do they reembody? Because they are still playing out the light they once had.

One's light does not expend itself in one lifetime. One could have extinguished oneself two thousand years ago and still be embodying as the living dead, without a spark of life but continuing to play out the residue of the spiral of their existence.

One thing is true: all children ages two to seven need to be exposed to the Montessori method. The Montessori method is like the resurrection flame. This is what Jesus wants you to know right now, that the Montessori method will resurrect the depths of being. The resurrection flame will resurrect some to everlasting life and others to everlasting damnation,[3] for it forces everything to the surface so that the soul may make a choice.

Jesus says that our current educational systems do not allow either the extinguished ones or the undeveloped ones to come to grips with their inner being, their soul or their inner potential, and, therefore, they are never able to make the choice between the living Christ and the mechanization concept.

Thus, the Montessori method is the resurrection flame that brings out the momentums of the child. It harmonizes and resolves the past. Through the method the child can work through his opposing subconscious momentums and ultimately, because all momentums are brought forth, make the choice as to where he will position himself in this life.

We have the ultimate opportunity in the last century of the Piscean age to make the choice to transmute those momentums of misqualified energy. The child represents an opportunity of God given to the soul to reembody and once again have the confrontation with the internal Guru, the Christ Self. Once again the soul may determine to love the Christ and be resurrected, or once again she* may determine to deny that Christ.

To me, this is a profound revelation, that the Montessori method and the materials are truly the resurrection flame that you bear to the little child for the purpose of the path of the ascension or the final judgment.

Jesus says that it is bad enough that education deprives the lightbearers of contact with the internal flame, but what is worse is that it also deprives the fallen ones of their judgment that is due. Therefore, it serves neither evolution. To Jesus, that is what is wrong with humanism and the teaching standards today: they deny the outpouring of the resurrection flame for the opening of the path of choice.

The Queen's Chamber of the Great Pyramid

You can look at the Montessori classroom as the Queen's Chamber of the Great Pyramid, where the soul is given the beginning initiations that will enable her to enter the King's Chamber for the ultimate initiations of the resurrection flame. Every Montessori

---

*We use the pronouns *she* and *her* to refer to the soul because each soul, whether housed in a male or a female body, is the feminine counterpart of the masculine Spirit.

classroom, Jesus is saying, should be consecrated as the Queen's Chamber of the Great Pyramid. There the Blessed Mother transfers to her children the footsteps of truth whereby they may ascend the stairs to the King's Chamber. These footsteps of truth remain for life; they can never be taken from the child.

We now return to the boundary line between lack of development and extinction.

> But one quality will be unquestionably indicative: Lack of development will or may be accompanied by the palpitation of devotion, but an extinct crater is full of cinders and brimstone. The Teaching does not refuse to expend energy on the undeveloped, but there is a degree of extinction at which the abyss is not to be flooded with a new substance. Only a cataclysm, with its terror of unexpectedness, can melt a congealed lava.
>
> Remember the treasure of the consciousness. Tremor of the substance of the Cosmos manifests the pulsation of the awakened consciousness. Indeed, the rainbow of knowledge flows out of the tremor of the consciousness—a visible stream from an invisible source.
>
> Through all experiences of the past and all attainments of the future, remember about the consciousness.

Devotion versus Human Sympathy

A consciousness in the state of extinction, that which is self-extinguished, is therefore in a spiral of disintegration. It is the logical conclusion of self-extinction when a candle is extinguished; all that remains is the shell. The shell has been given life by the candle, but when the candle is withdrawn, no new life is given. Therefore, the human shell goes through disintegration just like the remains of the shells on the seashore.

An individual in the process of disintegration because he has willfully, by free will, extinguished himself will have a momentum of anti-devotion that manifests as human sympathy. Sympathy becomes a replacement for devotion to God—sympathy for oneself, agreement with oneself and sympathy for others. There is a great human sympathy that replaces the pure stream of devotion to Almighty God.

The sympathy, then, becomes a very strong human magnetism. And because the individual now depends upon interaction with other human beings for his survival, he becomes, as the French say, "très sympathique." He's very sympathetic. In other words, he's a very likable person, and the likable quality comes from the fact that all his devotion that should be going to God is going now to the development of the human personality, the psychic personality.

Therefore, these people can even be considered to have charisma, charm, a great way with other people and great magnetism. They build a forcefield of magnetism, and behind all of this is still the extinguished self.

Save the Undeveloped Soul

The next statement then becomes the statement of the Law: "The Teaching does not refuse to expend energy on the undeveloped."

The teacher will go to any extent to save the undeveloped soul. The shepherd will leave the ninety and nine and go after the one. He will pursue the child of light who needs training to the ends of the universe, if necessary, to bring that one home. But there comes a time when the degree of extinction (another word for rebellion) is such that the cosmic law states that the abyss (the vacuum of the shell that is left) is not to be flooded with a new substance.

When an individual has denied the light, a time comes when the light will deny the individual. Mighty Victory explained this when he told us that if you serve the light, after a certain time the light will turn around and serve you.[4] This is absolutely true. I have seen it happen in my own life.

Sometimes you serve and serve and serve, and although you may be tired or weary, you can feel the return of the Great Central Sun coming into your being, flooding you with new strength and energy and love to go on. The experience of the light serving its own is an incomparable experience. It is like God expressing gratitude. It always comes when you have totally spent your life in service, and then the light is returned to you.

However, the light will not serve those who have created the abyss, the black hole in space. It is "not to be flooded with a new substance." What does the text say of such an individual? "Only a cataclysm, with its terror of unexpectedness, can melt a congealed lava."

If an individual has received all the teaching, all the light, all the love that the Great White Brotherhood and its emissaries can bestow, and has still rejected the Path, the light and the persons of the masters, then the only alternative is cataclysm. Thus, that congealed lava of rebellion against God is melted by the terror of its unexpectedness.

Do you know why God allows cataclysm? Not for mere punishment. He does it to break up the recalcitrance of someone who says that the seed time and the harvest will continue, and there is no threat of returning karma, no God who will punish their denial of the cosmic scheme of life. The only thing that wakes them up is a personal, private cataclysm, a planetary cataclysm.

Then they begin to have the fear of the Lord. And that is the moment when that fear of the Lord can become the bending of the knee, where the fear becomes another kind of fear: awe. And the awe becomes honor, and the honor becomes love.

I want you to understand the wisdom of the Karmic Board and of the ascended masters as you regard the planet and see what happens in the days ahead. You must recognize that many ascended masters and many fine representatives of the masters have worked for centuries with the people of this planet. Then you come along and work with them, and you wonder why they can't see the teachings that are as plain as life itself.

This is the problem: we live on a planet where there are many shells, many extinguished shells. The earth itself is almost like a shell, and as we look at its composition, we see that it is a dying world, a polluted world, a toxic world. It is a diseased planet, and the disease is this very quality of self-extinguishment of many of its inhabitants.

As a result, what does the Goddess of Liberty do? She passes to us the torch for transmutation into the new age. She passes to the world the torch of its own karma and its responsibility for self-extinguishment. She says, "You are the lightbearers. Do not pour your light any longer into the abyss of those who have denied the flame. Garner your light and use it to seal the community for the centuries to come."

This is the great wisdom of the Brotherhood. We really can't quite understand until we've experienced it. I urge you to be the wise ones who accept the experience of your teachers. You can save yourself many lifetimes by realizing that the ascended masters have experiences that we do not share; and by trusting them, we reap the benefit of their lifetimes of service.

How many of you think you know an extinguished self? Have you wept over that person as you have wept over humanity? It is the most difficult death to face. We weep more over the extinguished self than we do over the passing of a loved one, however much we may love that loved one who passes into the ascension.

It is much easier to smile at the transition of Lanello, because one knows that he is an ascended master, and therefore, he has become the sun. But when we see the death of a soul, when we see an extinguished self still walking around in a body that does not know that it is extinguished or that it is in a degeneration spiral, we mourn the death of that consciousness.

We mourn over what might have been, over the tragedy that could have been avoided, the tragedy that defies explanation because we cannot understand the psychology of an individual who chooses to become the hollow abyss when he could become a living temple of light. It is the enigma of the Path.

I also want to point out that we may consider such people harmless. But Morya says that not only are they infectious but they are also vampires. They are highly infectious, and therefore we must be careful. When I say that we are weeping for such individuals, who are we really weeping for? We're weeping for God, the God who has been aborted within that being, the God who has not become self-realized. Hence, another facet of the Divine Mind is not outpictured.

We weep for the life that is imprisoned in that temple. One does not weep for the human consciousness that has committed this crime against the universe. One weeps for the universe. One weeps also for a soul, a soul who is lost rather than a soul who is ascended.

How Do We Pray for Them?

The prayer for the self-extinguished ones is first to visualize the Cosmic Christ replacing that one. This calls down the matrix of the Cosmic Christ where that one is, and, therefore, you do not ever have to train your vision upon the extinguished self. You affirm the Cosmic Christ and give the option to the individual by free will to accept that identity. The Cosmic Christ both seals the infectious, vampire nature and continues the option of free will.

I would not advise long periods of time praying. I would pray for the will of God to descend with such intensity, such cataclysmic intensity, as to awaken the soul to its senses and cause it to return to the service of the light. That is the only true prayer you can make.

The way that prayer will be released is that you yourself contain such a momentum of God's will that your very gaze upon that individual will transform him in this confrontation of the light. Of course, those who are self-deniers of the light do not like to be around others who convey that much of the will of God. Therefore, your prayer needs to be from a distance, because you are a part of the light that has been denied.

When an individual denies the light within himself, he denies you as the keeper of that light. It then becomes a question of how God responds to those who have denied him. How does God pray for their souls?

How Does God Pray for Their Souls?

Ultimately, we see that God's prayer manifests as cataclysm of some sort, for God, the teacher, is telling us that there is no other way to awaken these individuals. It is as if he were saying, "Let them go their way, because ultimately they will be confronted by my Presence in the form of my Law and my will."

So the prayer for the will of God, in whatever form God deigns to send it, is the best prayer, as it is an impersonal prayer. It is not a prayer in which you are emotionally attached to the outcome of a situation or sympathetically tied to the person.

It is not lawful to be sympathetically or emotionally tied to people who have extinguished the God flame, because when you are tied to them, you are doing just that. You fill the abyss with your substance. Yet whose substance is it? It's the guru's substance. It is the light of Almighty God, and it is not yours to give away.

The guru gives you light so that you can multiply it and give it back to the guru. He does not give you light to give to those who have already denied him. It is not lawful. Remember the story of the talents. The master, the lord came along and gave out ten talents, five talents, one talent. And the receivers of the talents were supposed to multiply them and bring them back to the lord. They were not supposed to give them away to their favorite charity or have a good time with it. The lord wanted a return on his investment.

It is in your interest to keep in good grace with your mighty I AM Presence and with the ascended masters. Do you know why the ascended masters withhold light from some students? They can only give you so much light, and it is not lawful to give light to those who will give it to people who do not go after the light themselves and do not adore God.

If God cannot trust you to protect that light, he cannot increase your light. We who have the calling to serve are called to serve the lightbearers. We are not called to give our light to those who are in a state of denial of God.

Don't forget what I just told you. You may do everything else right on the Path and have perfect understanding, but if you cannot shake the human habit of giving away your light to relatives, family members, acquaintances of long-standing or somebody you just met, you will go only so far on the Path. Only so much attainment can then be given to you.

You need to think about that very carefully. You ought to sit down and write a list. Ask yourself, "To whom am I giving away my light through serving them, helping them, praying for them, taking care of them every time they fall? Every time these people get up, do they go back to their material existence?"

I call for the sealing of the Word of beloved El Morya within these hearts. May it be sealed in the diamond within the heart, beloved El Morya. And may the great truths that thou hast brought to us be there and waiting in the hour and the moment when each soul must make those very firm decisions in life on the path of chelaship under you.
Blessed master of light, we love you.

Camelot
March 19, 1980

The Chart of Your Divine Self

The Chart of Your Divine Self

The Chart of Your Divine Self is a portrait of you and of the God within you. It is a diagram of you and your potential to become who you really are. It is an outline of your spiritual anatomy.

The upper figure is your "I AM Presence," the Presence of God that is individualized in each one of us. It is your personalized "I AM THAT I AM." Your I AM Presence is surrounded by seven concentric spheres of spiritual energy that make up what is called your "causal body." The spheres of pulsating energy contain the record of the good works you have performed since your very first incarnation on earth. They are like your cosmic bank account.

The middle figure in the chart represents the "Holy Christ Self," who is also called the Higher Self. You can think of your Holy Christ Self as your chief guardian angel and dearest friend, your inner teacher and voice of conscience. Just as the I AM Presence is the presence of God that is individualized for each of us, so the Holy Christ Self is the presence of the Universal Christ that is individualized for each of us. "The Christ" is actually a title given to those who have attained oneness with their Higher Self, or Christ Self. That's why Jesus was called "Jesus, the Christ."

What the Chart shows is that each of us has a Higher Self, or "inner Christ," and that each of us is destined to become one with that Higher Self—whether we call it the Christ, the Buddha, the Tao or the Atman. This "inner Christ" is what the Christian mystics sometimes refer to as the "inner man of the heart," and what the Upanishads mysteriously describe as a being the "size of a thumb" who "dwells deep within the heart."

We all have moments when we feel that connection with our Higher Self—when we are creative, loving, joyful. But there are other moments when we feel out of sync with our Higher Self—moments when we become angry, depressed, lost. What the spiritual path is all about is learning to sustain the connection to the higher part of ourselves so that we can make our greatest contribution to humanity.

The shaft of white light descending from the I AM Presence through the Holy Christ Self to the lower figure in the Chart is the crystal cord (sometimes called the silver cord). It is the "umbilical cord," the lifeline, that ties you to Spirit.

Your crystal cord also nourishes that special, radiant flame of God that is ensconced in the secret chamber of your heart. It is called the threefold flame, or divine spark, because it is literally a spark of sacred fire that God has transmitted from his heart to yours. This flame is called "threefold" because it engenders the primary attributes of Spirit—power, wisdom and love.

The mystics of the world's religions have contacted the divine spark, describing it as the seed of divinity within. Buddhists, for instance, speak of the "germ of Buddhahood" that exists in every living being. In the Hindu tradition, the Katha Upanishad speaks of the "light of the Spirit"

that is concealed in the "secret high place of the heart" of all beings.

Likewise, the fourteenth-century Christian theologian and mystic Meister Eckhart teaches of the divine spark when he says, "God's seed is within us."

When we decree, we meditate on the flame in the secret chamber of our heart. This secret chamber is your own private meditation room, your interior castle, as Teresa of Avila called it. In Hindu tradition, the devotee visualizes a jeweled island in his heart. There he sees himself before a beautiful altar, where he worships his teacher in deep meditation.

Jesus spoke of entering the secret chamber of the heart when he said: "When thou prayest, enter into thy closet, and when thou hast shut thy door, pray to thy Father which is in secret; and thy Father which seeth in secret shall reward thee openly."

The lower figure in the Chart of Your Divine Self represents you on the spiritual path, surrounded by the violet flame and the protective white light of God. The soul is the living potential of God—the part of you that is mortal but that can become immortal.

The purpose of your soul's evolution on earth is to grow in self-mastery, balance your karma and fulfill your mission on earth so that you can return to the spiritual dimensions that are your real home. When your soul at last takes flight and ascends back to God and the heaven-world, you will become an "ascended" master, free from the rounds of karma and rebirth. The high-frequency energy of the violet flame can help you reach that goal more quickly.

CHAPTER 7

The Impetuosity of Striving

In the name of the light of God that never fails, I call to beloved Lord Maitreya, beloved El Morya. Enter now this forcefield and impart the fullness of your hearts to these chelas on the Path. In the name of the Father and of the Son and of the Holy Spirit, in the name of the Mother, Amen.

We are on *Community,* number 98.

> 98. When it is cold, even a dog warms one. There are unprecedentedly few people; therefore it is even impossible to drive away wretched adversaries, if in them the cell of the spirit has not been overgrown with weeds.

There are unprecedentedly few people that hierarchy can use. Therefore, it is even impossible to drive away the "wretched adversaries," and it is even less possible to drive them away if they have not been overgrown with the weeds that ultimately emerge out of their subconscious.

I'll read this passage to you again, and you can meditate on what you get from it:

> 98. When it is cold, even a dog warms one. There are unprecedentedly few people; therefore it is even impossible to drive away wretched adversaries, if in them the cell of the spirit has not been overgrown with weeds.

I have noted that the adversaries of the Great White Brotherhood are often those who cling most steadfastly to the messengers or to a center of light. This is ironic but true, because the adversary of the light is the one who must use the light in order to manifest his opposition. The adversary of the Brotherhood has no source of inner light, and, therefore, he must be in the community, is desperate to be in the community and is most desperate to be near the messenger.

The adversary is not a worshiper of the light; he is a worshiper of the personality. And such people always try to create a personality cult out of the living guru or out of the masters of the Great White Brotherhood. And, as the Brotherhood has told us, they erect their idols and ultimately must cast them down.

Although they cling steadfastly to the light and the lightbearer, they have an intense hatred of both. They have a hatred of the lightbearer because they do not have their own inner source of light, and so they hate the one who does. That hatred is actually jealousy.

I have noted the existence of jealousy of the lightbearers and of the messenger for years. It manifests itself in the sign of Gemini, opposes the throat chakra and opposes one's alertness and vitality. It is a draining force.

I experienced it through an individual's pattern of jealousy that became exposed. The person saw it, yet because he was an adversary, he could not manifest another vibration. Although he could see it, he may mourn it, he may have tremendous self-pity and feign remorse, yet the psychological patterns remain.

"Wretched Adversaries"

Morya and Maitreya call them "wretched adversaries." I say Morya *and* Maitreya because the thread of these two masters is intertwined in these books. Wretchedness implies a state of consciousness that is barren, unfruitful. And because of its barrenness, it becomes wretched, dark and dank. With adversaries who have not an inner light, it is even impossible to drive away, "if in them the cell of the spirit has not been overgrown with weeds."

One can observe adversaries for a certain period of time before their betrayal manifests. One can discern that it is present in the subconscious, but if that subconscious has not played itself out, has not grown and become the weeds that cover over the cell of the spirit (which is like the soul), then their betrayal is not physically manifest. Neither does their physical karma manifest. And so they cling to the light, and until there is a certain cycling of events, as is written here, it is practically impossible to drive them away.

We always have this in movements that are sponsored by the Great White Brotherhood, for the adversaries of the members of that Brotherhood who have been around for centuries always appear and try to get closest to the inner flame and close to the disciples. By their fruits you shall know them.

Therefore, they are the ones of whom the masters are speaking when they say, "When it is cold, even a dog warms one." And when it is cold, when there is an absence of chelas, let us say, we sometimes accept those who do not meet the full standard, and we allow ourselves to be surrounded by such people.

The Psychology of the Adversary

So this is a warning as well as an explanation of the psychology of the seed of the wicked. You must know their psychology because they are always present. It is not up to us to judge, but it is up to us to remain on guard and to know that there are cycles, periods, when the adversary can shine with light.

It is written that Satan himself can be transformed into an angel of light,[1] for it is the borrowed and reflected light of the Brotherhood. The appearance of the adversaries may be one of great light, but the moment the aura is turned inside out and their betrayal and conspiracy is manifest, they become totally dark. Then one sees that they never had any light of their own.

How somebody who appears to have light in his face can turn overnight to look as if he had two black holes for eyes and a totally black aura is one of the phenomena that I have observed over the years. You find that when people who are not of the light betray, they turn totally dark. All that they have gathered in the attempt to enhance their appearance has gone. And it is the most astounding thing to witness, because it may occur from one day to the next.

If you take a child of the light who is sincere, who would not for the world betray the Brotherhood, but who makes a mistake or sins, that child of the light will come to the altar, be chastened, be rebuked, be forgiven, repent and go on. There will not be a substantial loss of light to the core. There may be a temporary clouding of the aura with the burden of the sin that must be transmuted, but the lightbearer does not turn inside out and reveal the nature of a conspirator, because he is not a conspirator. He is then forgiven, and he moves on. And the whole outcome is entirely different. From the position I hold, watching this is really amazing.

So the "wretched adversaries" are the betrayers, the treasonous ones. They are spoken of continually throughout these books sponsored by Morya and Maitreya. Why is this? Because to have a Community of the Holy Spirit, one has to be on guard to know what assails that community. And who assails the community? Those who hate the light most, because the only place they can have the light is where they can warm their shins on the fire and hearth of the master and his disciples.

The Defense of the Community

The guru is obliged to look out for the welfare of every member of the community. While on a one-to-one basis with them, although one might conceive of continuing the relationship with someone who violates the masters' standards, one could not possibly jeopardize all the sheep in the community for the sake of the one who keeps on saying, "I'll never do it again. I'll never do it again. I'll never do it again"—but then he does it again.

What can I do but dismiss a repeat offender? I am very grateful that Mark and Morya and Maitreya have shown me cases where the line has to be drawn. You will see this in your teaching centers and study groups all over the world. Be aware of it, and know that the mercy of God belongs unto the lightbearers, and the mercy that endures forever belongs unto the child of the light.

Likewise, be careful of the sympathy and the self-pity of the fallen ones who are not sorry when they sin. When they are found out, they cry. But that's the only time they cry—not while they're sinning. They have no regrets about betraying the messenger or the Brotherhood while they are enjoying the fruits of their betrayal.

The minute they are exposed, however, they cry crocodile tears and tell you how sorry they are. But they are not really sorry at all. They are saying, "I'm sorry I'm caught. Now that I'm caught, let me back in."

Once when I had to deal with this, I picked up a book, *Mercy's Law,* that said, "It's easier to ask for forgiveness than to get permission." And that is the philosophy of the betrayers. Isn't that interesting?

Look at the Motive of the Heart

I wish to recall to you how the Blessed One [Gautama] showed consideration even for the adversaries. This book is read at the entrance to the community. The newcomer must be forewarned about many perplexities. It often appears that contradictions are insoluble. But, wayfarer, where are the contradictions when we see only an abundance of road signs? The abyss is barred by the mountain, and the mountain is bounded by the sea. Shoes for the mountains are not suitable for the sea. But those who enter are obliged to change hourly their armor. Not only mobility, not only quickness of thought, but the habit of changing weapons is needed. It is not so easy to become accustomed to a change of weapons. Beside the feeling of ownership stands habit, and it is difficult to replace addiction to objects by adaptability of consciousness. For superficial thinking it may seem mere playing upon words, but how necessary it becomes for the leaders guiding the destinies of nations to understand this distinction of concepts!

I think you can understand "changing weapons" to mean changing the different types of decrees to get at different conditions. Changing weapons also holds true when dealing with two individuals who make the same identical mistake, because their motives need to be understood. There are so-called innocent mistakes, and there are mistakes that are treason.

Whether the mistake is a lie, an infraction of the code of conduct or something that is an ultimate betrayal of the messenger, one looks at the motive of the heart. One looks at the soul. One looks at the entire karmic record, the whole life pattern, to see whether or not one is dealing with the tares or with the wheat.

Behind this mistake, was there intense hatred of the Mother, jealousy of the Mother or revenge? Or was it merely density that caused one to do thus and so?

This is why the Brotherhood has stressed, as Gautama Buddha stressed to his disciples, that the guru deals with each chela separately. The Law is the same, but the disciplines and the teaching may be different for each one. This has to do with the changing of the weapon, how you deal with the fallen ones. "A soft answer turneth away wrath"[2]—but on the other hand, sometimes a loud rebuke is necessary.

When to use a soft answer or a loud rebuke takes attunement with Morya. These are the things you only learn in life and through practice. That's what chelaship is all about. It can't be learned in the classroom, for circumstances are our teacher.

Distinguish between Slavery and Freedom

It is impossible for a poisoned consciousness to distinguish the moments of freedom and of bondage. The man who is lost in conjecture as to where is slavery and where freedom is unable to think about the community. The man who oppresses the consciousness of his brother cannot think about the community. The man who distorts the Teaching cannot think about the community. The basis of the community lies in freedom of thinking and in reverence for the Teacher. To accept the Teacher means to fall in line with the workers fighting the fire. If everyone rushes to the fire from the wellspring without any order, the wellspring will be trampled without benefit.

It were better to understand carefulness within one's consciousness; this will safeguard the concept of the Teacher. Definitely the Teacher, definitely knowledge, definitely evolution of the world—these will serve as paths to the far-off worlds!

About the far-off worlds We shall write in the book "Infinity." Now, let us call to mind that the gates of the Community lead to the far-off worlds.

There are people who have desired to be in the community because the light is here, but when it comes to making a hundred-percent commitment, they have been lost in conjecture as to where is slavery and where is freedom. In the process of debating whether such a commitment would lead to their slavery or their freedom, they totally lose the perspective of community itself because they become incapable of giving their life to the community because they were so concerned about themselves as a separate identity.

I notice that this state of consciousness poisons the community. I also know who the people are in the community who have this state of consciousness. And I have to allow them to outplay themselves even though I may know what is in their subconscious months or years before it manifests. I have to give them the freedom to make their decision for or against the service or the surrender that is required.

They desire a certain level of light outpouring as well as blessings and initiations. They will say, "Oh, yes, we know you are the messenger. We know that the dictations are real. We know the blessings come forth from you," and they are the first in line to receive them.

But when it comes to giving the required equivalent to receive that level of light, they withdraw and speak about slavery and freedom. Then it becomes my calling from El Morya to set the standards at a certain level, such that to meet the requirement of the Law, they will be required to give what must be given. And if they cannot give what must be given, they cannot remain in the community.

If I were to lower the standard and allow in the community those who take but do not give, I would be betraying the community as well as betraying the Brotherhood who sponsored me. And if I were to betray, then I would no longer hold the office. Therefore, there is a very real standard, a golden-age standard, that I must keep.

I don't make the rules; I don't set the standard. I have been accused by many people who live in various cities that I make the staff work too hard. The standards are too rigorous; it's bad for their health; they have no rights of their own; they have to do this, that and the next thing.

But if anyone were to go forth in the world and start their own business, they would find themselves working longer hours than our staff works. Americans are known for working hard and for investing their energy in various endeavors, whether it's becoming a great violinist or an artist, or doing anything they really want to do.

People think that it is my level of discipline that is unacceptable, but I don't do any of this. I simply carry out the orders of the Chief* and of Maitreya. I see the wisdom of these rules of order for the community because I have seen that those who aren't willing to live up to them shouldn't be here.

For those who are willing to live up to them, these rules are no hardship at all. They would live that way by themselves. They would live up to that standard because that's the kind of people they are. So, one of the great teachings of community is that those who do not love the sacred labor do not belong in the community.

It's an amazing process to watch. It's amazing to become aware of certain qualities of consciousness that Morya and Maitreya say prevent the individuals who hold them from thinking about

---

*El Morya, chief of the Darjeeling Council of the Great White Brotherhood

the community. And if we cannot think about the community, we can't really say that we are a contributing member.

Reverence for the Teacher

"The basis of the community lies in the freedom of thinking and in reverence for the Teacher. To accept the Teacher means to fall in line with the workers fighting the fire."

I have seen people who could not safeguard the concept of the teacher, and they would betray the teacher in the very midst of the community. The betrayal of the teacher is the betrayal of the nucleus of the community.

"The gates of the Community lead to the far-off worlds." This means that the disciplines we have within the community lead us to the initiations that enable us to gain entrance into the inner retreats of the Brotherhood and to higher octaves of light.

So, in all of my years here, what have I found? I have found that Morya, Maitreya, Saint Germain and the other masters know exactly what each of us needs to do in order to go where we want to go: to the feet of other hierarchs and adepts. They are so fastidious and so determined to get us there that they are willing to wrestle with us.

They don't allow us to get away with a thing. They know exactly what we must face in this life and in the next and beyond until we have the Cosmic Christ consciousness we seek. They don't tell us why they set up rules, why they do what they do, but we know that if they put it forth, it's for the defense of the individual, the community and the Path.

The Impetuosity of Striving

99. A seal is the guardian of a secret. Secrecy has existed in all times. Where the knowledge is small, secrecy must be used. It is fearful to reflect that a certain quality of the consciousness is in no wise different now from the level of the stone age. Alien thinking, not human, does not wish to move forward; indeed, does not wish it.

> The Teacher can pour out knowledge, but it serves far
> more for the saturation of space; therefore, a teacher is not
> lonely even without visible disciples. Remember this, you
> who draw near to the community! Remember the secret—
> not to despair.
>   The secret of the future lies in the impetuosity of striving.

Impetuosity means acting suddenly, on the spur of the moment. It is noted as a fault of the Aries temperament—impetuosity, doing something suddenly. As an Aries, I've always felt
guilty for being impetuous. This is the first time I've read that it
might be a virtue!

> The eruption of a volcano cannot be delayed; likewise, the
> Teaching cannot be deferred.

For me, the great blessing of observing that the teaching
cannot be deferred came from Mark. When a teaching or a discipline was to be given, everything came to a stop—the whole
activity, the whole heart center in Colorado Springs. If some violation of a cosmic principle or a rule of the household had
occurred, all were called together into the sanctuary.

What had been done was reviewed with the individual present and was laid bare before everyone. Everyone would learn the
lesson. Not until the whole question was resolved—sometimes
not for two or three hours—could anyone go back to work.

It's a bit difficult to do now, but we have our staff meetings,
and often we have to have them in the evening. However, the
teaching cannot be deferred. Teaching is the logical correction for
error, not condemnation. When a child is in the act of doing
something that is a violation of his integrity (the integration of his
own being), he must be taught then and there. If a horse needs to
be corrected, you've only got so many seconds before he forgets
what he did wrong. You have to correct him immediately, or he
has no idea what you are teaching him. An energy spiral release
has to be corrected then and there.

The fallen ones do not like to be corrected and do not take

discipline graciously. They rebel against it. They do not want their errors to be exposed before their peers. True disciples and children of the light are eager to have error brought out into the light. They are not possessive of error and, therefore, do not become engaged in a sense of injustice when they must admit their faults in common with their fellow classmates.

Truth Must Counteract Error

The indication of a certain time permits no delay—whether it flows into the chalice of the consciousness or ascends into space. It is impossible to calculate when the individual consciousness is the more important and when the factor of space. And in that moment when the nearest one does not harken, the echo of space rumbles. Therefore, approaching the community, do not despair.

Truth must counteract error. A lie must always be countered verbally, audibly or in written form. The individual must be corrected, and if the individual is not present to be corrected, one sends forth this absolute truth into space so that it is recorded in Matter. When the one who should receive the teaching does not harken, the echo of space rumbles. One can feel the very universe send back judgment upon an individual who does not accept correction.

Before I had my training from Mark, I might have been in the camp that says, "You don't have to correct error because truth is its own defense." But, you do have to state the truth, and you must state it thoroughly.

Loud Thoughts

The book "Call" knew no obstacles. The book "Illumination" is like a rock. The book "Community" is like a ship before the tempest, when each sail and each rope comes to life.

The manifestation of the community is like a chemical combination; therefore be pure, be penetrating, and forget the chains of negation. Through forbiddance and denial do not emulate tyrants and fanatics. Through ignorance and self-conceit do not become comparable to gilded fools.

Indeed, the community does not admit the thief, who through theft affirms the worst aspect of ownership. Manifest austerity, know how to respect secrecy so as not even to repeat a date to oneself—be as a wave which washes away a stone but once.

I notice that individuals do not realize how loud their thoughts are. Even within community, disciples can read others' thoughts, because some of them think so loudly. Their auras are constantly sending their thought emanations.

When you work for K-17 and Lanello and are aware of the projects of the Brotherhood, of dates, of places, of releases of light, you learn to wrap the information in a cloak of invisibility within your own mind. You learn not to think about that information lest psychics pick your aura and take from you that which is a part of the inner workings of the Brotherhood. This they will do.

Your tube of light and the great white cloud you establish around yourself through Saint Germain's teaching on the creation of the cloud should be adequate protection.[3] But you need to be careful about loudly projecting into space the plans of the Brotherhood, your own alchemy and projects that you are working on. Sensitive people, whether of the light or of the darkness, have a habit of reading the aura.

Overcome Babbling

100. Understand the Teaching; understand that without the Teaching one cannot get along. This formula must be repeated, for in life much is done without the Teaching. The Teaching must color every act and every speck. This tinting, as of a beautiful textile, will adorn the effects of speech. According to the effects must the quality of a sending be judged. One should become accustomed to the fact

that the sending itself can appear unintelligible, for only its inner meaning has a shield.

Accustom yourselves to placing significance in each speech, eradicating needless babble.

It is difficult to renounce the feeling of ownership; it is likewise difficult to overcome babbling.

Babbling and chattering! You can imagine El Morya, the chohan of the first ray, giving instruction on this, for the ascended masters are not comfortable in the presence of chelas who never cease their chattering. Chattering squanders the light in your power center* and depletes your power in the spoken Word— your power to give the commands of creation.

It is true that the more educated and the more serious people become, the less they talk. They value the Word. They have a certain humility and do not impose themselves upon others unless they have something of value to say. The truly wise stay silent more often than they speak. When you realize someone has wisdom, go after him to get him to impart his wisdom, for he often does.

101. Know how to take it when you are called materialists. In actions and in thinking we cannot be isolated from matter. We turn to higher strata or to the crudest aspects of the very same matter. It is possible to prove scientifically this inter-relationship. It is likewise possible to demonstrate scientifically how the quality of our thinking acts on matter.

Egotistical thinking attracts the lower strata of matter, for this form of thinking isolates the organism—as a single magnet which cannot attract more than its own intensity allows. It is another matter when thinking proceeds on a world scale; there results, as it were, a group of magnets, and an access may be obtained to higher strata.

It is easier to observe one sensitive apparatus which fixes the quality of thinking. It is possible to see spirals going upwards or descending into a darkish vapor—the most

*the throat chakra

graphic illustration of the materialistic process of thinking through the quality of inner potential. These simple manifestations have a dual significance: first, they detect the ignorant ones who imagine matter as something inert and lacking anything in common with the seat of consciousness; second, they have a significance for those seekers who will be responsible to themselves for the quality of their thinking.

It is instructive to observe how thought infects space— an analogy may be obtained in likening it to the process of gunfire. The bullet flies far, but the dispersal of the smoke depends upon atmospheric conditions. The density of the atmosphere forces the smoke for a long time to cloak the sunrise. Hence, take care about your thinking. Also, learn to think beautifully and briefly.

First we are told not to babble and to control the throat chakra. Now we learn to think beautifully and briefly.

Clarity of Thinking

Many do not see the distinction between thought for action and a reflex of the brain. It is necessary to know how to cut short reflexive spasms that lead to semi-consciousness. The development of reflexive activity is similar to intoxication.

The community is arrived at in clarity of thinking. The manifestation of thinking produces a clear, inexpressible responsibility. We are very solicitous that the realization of responsibility should not forsake you.

Clear thinking is the sharp line of logic of the Gemini mind. If you have a problem to solve, apply the Law you know, and given the situation, there are only two or three alternatives. You consider all three. You decide upon one based on experience. You go after it. You take action, and you accomplish it. The thought and the action are complete.

And then there is muddled thinking, a reflexive spasm that leads to semi-consciousness. People let their thoughts go round and round and let their emotional feelings cover over the thinking process. They are not disciplined to think logically. Perhaps they have not had Montessori training or geometry or math. Perhaps they haven't understood the laws of Matter and don't move from cause to effect. They have no mental discipline, and their thinking is not sharp. They can't figure out how to do a given task in the shortest amount of time at the least expense of money and energy. Hence, they are not leaders. They have to be told not only what to do, but also how to do it.

This problem is becoming epidemic in America because of our system of education. Therefore, going back to the foundations of logic themselves, plus having experience, plus being a chela under people who have learned to sharpen the mind, you can learn to make decisions that are effective for action. Then you are educated and you become professional and you can be successful.

I have pursued this discipline as part of my responsibility as a messenger. I never know when El Morya will want to send a message through me. If my body and mind are not alert, I definitely won't know when he contacts me. I have seen El Morya dictate in the middle of the night or at dawn. I've felt him nudge me when I was sleeping: "Get up. Take a dictation." I have a tape recorder at my side. I'm always ready.

If I were not careful about my diet, I would be so foggy that not only would I not hear him, but if I did hear him, I might not have the capacity to serve as a messenger at that hour. So, to pursue my office, I have had to be careful.

You also have an office. The worst thing that could ever come upon a disciple of El Morya is not to hear him when he needs to use you because of your neglect of the physical body or the mental body or not to get the proper rest on a regular basis so that you are too tired to respond with the impetuosity that he's talking about.

❧

Beloved El Morya, beloved Lord Maitreya, beloved Mother of the World, I call for the sealing in these hearts of this particular ray and piercing light of illumination's flame brought to us today for the edification, comfort and exhortation of these souls of light.

Beloved Mother Mary, instruct each one and bring them into alignment with the perfection of their inner matrix. In the name of the World Teachers, Raphael and Mother Mary, Amen.

Camelot
June 5, 1980

CHAPTER 8

Embody the Flame of Trust

Ln the name of the Father
and of the Son and of the Holy Spirit, in the name of the
Mother, I call to the Cosmic Council of the Four and
Twenty Elders. I call to beloved Jesus and Kuthumi, World
Teachers, Lord Maitreya, our Great Initiator, beloved Lord
Gautama and the Seven Holy Kumaras, beloved Sanat
Kumara—all who sponsor our youth and children, their
parents and teachers, for the ongoing flame of illumination.

Beloved Goddess of Liberty and the Great Karmic
Board, Pallas Athena, beloved Portia and beloved Kuan Yin,
O beloved hosts of the Lord, Cyclopea, Great Divine Director, beloved Nada, I call unto you now, and I call for the full
power and the action of the sacred fire to descend with
magnificent dispensations of creativity, genius and the gift of
hard work itself, enjoining the sacred labor and the fastidi-
ousness to daily service on the Path on behalf of these souls.

We ask for this bread of communion and this wine, the
essence of thy life from the heart of the God and Goddess
Meru on behalf of the sixth root race, from the heart of
beloved Vaivasvata Manu and beloved Lord Himalaya on
behalf of the fourth and fifth root races, from the heart of
the beloved Great Divine Director on behalf of the incoming seventh root race, the seven mighty archangels on behalf
of the root races remaining, and the embodied angels and
elemental life to give us the sponsorship, the light and life
and determination to set the captives free.

Therefore, let the Word go forth, O Maha Chohan, O Holy Spirit. In the name of Jesus Christ, let thy Word go forth, O God.

Happy Father's Day to you!

I am very grateful for the flames of the sons of God in the earth who bring to us the awareness of Father. It's a great joy to have you here. I know that the daughters of God also outpicture the masculine ray to some degree, but when we celebrate Father's Day, we are so grateful for the sons of light who carry the flame of Lanello and who remind us of God the Father, God the Son and God the Holy Spirit.

I feel that in our culture, although perhaps it is unspoken in some circles, there is often a lack of appreciation of manhood, sonship and the masculine ray, and a certain desecration of it. I think that the sexual stimulus we see in advertising is as much a desecration of man as it is of woman. Although woman is most often shown, it is always implied that sexual symbols will manipulate the male to buy the products. So both are degraded.

Unfortunately, as you know, this trains man to respond and to demean himself and not to have a sense of self-worth, of Christhood and sonship. And I think that we can trace the absence of self-worth of the American male to the doctrine of the virgin birth.

This doctrine indicates that man is not needed, that he is not pure enough to sire the Christ. Therefore, it builds up man's hatred of woman because he is not acceptable. He is not equal to the woman, and, therefore, he must be beneath her. Joseph is supremely unimportant in the whole situation, and, therefore, so is every husband. You see only the Madonna and child, and the child's father is God.

So, what happens to man? He becomes a second-class citizen. That understanding is in the subconscious of the entire human race, and Mother Mary told me that is why it is so diabolical. Psychologically the man's reaction is to get even with woman, and if he is not worthy to sire her child, he then goes to the harlot. He has the excuse to be exactly what this doctrine says he is.

He does not place supreme value on himself as the bearer of the seed of Alpha. And whether or not a man is ever a father, the very presence of the seed in the physical octave as the vibration of light holds the balance for the planet. The same holds true for the presence of the physical egg. Whether or not a woman ever bears a child, the moment the egg is released in her body on the day of ovulation there is the presence of the Great Central Sun egg. It's a very high vibration and ritual. Because the pill prevents ovulation, it deprives woman of her essential womanhood, which is the meditation on the egg during the cycle of ovulation.

Her meditation upon the Cosmic Egg, the Cosmic Womb, the Great Central Sun and the arcing of the light is one of the highest meditations a woman can experience. As a result of the pill, there is no ovulation, so woman's identity is destroyed. Her essential mission as a daughter of God is interfered with chemically. And, therefore, no value is placed upon the seed itself, nor is any value placed upon the egg.[1]

So, when I come to Father's Day, I am supremely grateful for the bearers of light, and the light that we bear is the seed of God. We are the seed of God, and we bear the means for his seed to be sustained in Matter. The seed in itself is a sustaining principle of life.

When we have the sense of ourselves as bearers of light and bearers of the seed within our bodies, we have a sense of exaltation about our mission. That sense of exaltation begets the self-worth and the self-mastery to contain and to have the God-control of these energies. And we gain an appreciation of just how sacred the sacred fire is. So fatherhood in the highest sense of the word comes down to us through the embodied sons of God.

You Can Do Everything

Let us turn to the book *New Era Community* now, and I will start with number 102:

102. It is necessary to guide the education of a people from the initial instruction of children, from as early an age

as possible. The earlier, the better. You may be sure that overfatigue of the brain occurs only from awkwardness.

We would define *awkwardness* as misalignment, as the Buddha's word *dukkha*. Chelas will tell you that a couple of hours of decrees are worth several hours of sleep, and that is because the decrees bring the four lower bodies into alignment. You require less sleep when the bodies and the chakras are perfectly aligned. Alignment creates flow, and where there is flow, the substance of fatigue is transmuted.

El Morya instructs you never to push this, however, but to get the full amount of sleep you feel that you require. The text does not say "fatigue," it says, or Maitreya-Morya says, "overfatigue." Overfatigue of the brain occurs only from "awkwardness." Some people have the problem of falling asleep, which may not be from fatigue but from an illness. We can see that alignment is most important, and alignment can be assisted by hatha yoga.

The mother approaching the cradle of her child utters the first formula of instruction: "You can do everything." Prohibitions are not needed; even the harmful should not be prohibited. It is better instead to turn the attention simply to the more useful and the more attractive. That tutorage will be best which can enhance the attractiveness of the good. Besides, it is not necessary to mutilate beautiful Images for the sake of an imagined childish nonunderstanding; do not humiliate the children. Firmly remember that true science is always appealing, brief, precise and beautiful. It is necessary that families possess at least an embryo of understanding of education. After the age of seven years much has been already lost. Usually after the age of three years the organism is full of receptivity. During the first step the hand of the guide must already turn the attention to, and indicate, the far-off worlds. Infinity must be sensed by the young eye. Precisely, the eye must become accustomed to admitting Infinity.

It is also necessary that the word express the precise

thought. One must expel falsehood, coarseness and mockery. Treason, even in embryo, is inadmissible. Work "as grown-ups" is to be encouraged. After its third year the consciousness easily grasps the idea of the community. What a mistake to think that one must give a child its own things! A child can easily understand that things may be held in common.

The assertion "I can do anything" is not idle boasting but only the realization of an apparatus. The most wretched being can find the current to Infinity; for each labor of quality, opens the locks.

103. The schools must be a stronghold of learning in all fullness. Each school, from the very primary up to the highest institution, must be a living link among all schools. Study must be continued during one's entire life. Applied knowledge must be taught, without breaking away from historic and philosophic science. The art of thinking must be developed in each worker. Only then will he grasp the joy of perfectionment and know how to make use of his leisure.

104. Each school must be a complete educational unit. In the schools there must be a useful museum in which the pupils themselves take part. There must be a cooperative, and the pupils must also be taught such cooperation. All phases of art must be included. Without the paths of beauty there can be no education.

105. The study period will be a most agreeable hour when the teacher justly appraises the aptitudes of the pupils. Only discernment of capabilities makes for a just relationship toward the future workers. Often the students themselves do not understand their destination. The teacher, as a friend, prepares them in the best direction. No compulsion is applicable in schools. Only persuasion can be suitable for stimulating learning. More experiments, more discourses— what a joy there is in the application of one's forces! Little ones love the work of the "grown-ups."

106. When the family does not know how, let the school teach cleanliness in all ways of life. Dirt comes not from poverty but from ignorance. Cleanliness in life is the gateway to purity of the heart. Who then is unwilling that people be pure? One should equip schools in such a way that they will be conservatories for the adornment of life. Each object can be considered from the standpoint of love. Each thing must be made a participant in the happy life. Cooperation will help to find a way for each household. Where one person alone does not find the solution, there the community will be of assistance. Not prizefighters but creators will be the pride of the country.

How to Penetrate a Book

107. The school must not only instil a love for the book but teach how to read—and the latter is not easier than the former. It is necessary to know how to concentrate thought in order to penetrate into a book. Not the eye but the brain and the heart do the reading. The book does not occupy a place of honor in many homes. It is the duty of the community to affirm the book as a friend of the home. The cooperative, first of all, has a book-shelf whose contents are very extensive. There will be accounts of the treasures of the motherland and of her links with the world. The heroes, the creators and the toilers will be revealed; and the concepts of honor, duty, and obligation to one's neighbor, as well as mercy will be affirmed. There will be many examples prompting learning and discoveries.

I think that this section is important, because just teaching children to read does not teach them how to penetrate a book. Even the simplest stories we read to our children contain facts that we should quiz them on. Children need to be able to walk away from a story and remember the facts as they were presented.

It's important to be able to do this. It's important for witness, for testimony. People have to be able to tell you what they did yesterday or the day before, and they should be able to give you the plot sequence of a simple story. It gets more complex as they analyze plays and operas, as the masters reveal many of the mysteries through these plots that increase in complexity, such as in Shakespeare.

The ability of a child to grasp a plot, to memorize how it unfolds is an important process in logic and in being able to think things through step-by-step. For instance, when you are deciding how to deal with a certain situation, you say to yourself, as you would in chess or in Chinese checkers, "If I do this, this and this, the person will react in this, this and this way, and then I will have to deal with this next set of circumstances." Chinese games are often based on this concept of strategy, and each person needs to learn from a very early age how to gauge what will happen if he makes a certain move.

For children, the basic ability of how to deal with facts goes along with learning multiplication tables and learning spelling. There are certain concrete blocks that must not be overlooked. Until a child can tell you the story of Cinderella or Snow White, don't take him on to the metaphysical interpretation of the story. Let him tell you the story of Jack and the Beanstalk before you start talking to him about how the son of God can conquer the fallen one or the Nephilim. Be sure that he can grasp the facts and become a master of facts.

Learning how to read with the necessary concentration is not something that children get simply by teaching them the mechanics of reading. Children like games and like to be questioned. They like to be praised when they do well and when they master a subject. So bedtime stories are an important communion between parent and child. If the child hasn't fallen asleep when the story is over, quiz him. Most children can give the story back to you almost verbatim. The next step is to teach them to summarize it.

Adults also have the problem of penetrating what they read. I see this all the time because I talk to a lot of people. Many adults cannot tell you something without going into a blow-by-blow account and including every detail: "He said this to me, and I said that to him," and so forth. They don't know how to summarize.

Once they finish their lengthy account, you have to ask them to summarize the story, which means they have to extract what is most important, what is necessary for you to hear to get the concept. Often those who try to explain something to me leave out the obvious, and I can never completely grasp what they are talking about. I am, then, required to ask them questions, and I will scold them and say, "Don't make me stand here and pick your brains. Tell me what I need to know about the situation." And you would be surprised how difficult this is for some people.

People should train themselves to list six important points about something that happened, like a car accident or a death or a stealing or a robbery. What happened? What time did it occur? How many people were there? Did you see the individual? What was stolen?

An excellent way to train the mind is in reading right from the very first stories. I like the Seventh Day Adventists' series of Bible stories and Bible books, because they tell exactly what is written in the Bible without interpretation, so that people of any faith can use them. And they are beautifully illustrated. Through them the child can learn the stories by the facts, even the Book of Revelation. It's not only illustrated, but the story is told as it is written. So he learns it at the physical level.

Later you teach him the interpretation level. But you have to be careful not to go to the abstract before you have dealt with the concrete—as in the Montessori method of teaching math, we do not skip the concrete steps.

Reading is both an art and a science. Your responsibility to yourself and to your students is to know how to extract information and how to retain it. This can also be seen as training to bring back memories of the inner retreats. People say, "I can't remember what I did in the inner retreats." That is because they lack discipline in their memory body.

The inner memory of the soul is actually little used by us, and what cuts us off from that memory is the effluvia in the lower memory body and in the astral body. We have covered over our being with so much substance and misqualified energy that the higher memory is not available to us, yet everything worth having is stored in that higher memory.

Mastering Information

The art and science of mastering information is something I seek to convey at Summit University. I suggest that you start by testing yourself on what you have extracted from an article or from something you have read. Although people who teach speed-reading do not believe in underlining, I do. I think it's important to underline, to outline, to read the section over several times and to set it in your memory, because when you are speaking spontaneously, you need to be able to pull facts out of your head.

On whatever subject you are speaking, you need to have ten or twenty facts that you have memorized, as well as dates and key quotes that other people have said. Some of the most convincing evidence should be right on the tip of your tongue. When you develop a repertoire of information, you'll be invited to speak on talk shows and be able to back up what you say.

After I give lectures, I'm not always able to come out later with the same facts. I have to study them again. It's difficult to keep a lot of information at hand, and it's especially difficult for me because the Brotherhood requires that I be a blank page at all times for them to write on. On the one hand, I'm not supposed to be cluttered, and on the other, I must know my subject. It is a constant test, a constant challenge. You can never let down. But it makes you more powerful people.

One of the nine gifts of the Holy Spirit is the gift of knowledge. Another is the gift of wisdom. The gift of wisdom is the understanding of the Spirit sphere, of all the octaves of light, including ascended master law. The gift of knowledge is knowledge of what is happening in the Matter sphere. It is something you work at by study, and you must teach your children to work at it.

I have noticed that some of our New-Age children have tremendous memories. To retain information is a great gift, and we must see that they do not lose that memory through the use of drugs, chemicals, marijuana, et cetera.

"Treasures of the motherland." The motherland is not only Lemuria but the place to which we all desire to return. It's even the God Star, Sirius. It's one's nation, the history of one's people, the history of bravery, "heroes, creators and toilers," the saints. All this must be a part of the curriculum—"honor, duty, obligation to one's neighbor, as well as mercy will be affirmed."

> 108. The school will teach respect for useful inventions, but will warn against a machine slavery. All forms of slavery will be destroyed as signs of darkness. The teacher will be a guiding tutor—a friend who points out a shorter and better path. Not the process of compulsion, but the smile of summons.

We summon the children, and we must teach them not to be the slaves of machines or mechanization but to be the master of all useful implements. This will result in the liberation of the individual for communion with God and for the highest service.

Treason

> But, if into the schools of life treason will have seeped, then the severest judgment will put an end to such madness.

Treason is spoken of throughout the series of Agni Yoga books by Morya and Maitreya as the most heinous of crimes. Treason is the betrayal of trust, and trust is the essential foundation of all human and divine relationships. The fallen ones wage their greatest battles in their war to destroy trust.

I have seen betrayers placed close to me or to Mark, and I have seen treasonous acts performed against the Brotherhood or against us personally. The purpose is always to destroy our trust in the chela, in God, in the community and in human nature. I have seen, by God's grace, that nothing done to me in any embodiment has ever been able to take from me my trust.

If trust can be destroyed, one can destroy the entire psychological base of the individual. You can destroy the individual's trust in human nature to the extent that he no longer trusts himself or the spiritual leaders of the community or the ascended masters. He doesn't trust God nor any friend. Trusting no man and not trusting himself, he begins to disintegrate. I have watched it happen.

Trust God

The solution for this, of course, is to trust God. Mark gave a famous talk in which he said, "Trust no man. Trust only God." When you trust the light in the heart of everyone you know, when you adore that light, serve that light, speak to that light, befriend that light, that light returns to you the sacredness of the trust you have placed in it. You will find people elevated and behaving at a higher level because you have contacted the reality of their being.

Treason, therefore, is the betrayal of trust. It begins with the betrayal of the guru, the guru-chela relationship and all other relationships. For example, treason in terms of marriage is faithlessness on the part of the husband or the wife that breaks down the entire circle of fire of the marriage, breaks down the lives of the children and causes them to lose faith in human nature.

Treason is the arch-tool of the fallen ones to destroy the interaction of God and man. Perhaps you have heard of the *Humanist Manifesto,* which declares its disbelief in a God who answers prayer and who can be summoned to enter people's lives. This is treason because it is the overturning of trust. Humanists have manifested treason toward the hierarchy of light, toward Almighty God—God the Father, God the Son, God the Holy Spirit and God the Mother. They now declare that there is no God, or if there is a God, that God cannot be trusted to intercede on behalf of man.

Trust is faith, it is hope, it is charity, it is love. It is the cohesive factor of life, and if you sense that you are losing hold of that ingredient, you had better sit down and fast and pray and get back into the very heart of God. The test comes on the two/eight cycle of initiations as fear and doubt.

What do you do when you doubt someone's sincerity, loyalty or love? You begin to withhold yourself. You begin to withdraw because you do not want to be fooled or hurt. Thus, you begin to have lip-service relationships in which you really don't give your heart either to God or to friends or to a community or to a nation. This is dangerous because now you no longer enter fully into relationships. You remain on the fringe as an observer, and if the other person does his part, you will give your equal part.

However, that is not true friendship with God. You always have to go all the way and give all the way and love all the way without the fear of being hurt or being fooled or being betrayed. We each have an obligation to bring to life our essential flame of trust in God and trust in the God in one another. And we must never, never be moved by people's betrayals.

When I experienced a betrayal of a most intense form, I said, "Though it was done to me, I had no part in it." I was not touched by it because I was innocent of its vibration and totally in the immaculate concept of giving trust even where trust was not deserved. Ultimately, however, I gave that trust to Almighty God and to Maitreya, and ultimately Almighty God and Maitreya, despite the treasonous acts of individuals, returned their trust to me.

If you are going to have community, if you are going to have love on earth, if you are going to have the fullness of the faith that we enjoy, sooner or later you will see treasonous acts against you personally or against a teaching center, a study group, your marriage, your family, your endeavors.

You have to be prepared to stand on the rock of faith and trust and not be moved. If you become cynical or begin to withdraw because of others' misdeeds, you may be tricked into betraying your own divine plan. And in the end, you may even find that you have not given enough to precipitate your ascension.

Embody the Flame of Trust

When you come into a classroom of children, you must be all trust. You must so embody a flame of trust and trustworthiness to your children and your family that it evokes the response: we are at peace and we do not fear.

When I worked in certain government agencies and at the United Nations, I had FBI clearances done on me after I left high school. They went back to my hometown and interviewed all kinds of people. It was reported back to me that, of all the people interviewed, no one had anything to say against me. They said that I was trustworthy and responsible in everything I did.

I had lived in that town since the age of two, so all they needed to know was there, yet I was surprised to hear it. As I look back on my life, I see that I have simply tried to do a good job in everything I did. I tried to be a friend to all people and defend those who were oppressed. And I realized as I looked back that whenever anybody wanted a job done, they came to me because they knew they could trust me.

What people remembered about me was an essential flame of faith that really was a contribution to their lives. I am grateful to God that he has so graced me with faith, and I realize that that faith is precisely what is missing today.

I have meditated on this a great deal in the past week and I realize why El Morya is committed to the first ray: because trust is the foundation that holds our money system together—"In God we trust"—and trust is a quality of the first ray. Morya himself, with his Gemini mind, is totally aware of people's psychology. He is totally aware that the whole conspiracy of the fallen ones is to break down people's faith in one another.

Look at what the deprogrammers do to break down people's faith in Almighty God and in the organizations they belong to. Someone asked a deprogrammed girl if she trusted the deprogrammer, and she said, "Trust him? No, I don't trust him. I don't trust anybody."

That's what he accomplished. She didn't trust him. She didn't trust me. She didn't trust her former church. The only person she could trust was Jesus, so she decided to stick with him. But the deprogrammer didn't even care if he broke down her trust in Jesus. In fact, that was part of his plan—"Don't trust me. Don't trust anybody." It becomes logical, and the person falls for it.

I'd like you to remember the times in your life when someone you trusted betrayed you. Look at the enormous pain you felt— a pain that you almost do not recuperate from. We talk about our first love as the special love of our life because we have no prior experience, so it is where we give of ourselves freely. We have no prior experience and have never been burned.

Subsequent to that, people never have quite the experience of that first love, as they resolve to give less of themselves the next time to avoid being hurt. That affects your relationship with God, believe it or not. Those hurts build a psychological mechanism in your subconscious that makes you give just a little bit less, with a little less fervor. You think, "If God doesn't answer my prayer, I won't be disappointed," and you no longer have the faith that every prayer will be answered. You do not trust God to the extent that no matter what adversity comes your way, you know that God is taking care of you, and you know that he is answering your prayer.

I'd like you to sharpen the sword of trust and faith in your world and see how it affects everything else that happens to you. See how much more you can give in every relationship without fearing that somebody is going to take something from you somehow. Do you see how cynicism creeps in and you don't even know it?

When I look into people's eyes as I am giving blessings, I often see fear. It is the main human vibration that you can see. Fear will lead to everything else—rigidity, ignorance, slovenliness, faithlessness. It all goes back to fear—fear that somehow God does not love you, fear of separation from him, dating from the time of the Fall. Sometimes it is fear that God will find out about a sin that you should have confessed and put into the flame.

"Strip Us of All Doubt and Fear"

When I first came into this activity and was handed the decree "Strip Us of All Doubt and Fear," I said, "Why do I want to give this decree? I don't have any fear."

I was twenty-two. I had no fear. I'd go anywhere, do anything, travel around the world, be alone. I had never encountered a situation where I had fear—or so I thought. Then I began to analyze what fear was, and I realized that all kinds of other things in my life that I hadn't called fear were the result of fear, patterns of the human consciousness. When I gave "Strip Us of All Doubt and Fear," those blocks disappeared, and I could feel a free flow of energy. Then I knew that beneath the surface, in my electronic belt, I had a record of fear.

When people form groups that are very rigid, they become little robots to some leader. This is a very intense form of fear. It affects the total personality.

> But, if into the schools of life treason will have seeped, then
> the severest judgment will put an end to such madness.

Trust in the Teacher

From hierarchy's point of view, the greatest crime against community is treason—a breach of trust in the relationship with the guru, another member of the community, with Almighty God or with an ascended master. It is the most heinous crime, because while it exists, it breaks down the community.

The entire community is compromised by the presence of treason. This is why a treasonous act is punishable by death in the military. Lately, there have been many treasonous acts in our government that have gone unpunished. We have become lenient toward treason in the United States—the betrayal of one's country, one's family, one's community, one's state, one's marriage and ultimately of oneself.

As you know, Kuthumi has said that the greatest test on the Path comes years into the Path. It is the test of trust in the teacher.

The vibration is doubt of the teacher and doubt of the teaching. Kuthumi wrote about this in Theosophy. He said that the greatest single test on the path comes when you begin to have this overwhelming doubt of the teacher and the teaching, and if you do not pass this test, you lose your foothold on the Path.

It's a very intense test, and it comes in the form of hearing gossip about the human qualities of the teacher that make you begin to feel that he is not worthy of being a teacher and has been pretending to be what he is not.

Kuthumi explains that this mistrust comes from within the individual himself as the individual's self-distrust arising from his own records of past betrayals where he once played the role of the hypocrite and the false one, and he suspects that what he has done to others will come back upon him.

To heal this situation, as I see it (Kuthumi didn't say this) we have to start on the premise that the ascended masters are real, the I AM Presence is real, the Christ Self is real. Therefore, if you have a crisis involving the embodied messenger, if you have such an onslaught to deal with, you don't have to throw out the activity or the teaching—you can go straight to the heart of God and begin to transmute your fear and doubt on the two o'clock line.

When you surface from prayer and fasting to heal your relationship with God and the masters, then you can come back from a higher vantage point of a higher attainment to look again at your relationship with the messenger. Trust in the messenger is not trust in the human consciousness or the human person, nor is my trust of you placed in the human consciousness. It is absolute faith in Almighty God, who will be the chela where you are, regardless of outer appearances.

The community cannot survive with treason in it, and this is why the ascended masters do dismiss various individuals from the community. Treason is infectious. It is a disease, a virulent disease. When you look at treason as the betrayal of trust, you see that it has its roots in the fear and doubt of one's own identity. And if you analyze the two o'clock line of fear and doubt, you realize that treason, or betrayal of trust, always results in death.

It may be the death of an idea, the death of a project, the death of an organization, the death of a relationship or even the death of a portion of one's own identity. I am sure you have experienced the betrayal of a very close friend as almost an experience of death. In your eyes, the friend is no more. A part of yourself has died. A certain joy has gone out of your life, and you must replace it with the joy and understanding that God is your true friend.

Often I see on the countenance of students the residues of previous betrayals going back many embodiments. I see a look in the eye of an absence of a certain luster of life that ought to be there. Get to the source of the problem, for it will deprive you of consorting with angels and entering in to the joy of the masters.

If someone betrays you, you must know that your love for that person has always and forever been your true love for Almighty God. If the person's matrix crumbles and you can no longer deposit your love in that cup, there is another cup that is the Sun behind the sun just beyond the veil. It is the cup of Maitreya and Morya and Mary, where your love always was from the beginning. And that is the secret of overcoming one of the greatest hardships we experience on earth.

All the great saints have had these painful experiences in their final embodiment—look at Thomas More or Francis Bacon—and they made it because they understood this lesson. I am certain that God is preparing you for this initiation, or I would not be discussing it today. Therefore, put all past records of betrayal into the flame, and say to future encounters, "Your betrayal cannot harm me because I'm prepared for it."

Laziness

109. The schools will determine where is laziness, where an unusual structure of character, where madness and where the necessary understanding.

Laziness is the archenemy of the unfolding genius. What do marijuana and the other drugs produce but laziness—laziness in the dharma, in the sacred labor. They also produce it in the genes, chromosomes and cells.

Perhaps you saw the illustration in the *Saturday Evening Post* of two monkeys—a mother and her offspring. The *Post* said that in a study of monkeys that were subjected for three years to a daily dose of marijuana, the mother monkey no longer breast-fed, groomed or protected her young. The baby monkey herself was visibly affected, as was noted by its lack of concentration on the objects in its environment. The picture in the *Post* showed the control monkey breast-feeding, but the marijuana-fed monkey was not breast-feeding or paying any attention to the baby monkey. The baby monkey wasn't too interested in her mother, either.

This image can be applied to the disintegration of the family today. One word describes it: laziness. It's like ignorant animal magnetism. The full potential of the cells of the body is not employed because of an alteration of those cells, either by drugs, karma or effluvia, and they are in a state of depression. Every cell has a threefold flame and a Great Central Sun, and it should be full-blown, like a full-blown balloon in its vibrancy.

When you see laziness in children, you have to study their habits. You have to see to it that they have the proper vitamins and food and not too much sugar. Otherwise faulty chemistry may cause fatigue or depression. Then you have to be sure that they have enough sleep, that their lives are ordered, that nothing in their environment saps their energy, such as lights that are too bright or too dim, ugly colors, discordant music, noise. All kinds of things affect sensitive children.

After eliminating all the possible physical causes, you teach them to discipline their four lower bodies. Laziness is boredom; boredom is selfishness and lack of appreciation for the very presence of God in their lives. Laziness can be one of the first signs of psychological problems that can become serious in later life.

Don't allow people around you to be lazy. Morya never

does. Those who are lazy don't stay long in community, for we must follow the principle that if you don't work, you don't eat.[2]

"... where is laziness, where unusual structure of character" —anything out of keeping with the character of the Christ— "where madness"—any form of insanity or psychological problem. You have to make decisions regarding the presence of these factors with the personality.

The Brotherhood gives everybody a certain span of time and space to make it in the community and on the Path. After that, if they have not become tethered, if they are not an active, vibrant part of the community, they are sent out. They have to go out into the world and make it there because, if they stay, they will become a detriment to the community.

I must be willing to say, "This is it. You have to go out." I say it in the nicest and most loving way, but I have to say it. If I don't, I am betraying every other member of the community. For even though they may not know that an individual is a detriment to the community, it weighs down everyone else.

One of the greatest responsibilities you have in a teaching center, a study group or your Montessori classroom is when you become aware that a certain individual, perhaps even a child, is destructive to the light of every other person in that group. Then, no matter how much compassion you may have for that person or that child, there comes a time when you may have to say that he should be sent out to work or to public school, that you cannot have him in the classroom.

If I had not done this in years past, we would not have the fine Montessori school we have today. Last year I faced the possibility of having to dismiss several students in one day. I didn't dismiss them; I asked them to write a letter stating whether or not they wanted to remain in school. They all wrote letters saying that they did not want to remain here and that they were only here because their parents wanted them here.

I told the parents that I could not keep children here who did not want to be here. What's more, they had to be policed because they constantly violated the rules. They had formed a clique, a clique of the rebellious ones, who tried to get away with the least amount of work. The rest of the students (who came to be known as the goody-goodies) wanted to do the decrees and attend the lectures, for they really loved the Path and the light. Then the sincere chelas began to feel as though they were the "squares," and the other kids, who were into all sorts of worldly things, were the crowd that supposedly had everything going for them.

Finally, a high-school student who had been here several years said, "I can't stay any longer," and left. He left because the other students were making life difficult for him, picking on him and criticizing him and saying the most malicious sort of gossip, and the energy became so heavy that he walked out. I said to myself, "By tolerating the others and hoping that they would come through, I am letting the true chelas be destroyed."

Some of these delinquent students had been suspended for smoking on the premises and received back when they begged forgiveness. Yet they really requested readmission because of their parents and because it's a nice place to be. They had violated the code of conduct in many ways. Some stole things, some were engaged in sexual misconduct, some drank. But I forgave all of this. I rebuked them and let them go on. But it didn't work.

I have borne this cross for about four years, and now I know that only chelas can be accepted in our school. They also have to continue to prove themselves chelas day in and day out. So we now have a fine group of students.

Special Cases

Once El Morya gave a talk to the students in our Montessori High School in Pasadena. A woman had brought her daughter to the school, a child who had been involved in criminal activities in her hometown. The girl was obviously possessed, and the mother could do nothing with her. The girl had vowed, among other things, to steal all my rings. She was very disturbed psychologically.

Morya called a meeting of the students, and he delivered a

very fiery lecture to them. And as a result of that, I developed a program for worldly students. If they're girls and they're into their bodies and into clothes, I might make them cut their hair like Joan of Arc, wear no makeup, dress in simple clothes, work in the kitchen and attend Astrea sessions. In a month or two, they surface absolutely filled with light and really ready for chelaship. I mean, it's fantastic! Either they turn out that way, or they leave because they can't make it.

I've had great success with this. I even have one student, a senior, whom I have allowed to take two years for her senior year. She spends half a day working in one of the departments and is all caught up in service and doing decrees. If you knew what she had been involved in previously, you would understand that this is not too severe. She had made and broken commitments to me several times, and the only way I could admit her again was under the most severe discipline.

But this girl is making it and has succeeded. On a number of occasions when I have seen her, I wept just looking at her, and so has she, because she has come out of the darkest of circumstances. I just praise God that he could provide a matrix of community that she could work through and make it on the Path. She knows I know everything there is to know about her, and yet she can look me in the eye with confidence, with a sense of self-worth because she earned her way back up the ladder. She has done penance, and she has no reason to look at me with fear or a sense of guilt, because she has been willing to pay the price.

When I talk to you about looking into older people's eyes and seeing fear, I know it's because they are walking around with a heavy burden of past sins. They do not feel that they have expiated or atoned for these sins. Nor have they really looked at God face-to-face and been willing to stand before him as the white-fire wrath comes out to consume that sin, knowing that when the fire passes through them they will survive and will still have an identity. For God is forgiving, and they can build from the foundation up.

We need to understand how to deal with students from pre-school to twelfth grade who come from varied backgrounds with different types of psychological needs. We must constantly pray for guidance, because if you try to ignore the foundation, if children come with problems and you try to build a superstructure of ascended master teachings on top of the child's unresolved psychology, ultimately that child is going to have to go down to the basement of his being and make things right. Otherwise, what you have built on top will not be secure.

The greatest gift we can give to young people is the clearing of what has happened to them so far in their embodiment so that when they graduate, they will go forth with the confidence that "God loves me. God has seen me for what I am. God has shown me how to deal with myself, and what I am right now, he will support."

So we come right back to the issue of trust. A person has to be able to trust himself before he can trust God, because trust doesn't exist without prior awareness. If you don't trust yourself, where is the clay with which to mold your trust of God or of other people?

Creating a Mask

When children lie or steal, you can't pass over it, because every lie is an escape from Reality. The child is attempting to create an identity that will receive your approval. He is saying, "You wouldn't approve of me if you knew that I did this, so I'll lie and tell you I didn't do it." At that point, the child has departed from Reality and has created another person that he presents to you that's not the Real Self.

Every time the child tells a lie, he creates a papier-mâché doll of himself, and that's the image that he brings forward. It's his mask. Pretty soon, if he tells so many lies, he can never undo them. He has built a pseudo personality, and he goes through life with the belief that if people knew what he was really like, he would not be acceptable. And so he has to lie.

In this way, you find whole personalities built on the structure of putting forth a false image or making themselves appear to be what they think everybody else wants to see. We do this to a greater and lesser extent in the way we dress and the way we present ourselves. And there's nothing wrong with putting our best image forward, in thrusting forward the image of godliness and our own Christhood, because that is what we are truly and that is what we are striving to be. But you cannot allow a false character structure to be built before your very eyes.

You have to have a loving faculty working together with parents. You may find that a child's psychological problems have a lot to do with his parents—perhaps everything to do with his parents. They don't want to admit that their children have psychological problems, and they become very difficult to deal with. "There's nothing wrong with my child," they say. And they get very upset about the whole situation of discipline, because you are obviously being unjust toward their child.

For instance, I have a mother here who has two sons and a daughter. The daughter is well brought up and disciplined properly. The boys are spoiled. Why are the boys spoiled? Because the mother hates men, and by reverse psychology, she is making misfits out of the boys by spoiling them.

She is not allowing them to attain their manhood because she has a momentum in herself of emasculating man, of stripping him of his manhood. Why? Because she hasn't resolved her womanhood, and she feels threatened by the manhood of the man. Therefore, by spoiling those boys, she's destroying their manhood.

I have not explained this to her. I have been in prayer for many months, and when the Holy Spirit and Mother Mary show me how, I'm going to explain it. I have to be very gentle. I must just tell her this without destroying her, without making her feel absolutely crushed. I can't overwhelm an individual who has much worth, many virtues, a desire to serve and all kinds of fine things in her lifestream. But her fundamental absence of resolution with men affects her husband as well.

The more you are in communion with God and the ascended masters and the more you are attuned to the Holy Spirit, the more God will show you these things about people. But God expects you to be loving and tender and sensitive to the fact that you are dealing with people who are not whole. So the prayer and the counseling you give has to be most tactful, understanding and supportive. In order to do that yourself, you have to have the ultimate love of God in your heart, because anyone who has a problem with power will immediately use such a situation and enjoy watching people suffer as the hammer of the Law descends.

Thus, when you are a teacher, you have a great deal of power over the lives of little children as well as the lives of their parents. And people who are insecure will abuse that position.

The Little Bird Held in Your Hands

I think you are coming to realize that to be a teacher anywhere in life involves the supreme responsibility that Gautama Buddha told us about when he gave us his dictation, "The Little Bird Held in Your Hands."[3] He said that every child, every student, every chela who comes to the altar comes like this little bird. Their hearts are beating, and they are naked before God. They come with fear, with hope, with trust and with all their scars. They are hoping that this altar is the place where God will receive them and where they will be loved.

You must have the sense that everyone you deal with is as tender as that little bird that is held in your hand. You have the capacity to destroy that person or to give him or her eternal life through one word that you might say. You are holding the ultimate power. So you must have a commensurate love that magnetizes the wisdom that says the right thing and not the wrong thing.

I'm sure that you all remember as children finding birds thrust from the nest and being very concerned about making a home for them, taking them home, trying to feed them with little baby bottles and helping them to avoid the cats and dogs in the neighborhood. We've all had the experience of saving some of them, yet some don't survive. We have to watch them die, and we go through the terrible experience of realizing that something more than human hands has to take care of these tender creatures.

Therefore, when you have that sensitivity to life, God will entrust not just a few but hundreds and thousands of people to your care. But until you do, he will not trust you with his little birds. When you have that sensitivity, you will have so many souls coming to you that you can scarcely care for them all in this octave. You have to do it by multiplying your bodies at inner levels, which is a great gift.

I hope that in your life as a teacher and parent, you will help to make up for all of the abuses of power of teachers and parents over thousands of years. I just pray that your flame, wherever you are, will so exude this love that you will atone for the sins of people who have abused children and youth. That is my heartfelt prayer for you.

Astronomy

110. Among the school subjects let there be taught the fundamentals of astronomy, but let it be presented as the gateway to the far-off worlds. Thus schools will stimulate the first thoughts about life in the far-off worlds. Space will become alive, astro-chemistry and rays will round out the presentation of the magnitude of the Universe. Young hearts will feel not as ants upon the earth's crust, but as bearers of spirit responsible for the planet. Let us fix our attention on schools, for from them will issue the affirmation of cooperation. There will be no construction without cooperation. There will be no security of state and union while outworn egoism holds sway.

111. Many warnings were given against selfhood. This deadly sister of ignorance smites and extinguishes the best fires. Do not consider a reminder about egoism out of place during the establishment of cooperatives. On the contrary, each statute must be written not for oneself but for others.

Among various appellations the word "friend" will be a most hearty one. Indeed, the heart does not admit egoism. The heart lives in self-abnegation. Thus, strong is the heart when it is concerned about the future, not thinking about self.

112. It is a most useful thing to be able to combine the tenderness of love with the austereness of duty. The new life will not be deterred by contrasts. It will not exert compulsion with one yoke, but will bestow breadth of receptivity. It is not fitting for people to sit in a chicken-coop. It is time to know the planet and to assist it. People cannot lull themselves by calculating how many years are yet left before the sun will be extinguished. A great number of various conditions may upset all calculations. It also cannot be forgotten that people can gnaw each other in two. This consideration must not be forgotten, since malice is deluging the Earth.

113. Cupidity is coarse ignorance. Only true cooperation can save from such a malignant mange. A greedy man has a stamp on his face. He is not concerned with the heart; his cup is a bitter one. And for the greedy man the Subtle World is only a source of torment.

114. People study the life of bees, of ants, of monkeys, and they are amazed at migratory birds, at their order and precision of course; yet from all this they draw no deductions for the betterment of earthly life. Natural history must be taught in schools as completely and attractively as possible. By examples from the vegetable and animal kingdoms one should give to understand what treasures are contained in man. If the comparatively lower organisms sense the fundamentals of existence, then so much more must man apply his efforts for a successful improvement. Many valuable indications are revealed everywhere. From the very first lessons let pupils rejoice at the wonders of life. Likewise, let them apprehend how to make use of flights and of clairaudience. Thus, clairaudience will be a natural condition. Likewise the Subtle World will be studied, along

with subtle energies. There will be no dividing line between physical and metaphysical, for all exists—which means that everything is perceptible and cognizable. And so superstitions and prejudices will be shattered.

The Purpose of the Embodied Guru

You may have read stories about Ramakrishna and others who would take upon themselves the diseases of their pupils. After healing a student, for an hour or a day they would bear upon themselves the full symptoms of the cancer or fever that the student suffered from. It would pass through them, be transmuted, and then they would be normal again.

Actually, each time I teach, I receive substance. Each time I come into a classroom and stand before a group of people for two or three hours, I walk away with the quantity of misqualified energy that the Law allows me to take on. I am aware of it for the time it takes to pass through.

Nevertheless, the opportunity for us to serve together is the great joy of my heart. I see tremendous acceleration in your beings and in your faces. I see the shortening of the cycles for the elect that was promised to us by Jesus,[4] enabling you to go forth and do great planetary service.

Therefore, the price I pay is very little for the joy received, but it involves the laws of chemistry and physics and matter and alchemy. The misqualified substance does not simply disappear. And the purpose of the embodied guru is to provide that focal point and that heart flame for the fiery furnace of transmutation.

115. No one dares to stand up against the school, but few there are who think about its improvement. School programs are not looked over for years at a time, and meanwhile discoveries are on the march. New data are rushing in from all sides: the air spheres and the depths of the oceans and the mountain treasuries all relate wonderful facts about themselves. Haste is needed, else excavations will alter the data of conventionalized history. In the new

schools prohibitions must be removed, in order that pupils may see reality—which is wonderful if truthfully revealed. Broad is the field of mental competition!

116. Shield children from everything false; guard them against worthless music; protect them from obscenity; protect them from false competitions; protect them from affirmation of selfhood. The more so, since it is necessary to inculcate a love for incessant learning. The muscles must not gain the upper hand over mind and heart. What sort of heart takes a liking to blows of the fist?

117. It is absurd to think that perspiration is only a physical manifestation. During mental work a particular emanation valuable for the saturation of space issues forth. If bodily perspiration can fertilize the earth, then that of the spirit restores prana by being chemically transformed in the rays of the Sun. Labor is the crown of Light. It is necessary that school pupils remember the significance of labor as a factor of world-creation. As a result of labor there will be steadfastness of consciousness. It is necessary to emphasize strongly the atmosphere of work.

118. It may be asked, "What signs in a teacher should be valued?" You already know about the quality of action, and thus can apply new methods in action. One should prefer that teacher who proceeds in a new way. Each word of his, each act of his, bears the stamp of unforgettable innovation. This distinction creates a magnetic power. Not an imitator, not a commentator, but a powerful miner of new ores. One should take as a basis the call of innovation. The time has come when it is possible to go only forward. Let us preserve the call of the will in an incessant run and not linger over the precipice.

One must tell the builders of life to find new words, forged by new necessity. Realization of the newness of each hour will provide the impulse.

Point out to friends what happiness it is to be eternally

new. And each electron of the New World will give new power. Apprehend the power of the new call. You can apply it in the life of every day. You know well enough that My words are for application.

119.   You think rightly that without the achievements of technic the community is impossible. Every community is in need of technical adaptations, and Our Community cannot be thought of without simplification in life. Needed is the manifested possibility of applying the attainments of science; otherwise we will become mutually burdensome. As practical realists We can boldly affirm this. Moreover, We can persistently reproach all pseudo-realists. Their subservient science and blindness prevents them from attaining that for which they are striving.

Precisely like the Pharisees of old, they conceal fear before admitting that which is already obvious to others. We do not love the ignorant, We do not love cowards who in their terror trample the possibilities of evolution.

Extinguishers of fires, haters of the Light, are you not all alike, from whatever side you come crawling! You wish to put out the flame of knowledge; but the ignorant community is a prison, because community and ignorance are incompatible. It is necessary to know. Believe not, but know!

Beloved El Morya, beloved Lord Maitreya, beloved great causal bodies of Nicholas and Helena Roerich, beloved Lanello, O mighty action from the heart of Maria Montessori, Mother Mary and the World Teachers, I call for the sealing within these hearts of the treasures and jewels of the white-fire core of the five secret rays, of all that God has deposited within my heart and out of the heart of Mother Mary, Jesus and Saint Germain.

Let these jewels of light give to each one now by the hand of the Maha Chohan this great gift that God has given to me, the great gift of sensitivity to life. Let each heart be prepared to be sensitive to the needs of all who are sent to them, the little children and people of all ages who are in need of love before they can even approach the teaching.

In the name of the Father, the Mother, the Son and the Holy Spirit, I commend you unto the keeping of your mighty I AM Presence and Christ Self, and of the Maha Chohan. Beloved Maha Chohan, be the perpetual teacher and enlightener of these souls of light. Let them go forth to engage in the mighty work of the ages, the binding of hypocrisy and the unreal and the exalting of every true child of God.

In the light of the entire Spirit of the Great White Brotherhood, may the mighty diamond of the heart of God's will keep you in perfect peace. Amen.

Camelot
June 15, 1980

CHAPTER 9

The Perpetual Labor of Love

In the name of the light of God that never fails, I invoke the flame of beloved Lord Maitreya, beloved Lord Gautama Buddha, beloved Lord Jesus Christ. In the name of Sanat Kumara, come forth now and clear the opacity, the density, the cause and core of all error in mind and heart.

I call for the sifting of the chalice of the desire body. I call for the sifting of the chakras. I call for the acceleration of light within them. I call for integration with each one's own Christ Self from the very heart of our own beloved Lanello.

I call for the mighty action of El Morya, the twin causal bodies of Helena and Nicholas Roerich. I call for the flame of community to descend. I call for the mighty action of its sacred fire. I call for it to be sealed within each one.

In the name of the Goddess of Light, the Queen of Light and the Goddess of Purity, beloved Archangel Gabriel and Hope, legions of white fire and blue lightning, draw now into the chalice of the heart the Divine Manchild as the Universal Christ of all. We thank thee, and we accept it done this hour in full power.

In the name of the Father and of the Son and of the Holy Spirit, in the name of the Mother, Amen.

In community it is important to recognize the indispensability of the individual. Without the individual, there is no community, and when the individual fails to exercise his right to be the embodiment of the Christ in the community, then he is no longer a focus of that community. When the individual fails to exercise his right to be the embodiment of the Christ, he takes from the community instead of giving to it.

The community can be destroyed by having such individuals within it. Some of these individuals are the fallen ones and the betrayers whose light has gone out. They make a very intense and frantic attempt to be seen as lightbearers. Consequently, they will have a veneer, a patina or a coating of light. They may do all the right things and say all the right things and work very hard, but we find that just beneath the surface is the extinguished self.

If you do not have a messenger or an avatar or the incarnate Word or the authority of the Brotherhood within the community, the community does not survive. This has been seen over and over again through the ages. "Smite the shepherd and the sheep are scattered"[1] is a true statement, because the shepherd is the only one who can recognize the wolf in sheep's clothing. He is also the only one who has the power and authority to bind that wolf in the midst of the sheep.

One of the qualities of sheep is their gullibility, their non-awareness of the anti-self. We have Summit University in order to teach this awareness, but even when we teach it, people often do not have the awareness. They still go out with a dreamy, idyllic sense of the masters and are often unrealistic about what the Great White Brotherhood is and what the battle of Armageddon is about. People's perceptions are often far from the mark.

You can hear these teachings, but unless you integrate them with the heart, they are of little use. Some people take in and give out the teachings like a computer. Because they have a computerized consciousness, they can sound very proficient. They can deliver the teaching with emotion so that their emotions and intellect combine as the imitation of the mind of Christ and the heart of Christ. But these people cannot endow the living Word with the flame of the Holy Spirit.

Unfortunately, the untutored do not know the difference

between one endowed with the Holy Spirit and one simply carrying on through human emotion. Until you reach that point of discrimination, you cannot go very far on the Path. Lack of discrimination is what concerns me about our students throughout the world. I have noticed that some are very astute, and some are not. Therefore, when they trust those whom they should not trust, they give their light away.

Imitation, Not Idolatry

I have been listening to the lectures on "Idolatry and the Fiery Trial."[2] I have taken the teaching to heart as I listen to what the Holy Spirit gave, and I am mindful of it in terms of assisting those in the community to live up to it, because it was the announcement of a certain pre-judgment. It stresses the need for harmony as the key to obedience to the laws of God. Since the release of that teaching, I have seen community members lose their harmony and not take the teaching seriously.

I must simply point out how you can fall into a state of human consciousness about life and not realize it. Idolatry causes you to lose your perspective on life, and you don't even realize that its venom has been injected into your veins until it comes upon you. It is the very thing that Jesus feared—to become an idol. I also fear it. The least important thing that could happen to you is not to have me with you physically.

When I went over Lanello's sermons to make our tape albums, I heard him say that worship of Jesus is not the way. The way is the imitation of Christ. Idolatry of Jesus is the formula of the fallen ones who corrupted Christianity, and Jesus was very concerned lest this be the result of his mission.

I also am concerned. I have the self-respect that comes from knowing that God lives in me. It's respect but not idolatry. I comport myself with that respect, as you should also. If you respect yourself and know that God is in you, you will treat me the same way. People should act as though they knew God were present in all of us.

We should cast out the idols from our hearts. I am conscious that God is the only thing that amounts to anything. Where I am is God and Christ. The more God is where I am, the more I am helpless without that God. And if I have a sense of "I" apart from that God, that "I" is totally aware that to function, it must be integrated with God at all times.

Therefore, functioning solely on God and on the living Christ, one does not develop and exercise the human faculties. One becomes less and less able to do anything, and is therefore, more and more dependent upon God. The more we depend on God, the more dependent we are on God.

My experience with the Brotherhood is that of oneness. When Jesus acts and speaks through me, I am aware of what he says after he says it and not in the manner of a teletype communication. In other words, I AM that Word. I AM that Christ of Jesus. He speaks. He does things. He talks to people. When I approach a situation that seems insurmountable, he gives the solution. I send someone to solve the problem, or I solve it myself and, miraculously, it is the Holy Spirit solution, and everyone is happy.

There are very difficult problems. I face difficult problems every day that I have no idea how I'm going to solve. And I have no idea how I'm to solve them until I open my mouth and God speaks.

So there is a period in your life of bhakti yoga in which you adore the Virgin, but you adore the light within her. You adore the Christ within Jesus. You adore God within Archangel Michael. You don't adore the emissary. You adore the one God, and you have that twofold experience. Then comes the internalization of the Word where you really do sense God where you are, but that God is not an idol.

God Is the Actor Where I Am

Of course, the part of me that is this vehicle has a physical apparatus. We know how it functions, how the mind works. It takes in information. It sorts it. It has discrimination. It makes decisions. That part of me is not the actor. God is the actor where I am, and I move as he moves me.

In your interaction with me, it is important not to set up blocks to dipping into the fount that God has placed where I am. What is walking around is simply a marvelous fountain of light! But I cannot teach idolators; I can only teach friends and servants—servants of God and friends of mine. When such a one is present (and there need be only one) the Word will flow all day. It will never stop. I can teach or write all day in the presence of one person who has the clear perception of what I am trying to give.

It was necessary for Jesus to exact from the disciples and from Martha a statement in answer to his question, "Who am I?" Those who could understand who he was could then be the electrode—the negative, or Omega, polarity—of his message and of his healing.

Mark commented in one of his lectures on how Jesus went to Nazareth where his parents and his sisters and brothers were known, and he was rejected by the people. They had a severe case of unbelief. Jesus could not do many mighty works in Nazareth, for you cannot work in the presence of those who do not recognize Reality.[3]

The greatest sharing between people is when the two halves of the whole know that there is this intense love. This love is pure, like an arrow, and it goes to the heart of the Christ and of God, and, yet, it is love for the total person. It's like loving the rose and loving the trellis and loving the vine and loving the heart of the rose and loving the matrix behind it and understanding that all of this is still God.

Yet one can personally love the person. If we talk about idolatry and then you think, "I will be an idolator if I love Mother personally," then we've also lost the point of our divine awareness. Hence, there is simply a necessity to transmute fear and doubt, to establish one's own inner base—that foundation of oneself who is Christ—and to be friends with your Christ Self, understanding that ultimately you are in the process of being assimilated by that Christ Self. And one day you will no longer say, "Here's my Christ Self, and here's my soul."

Sometimes people tell me, "Well, you know, I saw your Christ Self speak through you." And I always say, "Good," because whatever people perceive is what they can know. I know that I AM the living Christ. But I know it as *I* know it. And it would do no good for me to affirm it to anyone else, to all of you least of all, or even to ask you to accept that fact.

There is only one person who can confess that Christ is Lord and that's the Holy Spirit within your temple witnessing to the light. There is no righteous statement of truth unless the Holy Spirit is speaking it through you. Thus, in your state of idolatry, I don't want you to say that I AM the Christ. It does you no good. It does me no good. What good does it do? "You might as well call me anything," as Mark says, "as long as you call me for breakfast."

There is no need to have a discussion about who is the Christ if, in finding out who Christ is, you leave your own Christhood behind. Jesus called disciples to follow him and leave everything. They left what was unreal, took what was real, followed him and then internalized it. But for you to leave the moorings of your Christ identity to follow me will never work. We will never have a Community of the Holy Spirit. We'll never have a viable chalice for the Brotherhood.

If you worship the Christ where I am and not where you are, you will come to despise the Word. If it isn't where you are, you will become jealous. Nobody can stay in a state of idolatry very long before they have to topple their idols. There's a tremendous hatred in idolatry. It's a terribly unnatural state to worship something you are not. It's the whole Nephilim god consciousness and their brand of religion that they have injected into Christianity.

People worship Jesus instead of adoring and internalizing the Christ by works and deeds. Because we have talked about it a great deal, we often think that all this is behind us. In fact, it isn't behind us. It is right here and now, and it is your mighty work to internalize the light of your own salvation, your own self-elevation, your own self-awareness in the Word.

The Individual in the Community

We started out by talking about the importance of the individual in the community. The only true individuality is the individed Word, as Above, so below—the I AM Presence Above, the Christ below incarnate in you. The Christed ones are the only ones who have any ability to hold the chalice of community, to hold its grid. So that is where the line has to be drawn in a Community of the Holy Spirit.

You have to be aware of the Real Self and the not-self. Be aware when the not-self is acting in someone else. Be aware that you cannot have sympathy in your life for the extinguished self, for the individual who remains a shell and who is living off your light personally or who is living off the light of the community.

The myth of equality is something that Mark used to talk about—the myth that everyone is equal and that if someone says and does the right thing, the gates of paradise should open to him. The easiest thing in this world is to do and say the right thing. The human mind is a computer that finds it very easy, especially when one has no tethers or moorings to God and is about to be extinguished.

The hardest thing of all is to have a right heart with God and an internalization of the Word. The fallen ones put all their efforts into recording the Word, becoming experts on the Word and giving it out. As they are highly intellectual, they gain professorships or doctorates three and four times over, they become doctors of theology. They love to pontificate, pronounce doctrine and dogma and take the light of those who sit in their classes and receive that which is not the true teaching.

Many of the extinguished ones are in positions of power because they are to some extent the seed of, or the interbreeding of, the Nephilim. Therefore, the main thing they have going for them is a very sophisticated and complex carnal mind—like the vastness of modern computers. You will be amazed at how these people, even with the ascended masters' teachings, can so teach the Word as to appear to be the experts, the best chelas, overlooking totally the silent ones who are the real devotees.

The real devotees work hard and serve with love. When you come into their presence, you almost feel an aura of roses. You feel an aura of sainthood, for beauty comes from their souls, from their hearts and their minds and through the work of their hands. Their sermon is a psalm of life. They are up and doing and are the real pillars in the community.

Obviously, we are here to train people to bring everything to the consummation of preaching the Word. But how can you preach the Word when you don't have the Holy Spirit? You have to exercise the heart chakra. This is why I make it a requirement after Summit University to work or go stumping for three months. Only when you get in a work situation do you find out how much you love God.

A Disciplinary Matter

I had a disciplinary matter with a secretary recently, and I said, "Do you desire one hundred percent to be a secretary?"

She said, "No, only eighty percent."

I said, "Well, I will have to give you a certain discipline until you can live in the interior of your being rather than on the surface. You need to come to the place where it doesn't matter what you do—whether you are scrubbing floors or working in the garden or typing or accounting or whatever it is—where you can do all things with equal joy because your joy doesn't come from what you do on the outer, it comes from your contact with God."

I had never experienced such a thing as not serving the master wholeheartedly in my own life, but I have seen it many times in this organization. It's astounding, and it is a colossal defrauding of God by the individual.

You can go nowhere on the Path without studying *Quietly*

Comes the Buddha and embodying those ten perfections.[4] In all my years of service to the Brotherhood I have never done a task I didn't like, whether it was cleaning toilets or grocery shopping or doing the laundry or changing diapers or getting up and giving a talk before people who were belligerent or traipsing around the world and all the different things that I might not have chosen to do.

But I can assure you that it has never occurred to me to want or to not want to do something. It's just the next service, the next spiral, the next cycle, the next need God has. If I am called upon to do it, I do it. It's just automatic.

My joy is perpetual. I don't know about joylessness. I am constantly joyous. I am bubbling over with the laughter of the angels. It doesn't matter what I hear—lawsuits, newspaper articles, this or that calamity—it doesn't make a bit of difference to me. Nothing can move me from the joy of God.

I see people moping. I see people who are discouraged and depressed because they are working on a job outside the community that they don't like. But I will not invite someone to work at Camelot who doesn't like working downtown in a department store because it's too dense. Where are you going to gain your mastery?

I don't understand someone who says, "I'd rather do this than that. I'd rather further my own talents." I have never heard of such a thing—yet we heard about it in the reading from *Community*.

A Labor of Love

Community is for those who love the sacred labor, not for those who are frightened of perpetual labor. The meaning of community is perpetual labor. The heart perpetually beats. Its perpetual exercise is a labor of love for God. Without that exercise the heart loses its muscle, loses its life and begins to deteriorate. You have to constantly pump light through you into God's life. If you are not in the state of giving and receiving that is the whole pattern of the flow of energy to the heart, you begin to decrease until finally you are no more.

That is the law of life in the community, and those who have not internalized enough of the Christ to want that much striving should just be friends of the community. As they can contain so much and no more, they should be disciples who live with their families, come to services, read the teachings as they are able, decree as they wish and hopefully get the most and the best out of what is produced by those who are on the immense cosmic wheel of the perpetual labor of God.

To internalize the Word you hear in the classroom and to preach that Word requires the third increment, which is the perpetual labor of love. When you have that labor and that love, you are constantly on fire for God. All I need to do is speak about it, and the fire bursts and burns and creates a physical sensation of burning in me. My love for God and every individual master is so intense that I can hardly bear it.

I can hardly bear in this octave the love that is in my being for any master. I think about El Morya or Kuthumi, and I fairly melt. I have to discipline myself not to think about the masters because I will simply dissolve in the very fire of the love I have for them.

So I occupy myself thinking about the chelas and the staff members and the organization—all that doesn't have quite as much God in it for me to fasten onto as I fasten onto God through the Brotherhood. I enter into an ecstasy of pity where I meditate upon the chelas and feel their absence of fire. Then my sacred labor is to keep on infusing them with fire. In that way, I can dissipate some of the fire, and I will not melt from too much fire. That is the dharma of the Path and the great joy of being.

The best way to really discover your own personal psychology is to get into perpetual labor within the community. It is the fastest way to encounter the selfish self, the unreal self, the synthetic self, the resisting self, the unknowing self, the ignorant self, the dense self, and so forth.

When you labor until your body will simply not go any further, then you find out whether you love God enough to be

re-infused with love, or you say, "I will not go any further."
Now this has nothing to do with being sensible about getting
your sleep, eating properly and certainly not sacrificing spiritual
treasures, as Mark has taught us.

Yet moments come when something more has to be done and
you have spent your batteries for the day. You have such intense
love, however, for the person who will benefit from your service
that you actually open a valve. By the fervor of love, a valve
opens to the reserves of the causal body—not the physical body
—and you receive an increment of fire and light to finish the project on time for the victory.

An Explosion of Love

I can remember when I was the only one running the print-
ing press. I ran it long hours, sometimes eight, ten hours a day.
I remember finishing a job one day and not being able to move.
I lay down on the concrete next to the press, for I actually could
not carry my body to the next floor. But I was happy, as happy
as a lark. I had pushed to that point. Then I lay down on the concrete and meditated and was rejuvenated, and I went on to the
next task at hand.

I don't often talk about myself because I do not want to give
you any reason to elevate me above yourselves. But I must give
you a few examples so that you will understand where you are
and where you can be with a little bit more cosmic consciousness
—and how much more of an explosion of love in your heart you
can have.

Some people must depart from the community because they
have not internalized love. They need to go out and do something
to develop the heart chakra, for if the heart chakra is not developed, there's a point beyond which you cannot go. There's no
capacity to internalize light. There's no capacity to deal with the
increasing return of karma.

Karma accelerates when you have more light and when you
ascend the Path, if you have the necessary heart to deal with it.

In other words, you should, as you mount the spiral of attainment, be able to take more of both your past karma and of world karma than you could have before you had that attainment—but you can do so only if your heart chakra is developed.

The heart chakra develops through wisdom, love and the extreme exercise of will—God's will to be his will in action. Mark often quoted, "This is my body which was broken for you."[5] And we all need a fragment of that body, any fragment. We can have the body of Jesus as strength, as purpose, as zeal, as holiness, as will. Whatever quality we need, the body is broken, and each one's Christ Self is a portion of that Universal Christ whose body was broken and divided among us.

The teachings are mystical. You cannot understand a mystical teaching without a developed heart chakra. You can repeat the teaching, but you'll go out and steal or lie or cheat or murder and still say you know the teaching. Yes, you can hear it. You can study it and get A's on your papers. But if it hasn't changed your life, then it is because the block surrounding the soul and the heart has not been removed by fervent love. Waiting patiently upon the Lord, the Bridegroom, is an act of faith. And if you don't have a magnanimous heart, you begin with the quality of faith.

Believing in the One Sent

What is faith? It's an unbroken stream of love toward the object of one's faith. Believing in the One sent is not worshiping that one. Believing in the One sent is having the faith that the Christ is there and then pouring out love to that Christ and thereby internalizing more of that Christ where you are.

Faith, the absolute certainty that the Bridegroom will come, is a connection that literally draws the Bridegroom to you. The fruit of the divine union of the soul (the Bride) with Christ is always the birth of the Universal Christ consciousness.

The Brotherhood has spoken a lot about love. This Easter the masters released the fourteen-month spiral of the ruby ray. The ruby ray is the intense fire of the heart. Therefore we have the opportunity to expand the love in our heart in these fourteen months. It is a great opportunity, and yet in the midst of it, Jesus said, "Depart from me, ye despisers of the Word."[6]

Those who despise the Word are those who come and are already their own idols. An individual can set himself up as an idol with the authority to judge the next idol who is the messenger. So we have the situation in which no one can be an idolator unless he has first set up an idolatrous condition in his own consciousness and therefore establishes himself as the authority to judge.

So, I recommend that you lead with the sword of love, a ruby sword, and that you combine the action of this ruby-ray spiral with the necessity of exposing the unreality in yourself. When you see what is unreal, you can begin to take apart the mechanization man that the carnal mind has set up in your temple. And at the same time you can begin to construct the great pyramid of your Christed individuality.

You have time. You are in physical embodiment. We are not in the etheric octave. This is not the Karmic Board. We are not seated with the Goddess of Liberty having a final judgment for an individual incarnation. Most of you are young enough to be transformed many times over. Everything is in a state of renewal.

The value of our being together is that you suddenly have a greater awareness of what the internalization of the Christ means. Therefore, no matter what your sense of lack, I hope that your love for me will be a pure love. I hope you will not be a despiser of the Word, someone who despises me for having something you do not. I hope that you will have enough self-esteem to be happy that you found someone just like yourself who has realized a little more of herself than you have.

You can do the same thing this very minute, and that's what every one of Mark's sermons tells you. They are a self-help, law-of-success kind of teaching: "Anything I can do, you can do better." And that is the whole point of love, isn't it? We love the

things we admire in people when we have good sound relationships in our families and in our friends. We like to have friends
in whom we can admire an externalization of a facet of the
Christ we don't have.

It's all right to love and worship the Christ who externalized
that quality in your friend. I praise my friends for their diligence
and faith on their particular ray. I praise Lanello. Sometimes if you
say, "Praise the Lord," in the wrong way, it can be a denial. A person can feel a letdown and say to himself, "I did all this work.
I worked very hard for a week, and somebody comes in and says,
'Praise the Lord.'" The individual deserves praise as long as we
understand that we are praising the internalization of the Word
where he is rather than, "Praise the Lord, but never mind you."

Do you know that when Jesus healed the blind man, the
Pharisees tried to get the people and the man who was healed to
say that God had done it? They said, "Give God the praise. We
know that this man is a sinner."

The man born blind said, "No, this man did it. This man
healed me."[7] He had the real concept of the Christ incarnate. He
had been waiting for the Christ to come. And Jesus said, "I AM
that one." And the man believed that Jesus was that one.

Jesus would not have told the blind man that he was the
Christ if he hadn't passed his test and affirmed before the
Nephilim, "He hath opened mine eyes." It's a marvelous thing.
He was healed and did praise the Lord, for he had internalized
long ago the concept of the incarnation of Christ. There is an
integration, and there is the point of Reality.

Cast Down Your Idols

It is lawful to worship God as the center of one's individuality as long as one is not in idolatry. The surest guarantee of being
free of idolatry is your developed heart flame. When your heart
flame is developed, you can love a person totally and intensely
because you know that that person is God. You do not have a
flesh-and-blood consciousness of that person.

So, I'm not telling you to love less but to love more. You love your Self, your great God Self, and you are not separate. You're not a flesh-and-blood chart* in which the flesh and blood is down here and the Spirit is up there. You love this being that you are as a continuous stream of light.

Why, you exist on many octaves just like the little men you pile up as a child when you do blocks that hook into each other. You exist on all those planes. You have a grand identity, a vast inner being, and you should love that being. What outcrops here on earth is the unresolved portion of that being—the portion that has not resolved itself in time and space and that has its karmic pattern. But the vast part of us is the cosmic consciousness of the whole universe of which we are a part. And it is all integrated, all One.

We need to love that Great God Self and say, "That's me. I just have to get rid of this unreal self of me, this illusory self of me. I have to dissolve the sugar cube by bringing down more fire."

My great desire is to impart to you this teaching, to come at it from many directions so that it can get past your self-condemnation. So we did the wrong thing. That's unreal, too. It's all unreal. If you're going to go into a depression because you did the wrong thing, you're locked in. The idol of yourself did a bad thing, and now you're displeased with the idol of yourself.

Cast down your idols. Then you will not be disturbed, and you will not take on the vibration of self-pity or self-condemnation. There's only one true consciousness where you are—the Universal Christ. It is supreme. It is blissful. It is joyous. It inundates you with light. It has no other self-awareness. Each time you step out of its fountain of joy, you go into total unreality. Where you go does not exist. And if you don't get back into the center, you will not exist either, for that's what happens to the extinguished ones. You can't hold the light if the light isn't Christ. The light that is not the unfed flame will go out.

In every news bulletin about a blackout you will notice that the newsmen delight in saying, "The light failed." I've laughed at

---

*refers to the Chart of Your Divine Self, facing page 178.

this on several occasions. I turned on the news in the car this morning, and the announcer said, "Here is a story about the light that failed." It seems that the U.S. tested a laser beam that failed to hit an incoming missile. And so it was the light that failed.

There is a light that fails. It's a human light. It's a mechanical light. The only light that doesn't fail is the unfed flame, the threefold flame. So if you ever have a vibration that is not the vibration of your threefold flame, you're in outer darkness. If you stay there, it's your fault. And if you stay there too long, it's like going out on a long string from the mother ship, and you may not make it back. You may not get back to that flame. Therefore, you cannot be indulgent of vibrations that are not ensouled and embodied by your threefold flame.

What is your motivation? Love. It all goes back to love. There can be no motivation without pure love for God—for the God who is burdened here below, not for the idolatrous god you have put in heaven.

You have all launched your satellites, and then you worship them. We launch our gods in space. We launch Mother Mary, and we fall down and worship her in church because we've launched her. But what we are worshiping is a concept of Mother Mary that has no bearing on the real Mother Mary or Jesus or Gautama. So when we get into the teachings and we have some idea of who El Morya is, we launch him and are then forevermore down on our knees begging gifts and favors from him.

No wonder philosophy courses in college talk about belief systems being the product of people's needs and fears, because when you analyze a certain segment of the population, you find that it is true. You find that the Nephilim gods erected themselves as gods for the benefit of their own creation, their own mechanization man.

Why Have the Masters Receded?

Perhaps now you realize why the Brotherhood has receded to a dimension where you cannot actually see an ascended master.

You must realize that your inability to see an ascended master and your noncontact has to do with the fact that people have heaped idolatry upon the masters to their own hurt. The masters have had to recede beyond the veil to force the individual to make it on his own, to strive, to externalize a will and to experience enough pain to know somebody else's pain and know how to love.

In the last twenty years I must have asked the masters over a hundred times why they are beyond the veil. And each time I ask, I receive a different answer, as the answer you receive from a master depends on where you are in consciousness. If you feel very burdened you may say, "Why have you gone and left me here?" Or you may have compassion for an ascended master and realize that something must have driven him from this octave.

What drives a person of attainment out of embodiment, when in that very attainment he has the full compassion of a bodhisattva, of Avalokiteshvara, to remain in this octave? It must be idolatry. No one can live as the object of someone else's idolatry. You have to run and hide in a cave, go to the mountains. You cannot stay around people.

Idolatry has its push and its pull, its plus and its minus. Some people fawn over you with their human love. Others will destroy you with their human hatred, but human love and human hatred are one and the same thing—two sides of the same coin. So the people who hate you are actually voicing the other side of human love. Between the two they drive the masters from embodiment.

What drove Saint Francis out? The brothers came along and changed his order. It was no longer the order Christ gave him. He no longer fit in his own order. While he was away, the brothers got approval from Rome to do what they wanted. When Francis returned, they told him it was impractical to have a path of poverty, for they had now accumulated lands and possessions.

It broke his heart. It literally broke his heart. People do die of a broken heart. The very pain causes the heart to break.

Holding the Light

Thus, people have not left room for the ascended masters in their lives. They can tolerate them a little bit. They can afford to have them around for a little while, but they are not ready for them as a steady diet. I am grateful for the people who can stand me on a regular basis. It's wonderful.

The Book of Enoch describes how the Mother came down to earth but couldn't stay. She had to go back to heaven. It is an astounding record, for she came and she left.[8] Here, we have the Mother flame, and she is welcomed and made to feel comfortable. However, I have found that many people become weary after minutes or hours in my presence. It is totally understandable given their state of consciousness and their karma. They cannot stay any longer, either in service or listening to teaching. When they are able, they will come back on a regular basis or to a Sunday service from time to time. They will stay in my presence just so long and then go away.

What happens to me when they go away? Fortunately, there are enough friends around me who can take me all the time. If there were not, I can tell you that for someone who carries the amount of light I do, when all who come to a conference go home, you stand there alone with the intense light that is the greatest light of heaven and of the Brotherhood. You feel more in heaven than on earth. You identify more with heaven than earth, yet you have to stay on earth. It's very difficult. Where are all the people? They have had all they can take of the light, and they'll be back in three months or so.

When you are the instrument of the Word, you need training to get through these periods and re-assimilate levels of the earth without losing the light or losing your contact. By the very nature of living day to day, you have to take all the light and then put it in a compartment and seal it. You couldn't exist in the flesh as a messenger if you stayed as high as you were at the conclusion of a Zarathustra dictation or an Elohim dictation. It would be impossible for me to exist in the flesh, for the flesh itself would become weary of the light.

The moment those dictations are released and concluded, the flesh is spent and at its extreme point of weakness or vulnerability, whereas the Spirit is at its moment of intense strength. The full mighty I AM Presence is open and blazing, and all the people present are drinking in this stupendous light—each one as he is able. A conclusion has to come to that cycle, otherwise the adjustment is too difficult.

When to Take a Break

You also reach points of great highs and saturation when you serve and live in the Word. Therefore, it is important to take a break, take a vacation, go out to dinner, see a movie that's tolerable, that has some redeeming social value, as they say.

I saw a movie last weekend that was called, "Breaker Morant." It is the true story of Australians who fought in the Boer War in South Africa. They fought on the side of the British against the South Africans.

The policy of the British high command was not to take prisoners but to kill them. At some point, it was to the advantage of the high command to bring to trial certain officers and accuse them of murdering the prisoners. The high command wanted to get on good terms with Germans who were vying for control of South Africa. So the whole story is the trial of the men and how a kangaroo court of Nephilim succeeded in finding them guilty of murder when all they were doing was following orders in the call of duty.

It was an excellent story, and it gave one the opportunity to consider the play of human justice and injustice and how the Nephilim will always use the lightbearers for whatever ends they desire to accomplish. It's a very good lesson.

That's the kind of break I'm talking about. When you go to a movie, you can be anonymous. You don't have to counsel anyone or give them light. It's a neutral period when you can reestablish an interaction with the world. You cannot perpetually knock yourself out without sensible periods of rest in motion. That was a rest but it was also edification.

I try to go to movies that teach me something, even if it's learning about the wrong way to make a movie! It's an educational process that might be entertaining as well. But it's a great way to interact with the society we live in. It is important to find out what people are thinking and how they're portraying those thoughts on the screen. Social trends are indicated by movies and the theater, and in that way we can understand what people are relating to.

Don't be a rigid or an artificial chela. Don't try to stereotype yourself or model yourself after some mechanical image of what you think a chela should be. Be what you need to be, and discipline yourself strongly by recognizing that what you need to be is Christ. If Jesus was hungry, he ate. If he wanted to eat on the Sabbath, he did. If he wanted to go to sleep in the head of the ship, he did. He was a very natural person. If he wanted to sit around and talk, he would sit around and talk.

There's something very natural, very wonderful about Jesus. Mark had the same quality. It's wonderful to be with Jesus. The great thing about getting rid of idolatry is that you really do walk and talk with the masters. Then you really know what the witness is of the resurrected Lord. I can tell you things about masters I haven't seen in thousands of years. Yet they are with me. I walk and talk with them daily. It's a friendship that is beyond friendship. It's a very deep personal love.

When the masters walk and talk with me, they are very natural. They remark about events in life, and they are very real and warm people. They are not gods. There is some terrible indoctrination on this planet about the concept of gods. That is not the way the masters are.

Inventors and Invention

So, Maitreya says:

120. We are ready to support each inventor, for even the smallest inventor is trying to introduce an improve-

ment into life and is anxious to bring about economy of energy. The Teacher recognizes guaranty of and care about the conservation of energy. This persistent economy warrants trust in the disciple. Indeed this economy is far from stinginess. The general who is careful in guarding his select troops is acting advisedly. Each possibility becomes our warrior, but one should understand things in the larger aspect.

Innovation is drawing forth from the heart that which is needed to accomplish a certain task within the community. If a job needs doing and you don't know how to do it, invent a way. In all the things that Mark and I have done, we have had to invent constantly because no one told us how to do it.

For instance, when God gave me the matrix for the chapel at the Ashram, he gave me the magnificent concept of an egg. He said that the shape of the egg is the most profound and magnificently glorious shape in all of cosmos. God showed me that the yolk in the center of the egg is the Christ in Jesus. Christ is the Central Sun of the egg. Therefore, he is in the center of the egg.

Before I received the revelation about Jesus being the yolk, I kept thinking that I was going to put his statue at the head, at the top of the egg where it comes to a point. And that's when I received the revelation about Jesus being the yolk. But once the chapel was built, it was obvious that the statue of Jesus had to be in the center.

However, before we built this egg-shaped chapel, nobody knew how to design it. So they asked me, "How do we measure an egg?" I said, "I don't know how to measure an egg because I'm not that advanced in calculus. But take a dozen eggs, hardboil them and peel them. Cut them down the center and take the average size of the egg, trace them all and calculate what is the norm in the shape of the egg."

That's what they did, and that's how they got the shape of the chapel. Very simple invention, right? I told them that's how Saint Clare or Saint Catherine would have done it, for they weren't educated, either. Especially Catherine—she wasn't educated at all. Nobody has told me yet how I should mathematically determine the shape of an egg.

One thing about running a community is that you perceive a need, and then you go do it. I walk around this community and see what needs doing. Then I do it, or I get someone else to do it. Other people walk around this community and see the need, but they may sit there for two years and do nothing about it. You have to have heart, and this is the point.

"We are ready to support each inventor." And I'm certain that means inventor in the truest sense of the word, the person who will draw from his heart the mystical teachings of Christ and come up with a gas-saving device for an engine. That's what you draw out of your Christ consciousness.

Your Christ consciousness is your genius. Somebody asked me the other day if a particular child was a genius. Everybody's Christ Self is a genius. The child is a genius.

Economize Energy

"Even the smallest inventor is trying to introduce an improvement into life and is anxious to bring about economy of energy." Everything we can do to save energy is a good invention. The stress on economizing energy is very interesting. It means that the master can see that a disciple who does this warrants his trust. No ascended master will trust an individual who is not frugal with energy, with money, with time, with space, with turning off the lights or saving oil, or figuring out how to make fewer trips with a car, buying food wisely, and so on.

People who have an extravagant consciousness and do not have a co-measurement of what things cost and how to make do with the least amount of expense are not trusted by the masters because these people are very unreal, very impractical. They have a welfare-state consciousness. They think the community should support them and that it doesn't matter whether they leave the water running or take three times the normal length of a shower. That kind of person is just a misfit, and they eat up everybody else's gain.

There is a net gain to your investment of work in the community. It brings forth the fruit of an increase, which may allow the acquisition of Camelot. Because everybody worked hard and made sacrifices, we have Camelot. But if somebody wastes Camelot or wastes time and space at Camelot, they're eating up the multiplication for a future investment.

I have noted how certain people will waste money on the phone. On long distance phone calls they will eat up the money that they could use to buy themselves a decent pair of shoes or vitamins or a new piece of furniture for the office. Then they want the community to supply them with what they could have had themselves had they been frugal. You have to be conscious and conscientious about the energy in your life, or you may find that that is the reason why the Brotherhood is not interacting with you.

As the text says, even the general guards his select troops through the general economy of life. I have had to remove people from leadership who improperly treated the people under them. They did not guard their life or their spiritual health. I have had to remove them because of their hardness of heart toward the people working under them.

It is an amazing thing, but people misuse other people's lives dreadfully. You have to recognize that trait. Do you expect your family, your relatives, your loved ones to do for you what you ought to be doing for yourself? Do your friends exist to meet your needs, or do they exist because you have a real heart tie and heart exchange?

Resoluteness Must Not Be Deceived

How important it is to be circumspect with inventions in order not to deprive them of direct goalfitness! Let a consciousness of world evolution help to find the proper arrows. Your ears must harken to the steps of evolution, and resoluteness must not be deceived.

You can be so resolute about doing something that your intensity can eclipse the Holy Spirit's speaking to you to give you the spherical awareness of getting to the goal. Resoluteness, determination, is a very important quality, but you can be so determined that you walk right past the living Christ in your determination. Do not allow resoluteness within you to be deceived.

I've seen people so busy following and studying the teachings that they're too busy to talk to me when I come to visit them. I remember we had a group in Washington, D.C., years ago, and the head of this group was eventually expelled from the movement. When I arrived at their focus after a long journey, she did not even offer me a cup of tea or a piece of toast, which is the common thing to do.

I went in to sit down at the kitchen table, and I was there for a long time. Finally, I had to ask for a cup of tea. She was too busy running others' lives. We become too busy for Christ, too busy to let him enter our lives and establish a friendship with us.

Errors of Ignorance

> How wrong is slovenliness in an inventor, how pernicious is an ill-considered reaction, how inexcusable is an error of ignorance!

That is a very important point about errors of ignorance. If you make an error because of your ignorance when you have a big responsibility with the Brotherhood, it affects thousands and millions of people. It affects the finances of the organization. That's why a community has to listen to experts. Those who run the community have to listen to experts who make it their business to know certain things, like organic farming or lumbering or raising sheep and cows.

I don't know how to raise sheep, but I know that certain people on my staff do. And I'm at peace that it's being done right. I'll check into it. I'll listen to what they're doing, and I'll have other people who are not raising sheep listen to how they do it. You can spot-check a situation in the Christ consciousness and know nothing about it, yet you can give the right answer. I saw Mark do this all the time. He'd walk through the staff and come up with the single error that a person had made in three weeks.

For instance, through disobedience, someone didn't put water in an engine, and the engine cracked. He decided that he was going to fix the engine by replacing all the parts. I said, "That engine is ruined, and you should replace the engine."

"Oh, no," he said. "I can fix it." He considered himself to be an expert mechanic, and then he spent many weeks fixing the engine. It ran a couple of months, but it just blew up the other day. The engine happened to be in my son's car, and now this person has to go back and put in the new engine that he should have put in three months ago.

I'm not a mechanic. I wasn't even there. I didn't see the car. I just went within to Lanello. I received a reading of the Christ mind. "That engine is no good. The car needs a new engine."

You can do that all the time, but you have to do your inner reading. It is not a psychic thing, for your Christ Self does know. When you think of everything that goes on here that I couldn't possibly know about professionally, you can see that I would have to have the Christ mind for the place to even be running. A lot of people would have to have the Christ mind.

It's amazing how you can tell when there are areas where things are not going right in the community. You can tune into it, and you can also tune into the people who may appear to be working but who have so much inharmony internally and such anger toward the Divine Mother that they are the very sand that gets in the gears of a whole department. You realize that it would be much better for them to pursue the Path in an area of less light, because the light only aggravates the subconscious.

In a less tense environment, the individual could work at the Path more slowly.

When you give such people an opportunity to serve elsewhere, they are greatly relieved, often because they couldn't figure out where they should serve. Yet when you provide them with an opportunity to render service in a different situation with fewer demands, less light, less concentration of the Brotherhood, they accept it and they do well. They have a chance to make it, whereas if they stayed around much longer, they wouldn't make it at all.

So we have to realize that whatever blesses the community blesses everyone on the inside or the outside if we adhere to the basic law of the nucleus. The Community of the Holy Spirit is the nucleus of a worldwide movement. The nucleus must be sound, and every component of that nucleus must have a blazing heart chakra. Then it will prosper.

What the fallen ones try to do is to ring the nucleus with their counterpoints, their implants, and then you get a ring of people who do not have the heart fire. They manage to separate the nucleus of the heart chelas and the messenger from the people in the field. They manage to get into positions of responsibility because they have mechanical, intellectual attainment, but they have no heart, and they do not make decisions based on heart.

Once you assign a person to an important position, they have a certain autonomy in that position. And unless you are really sensitive, you don't realize that things are going wrong and can go wrong for years unless you make the calls. So it's very good when people in the field complain, because then we find out what is not happening properly in the interaction between people here and in the field.

I have seen people come to the community to gain the power of the Word. They get into important positions and become the shadow between the messenger and the chela on the outside, and sometimes even the messenger and the chela on the inside. Sometimes I have not been able to get past these hard-hearted people to enjoy community life itself because I'm so busy holding the balance for their hardness of heart.

We can evaluate the work of the inventor on a world scale through realization of the direction of world evolution. It will be difficult to understand the applicability of the laws of dynamics so long as the fundamentals of matter have not been assimilated.

In other words, is the invention of the inventor relevant to the evolution on the planet, and does it enhance spiritual as well as material evolution? To assimilate the fundamental laws of Matter is important. Whatever field you are in, it's important to become proficient in that field if you are going to bring forth something worthy in it.

121. The new consciousness supported by technical means will give a powerful impetus to knowledge. Indeed the community must be a most sensitive apparatus for the process of evolution. Indeed, in a conscious community no individual can make affirmation about an already molded world-study. Every dull barrier is swept away by the sharpened vibration of the collective.

The "dull barrier" may be a system that is wrong. It may be a group of people. Anything that is a barrier to the unfoldment of the heart is swept away by the sharpened vibration of the collective, the total collective, through our decrees, our awareness. It becomes very apparent to the collective awareness of the community in divine harmony what is out of vibration with the central harmony of the community. Those who are truly integrated into the heart of Maitreya and the World Mother within a community are sensitive to that which is for community.

Even a hint at completion makes sojourn in the community impossible.

In other words, the idea that we're going to finish building the community, for it is an ongoing, ever transcending spiral. There's no end to the community.

Who then will assume the stigma of stupidity?

Not me, not me, not me!

Don't Fear Your Karma

Even a worm will set no limits to his passageways of darkness—and you, looking into Infinity, you cannot resemble the worm!

The imperfect ingenuity of some people has guessed at invisible rays and inaudible rhythms. With crude imagination, with crude implements, nevertheless certain cosmic currents have been apprehended. But even a fool knows that the imagination can be refined and apparatuses improved. Starting with self-improvement you proceed toward Infinity. I shall repeat about the possibilities of improvement so long as the most obdurate one remains unashamed of his limitation.

One cannot be a community member who limits his own consciousness, thereby emulating the female foot of old China. The darkness of habit evoked also this ugliness.

What community member could wish to cover himself with the mold of superstition? Certainly, one does not now make use of the inferior, primitive type of locomotive. It is equally certain that one cannot remain in an infantile understanding of reality.

A childish materialism proves to be a narcotic for people, but enlightened knowledge will be a ladder of victory.

Without negations, without superstitions, without fear, proceed to the true community. Without any miracles you will find serene reality, and as with the prospector's pick you will discover hidden treasure in the depths. Grow to love the fearlessness of knowledge.

People fear self-knowledge, you know. They greatly fear to find out the untransmuted substance. There are some pretty fearsome records in the deep electronic belt, records of slaying the Christ, the four parts of God (Father, Mother, Son, Holy Spirit), records of the denial of God. But when we have the fearlessness of knowledge, we find it all goes into the flame all the more quickly.

Contemplate not fearing your karma. Some people fear what is coming upon them astrologically or karmically. We should leap as knights and warriors of the flame to slay those dragons. Nothing is unknown because God has been there. Even the worst karma will submit if you simply declare that it is a bunch of nonsense and if you have a sense of dominion over it, a sense of the authority of your Christ Self.

Mark talked in a lecture about how different people deal with their karma. Some people constantly beg God to spare them every pain, every symptom, every displeasure, everything that might disturb their perfect little idolatrous world.

Some people who study systems of metaphysics are this way. They use Unity or Christian Science to gain wealth. They have beautiful homes. Everything is perfect, and they keep on affirming it so that nothing imperfect will come into their lives. They deny pain. They deny matter. They deny disease. They deny death. They never allow themselves to experience enough of their karma to actually balance it. They just keep pushing it back. They live in this little narrow room of themselves and their friends, constantly discussing metaphysics.

Mark said that people push away their karma by the unreality of their intense mental belief systems—their minds actually push away that karma. They build up a mountain of karma, which all comes down upon them at once, and they say, "Save me! Save me!" They can't deal with it.

I realize that we all have different attitudes. You can test your attitude toward your karma by testing your responsibilities in life. Do you let huge debts pile up and not worry about them, or are you conscientious in paying your bills? Do you have a sense of responsibility to your community, or do you lack a sense of responsibility?

How you interact with yourself and with others is how you interact with your karma. Saint Germain's training and his great gifts and examples to me have placed uppermost in my mind the necessity of balancing every piece of karma I could find. He taught me to go after it voraciously, like you'd go after an enjoyable meal. Every little speck of karma that you leave untransmuted limits your cosmic consciousness.

I can remember once when we were traveling—I believe we were in Holland or Denmark—and a waiter was serving us breakfast. I disliked him instantly. It was an instantaneous clash of energy and a very difficult breakfast. It was a difficult interchange, and I sensed that I was encountering a karmic situation.

We left and got far down the road in our camper. When we went to buy groceries, we couldn't find the money that we had changed into the local currency. It was not a large amount, but it could have been anywhere from twenty-five to fifty dollars. So we had to put all our groceries back on the shelf and go without, for the currency exchanges were closed.

Mistakenly, I had left that money on the table and, of course, the waiter received it as a tip. What I saw very clearly and what Saint Germain said to me was, "Better to have lost the money than to have the karmic debt." Thus, by leaving that amount of money there, whatever friction needed to be resolved was taken care of. The debt was paid. I could be free forever from that ridiculous fellow.

Of course, at the time I was annoyed, and I thought of it many times. I gained a lesson from it and reached a point of extreme gratitude that I had such a relationship with a master. Because he knew my free will was utterly committed to him, he could take the liberty of dipping into my pocketbook and putting my debt to this man on the table—for his service was so terrible I would have never left him a tip!

It was a very good lesson. I have seen the masters do this in many situations. They know the intense willingness I have to bless all life and especially to bless life that I haven't blessed in the past and that I owe a blessing to. So I find myself in all kinds of situations of interacting with people and doing something for someone that I never thought I would do when I got up that day.

I don't think at the time, "Oh, I'm paying a karmic debt

now." It doesn't cross my mind. But in the total framework of this lifetime I can see that without that guidance, without my responsiveness to the Holy Spirit, letting it take me where it would, I might not have done it. When God tells me to go do something, I do it. I don't know why I'm doing it. I arrive. There's this person, that person, another person. All kinds of things come out of it, and life is blessed.

I have been doing that at top speed, a mile a minute, since the day I was born. That's how you accelerate balancing karma. If you think about it, my balancing karma became indispensable to the mission of Saint Germain, El Morya and Lanello. They could not have done what they wanted to do on this planet if it hadn't happened.

So what did they do? They trained me for many centuries. They anticipated this cycle. They know the law of cycles. They knew this moment would come. So embodiment after embodiment they have seen to it that I learned this law. I've been paying as I go. What I could finish up, I finished up quickly and then came to the place of being ultimately useful to them.

I can remember being burdened by karma twenty-five years ago. I wanted to do things for God or for people, and I couldn't do them. I sensed my limitations and said, "What is this limitation that I'm up against? Why can't I get through this to do what I want to do?" Now that I'm on the other side of it, I know what that limitation was. It was my karma.

You should be intense about balancing karma. It is enlightened self-interest, because you can do more for God, hence, have greater attainment, if you labor a while, do some dirty work, toil in the fields—do whatever you have to do to get that karma behind you. It's very important.

I rarely miss an opportunity to give somebody a gift of the teaching, a concept, a book, a picture or just my love. If I meet someone, as far as I'm concerned, I'm on the cosmic highway, and I'm meeting them for a purpose. Nothing is an accident. Nothing is unimportant. Everything has to be considered in the light that God is leading me, and I have to give my best offering to this part of God. As a result, you hear judgment come out of your mouth, and you hear blessings come out of your mouth. You hear it after it is said. And you come to the point where you have to trust God, trust your master and trust yourself. Trust those responses.

Don't overlay what God is doing through you with the idea, "Well, that really isn't the way to do it, so I won't do that," and then you suppress the flow. If you really have the flow of God, then let it work through you and trust it.

I have been astounded, almost aghast, at how I've heard God talk to people, whether total strangers or chelas. But I would not turn off the flow. I would let the Holy Spirit speak. Then I'd find out in the end, when I was through speaking, that people would thank me and tell me that it was just what they'd needed to be told for the last ten years.

In the name of the light of God that never fails, I call for the sealing of the third eye. I call for the sealing of this forcefield. I call for the sealing of the light in the servants of God. I call for the mighty action of the sacred fire. Sheets of white fire and blue lightning descend from the heart of God in the Great Central Sun!

I call for the white-fire, blue-fire sun. I call to the heart of beloved Surya and Cuzco. I call to the Great Central Sun magnet. Clear the way now! Clear the way for the crystal clarity of the mind of God. Clear the way for the crystal clarity of the mind of God. Blaze blue lightning from the mind of God! In the name of the Father, the Mother, the Son and the Holy Spirit, Amen.

Camelot
June 2, 1981

CHAPTER 10

The Community of the Holy Spirit

What is community? What is its purpose? The Community of the Holy Spirit begins with our communion with the inner law of our being, our communion with our God flame and with our Christ Self. Community is wholeness, and wholeness begins with one—the one God flame that we are.

Community is dependent on whole people coming together to complement each other, not on incomplete people fulfilling the incompleteness of one another. Even if we are the wholeness of God, we manifest only an aspect of that wholeness in time and space. Therefore, our needs are based on fulfilling the grand design of creation. That is how God planned it. God has said that no one should be an island sufficient unto himself lest he become proud and ambitious. Instead he should humbly acknowledge his need for others.

Community is the great dream of the ascended masters of the Great White Brotherhood. On the etheric plane, the heaven-world, the masters create ashrams, or retreats. And souls who need to work out karma together, who have certain lessons to learn in self-mastery, are drawn into these retreats. Each retreat of the Great White Brotherhood on the etheric plane, and even on the physical plane, is an archetype, a pattern of community. And each community has three, five, fifty, or a hundred or more souls working together.

The basis of the individual community and the world community is the individualization of the God flame. Few people attain self-mastery in a vacuum, for in a vacuum we have no sense of how we relate to the other parts of God. Without feedback, we don't know whether we are selfish or selfless. But when we start working with people, we find out what our level of irritation is. We find out what upsets us, and it is usually something small or petty. When we live night and day with a small number of people, our toes get stepped on very easily. And each one is required to give up something for the good of the whole.

If we aren't able to live in a community while we are in embodiment, chances are that as soon as we leave this life we will find ourselves in a community on the plane of Spirit. And we will be with all the individuals we ran away from when we were in physical embodiment—the spouse we divorced, our mother-in-law, the man down the street who cheated us in business, the person we sued in a lawsuit, and so on. The people we have the greatest antipathy for on this plane are the ones we will find ourselves inextricably united with on other planes of being. We have heard that hatred binds and love liberates. So when we have any form of hatred, mild dislike or irritation for anyone, we create an iron chain between us. Sometimes, somewhere, we will have to work it out.

The ascended masters who guide their chelas in physical embodiment do all they can to draw lifestreams together on this plane before the conclusion of this life so that they can work out their karma, be free to enter the temple of the ascension as a candidate for the ascension at the close of this embodiment. And so, they have created their Community of the Holy Spirit by drawing together lifestreams to work out the process of individual self-mastery. This is an important process, because in this exchange, in this interaction, people get to know what they need to master in themselves.

The teachings of Christ and Buddha outline the format of community. Gautama taught his disciples the three principal aspects to which they must cling: the Buddha, the Dharma and the Sangha. The Buddha is the lawgiver, the Father aspect of the

Trinity. The Dharma is the teaching, the enlightenment of the Christ, or the Son. The teaching sustains us. It enables us to understand the Father aspect. When these aspects are established, when we acknowledge the Buddha as the teacher or we acknowledge the Buddha within, we have the Sangha, the community, the order of monks and nuns and disciples.

The Sangha is the fulfillment of love as the Holy Spirit. The community cannot come until the teacher has come and the teaching has come. Buddha said that these three were necessary to the attainment of nirvana, and the masters of the Great White Brotherhood tell us today that they are essential to the attainment of the ascension. The community is the place for the realization of the Buddha within through the Dharma and the Sangha.

A great benefit of the Community of the Holy Spirit is the fusion of creativity. Group attainment is the multiplication of individual attainment. Group attainment has the plus factor of the Holy Spirit that is generated by the communion of hearts in the love, the wisdom and the power of the Law. A squaring action takes place that is the multiplication of the individuals involved.

Why did Jesus say, "Where two or three are gathered together, there I am in the midst"? Because the community draws down the flame of the Holy Spirit. A group mandala, then, is effective on a world scale for holding a forcefield, offering a service and setting a certain pattern. Each retreat, each community has a special flame, a special purpose for which it was founded. It is a spiritual center for the release of a specific energy, a special realization of God consciousness.

A Community of the Holy Spirit is something we can form here and now, right where we are. It starts with you. It starts with each one of us. It starts with our family, with our home. Community places emphasis on the third person of the Trinity, on love, on sharing, on self-sacrifice and on the path of initiation through love. When there is a flow of harmony between initiates working together under the masters, much more can be accomplished together than by a solitary individual.

Community is the place at the nexus of the cross where not one, but a number of individuals come together to sacrifice the lesser self to the fulfillment of the Higher Self, the fulfillment of the creativity of the Christ consciousness.

Notes

INTRODUCTION

1. Pallas Athena, *Pearls of Wisdom*, vol. 3, no. 29, July 15, 1960.
2. Nicholas and Helena Roerich, *New Era Community*, (New York: Agni Yoga Society, 1951), p. 99.
3. The Maha Chohan, "The Spirit of Community," *Pearls of Wisdom*, vol. 26, no. 46, November 13, 1983.
4. Mother Mary, "I Return to Glastonbury, *Pearls of Wisdom*, vol. 23, no. 42, October 19, 1980.

CHAPTER 1 ∞ *The Dream of Community*

1. John 5:17.
2. For more on the Cosmic Clock, see Elizabeth Clare Prophet, *The Great White Brotherhood in the Culture, History and Religion of America* (Corwin Springs, Mont.: Summit University Press, 1987), pp. 173–206.
3. H. P. Blavatsky, 1831–1891, founder, under the direction of El Morya and Kuthumi, of the Theosophical Society.
4. John 15:15.
5. On April 4, 1971, Archangel Uriel said: "Tonight I want you to understand a certain condition in the consciousness of men that is very, very important to each of you. Let there be, for example, in this room or in the next one, or even in an entire city, a whole city of devotees that love God and are most willing to be obedient unto him and the golden rule. Bring one person into that group who has in his consciousness the design of disobedience, and the entire city becomes tainted by it and affected by it. So powerful is this force of the mind in man that even one discordant note can affect the entire orchestration."
6. See Mark 5:7; Luke 8:28.
7. Aimee Semple MacPherson, *The Story of My Life* (Waco, Texas: World Books, 1973), pp. 98–99.
8. Matt. 16:18.
9. *Animal magnetism* is a term used by the ascended masters to describe the density of the human consciousness not tethered to spirit. The masters have named four types of animal magnetism which correspond to the four lower bodies of man. They are: malicious animal magnetism, the etheric body; ignorant animal magnetism, the mental body; sympathetic animal magnetism, the emotional body; deli-

cious animal magnetism, the physical body.

10. America entered her third century in 1976. In the first century (1776 to 1876), we see the laying of the foundation. This represents the ray of the Father, the I AM THAT I AM, and the blue ray. The second century (1876 to 1976) had a tremendous burst of science as illumination. This we call the yellow ray. It represents wisdom. It is the energy of the Son or the living Christ. The third century (1976 to 2076), is the love flame. It comes under the Holy Spirit, the pink ray, and it is the century in which we must resolve our differences. We must take the very first step on the path of mercy and forgiveness, forgiveness of ourselves and of one another, of all who have ever wronged us and all whom we have ever wronged in all previous lifetimes.

11. For the story of George Washington's vision, see Mark L. Prophet and Elizabeth Clare Prophet, *Saint Germain On Alchemy* (Corwin Springs, Mont.: Summit University Press, 1995), p. 138ff.

12. The ascended masters teach that America is the land set aside for the fulfillment of the prophecy of the gathering together again of the twelve tribes of Israel.

13. See John 3:17.

14. The Dark Cycle of the return of mankind's individual and collective karma began April 23, 1969. In this period of transition from the Piscean to the Aquarian age, the Great Law requires that the evolutions of planet Earth deal directly with the momentums of personal and planetary karma set aside for centuries by the grace of God through his Sons incarnate (i.e., Jesus Christ and other avatars). Earth's karma is, therefore, currently being delivered to the doorstep of the people and the nations for balance, according to the cycles of the initiations of the Solar Hierarchies, through (a) transmutation by the violet flame and (b) mutual service to life.

15. Helios and Vesta are divine beings who ensoul the physical/spiritual sun at the center of our solar system.

16. Paul the Venetian is the chohan of the third ray of divine love and sponsor of artists and divine art.

CHAPTER 2 ∞ *Striving to the Far-off Worlds*

1. Matt. 8:20.

CHAPTER 3 ∞ *Keepers of the Lightning*

1. The Hindu Trinity of Brahma, Vishnu and Shiva is parallel to the Western Trinity of Father, Son and Holy Spirit. The three form the triad for the creation, preservation and destruction of the universe.

Shiva, the Destroyer (also known as the Restorer), is the fearsome one who drives away sin, disease and demons of delusion. Shakti is the feminine principle of the deity and appears in many forms. She is the "negative" polarity who releases the "positive" polarity, the creative energy of her Lord. Without Shakti (the Matter-force), Shiva (the Spirit-force) is powerless to create or destroy. Shakti is that point of the feminine principle within us who releases the potential of God from Spirit to Matter.

2. Mother Cabrini, 1850–1917, founder of the Missionary Sisters of the Sacred Heart, and first United States citizen to be canonized.

3. Rev. 22:1.

4. Mark L. Prophet, *Cosmic Consciousness: One Man's Search for God* (Corwin Springs, Mont.: Summit University Press, 1986).

5. On November 4, 1979, Lord Lanto requested that Keepers of the Flame speak out in defense of the community of lightbearers. He said: "Let the children of the light position themselves, then, in points of service and understanding where there is a meeting of the mind with some segment of the community that for each individual may be a different segment according to your calling, your education and the leaning of your heart. Let there be expansion through friendship, through brotherly love, through contact, through communication, through a willingness to work together with the community at large to solve its problems."

6. See Lanello, October 7, 1978, "More Light: The Tolling of the Great Bell for the Mission of the Two by Two," in *Pearls of Wisdom,* vol. 24, no. 39.

CHAPTER 4 ∞ *Guard the Outpost of the Great White Brotherhood*

1. Rev. 12: 13, 14.

2. Ps. 139:8, 9.

3. Rev. 3:12.

4. The Keepers of the Flame Fraternity is an organization of ascended masters and their chelas who vow to keep the flame of life on earth and support the activities of the Great White Brotherhood. Keepers of the Flame receive monthly lessons in cosmic law dictated by the ascended masters to their messengers Mark and Elizabeth Prophet.

5. See Elizabeth Clare Prophet, *The Opening of the Seventh Seal* (Corwin Springs, Mont.: The Summit Lighthouse Library, 2001), pp. 233–37.

6. Elizabeth Clare Prophet was embodied as Martha, sister of Mary and Lazarus of Bethany.

7. Luke 10:38–42.

CHAPTER 5 ∞ *The Education of the Heart*

1. Dr. Elisabeth Caspari studied directly under Maria Montessori in India during World War II.
2. Matt. 23:37.
3. Matt. 23:38, 39.
4. Elohim Purity, "Blessed Fragments of Purity," July 27, 1968, *Pearls of Wisdom,* vol. 21, nos. 22, 23.
5. John Dewey, 1859–1952, a leader of the progressive movement in education in the United States.
6. Gen. 1:26.
7. See "Shaping the Hard Wood," Mother Mary, March 3, 1968, *Pearls of Wisdom,* vol. 11, no. 9.
8. 2 Cor. 12:9.

CHAPTER 6 ∞ *The Extinguished Consciousness and the
Undeveloped Consciousness*

1. Rev. 12:16.
2. See John 15:5.
3. John 5:29.
4. Mighty Victory said, "Let me assure you that the moment a man repenteth or a woman repenteth and turns to serve the light with all his heart, the light turns around to serve him. And what takes place? Why, an entire transformation, of course!" From "The Indomitable Greetings of Cosmic Victory," November 7, 1976, *Pearls of Wisdom,* vol. 19, no. 45.

CHAPTER 7 ∞ *The Impetuosity of Striving*

1. 2 Cor. 11:14.
2. Prov. 15:1.
3. Saint Germain teaches how to magnetize millions of "focal points of light" into a "brilliant pulsating cloud of infinite energy" that can be directed into personal and planetary problems for the healing of specific conditions, including disease, pollution, crime and war. See *Saint Germain On Alchemy,* pp. 191–251.

CHAPTER 8 ∞ *Embody the Flame of Trust*

1. The Goddess of Liberty has stated the position of the Karmic Board that parents ought not to bring forth more children than "you are able to care for and for whom you may adequately express your love." Means to predetermining the family circle must be intelligently studied and applied, for when life is at stake, one does not act haphazardly as though the bearing and rearing of children were a

matter to be left to the fates or the gods. Abortion as a means to birth control is deemed a violation of the sacred flame of life which every Keeper of the Flame has vowed to keep. When considering birth control, it is wise to choose a method that does not affect the health of the parents or interfere with the cycles of life.

2. 2 Thess. 3:10.

3. Gautama Buddha's dictation of October 11, 1970, "The Little Bird Held in Your Hands," is published in the *Pearls of Wisdom,* vol. 26, no. 17.

4. Matt. 24:22; Mark 13:20.

CHAPTER 9 ∞ *The Perpetual Labor of Love*

1. Zech. 13:7; Matt. 26:31; Mark 14:27.

2. Sermons by Elizabeth Clare Prophet, "Idolatry and the Fiery Trial," parts 1 and 2, May 17 and 19, 1981.

3. See Matt. 13:53–58; Mark 6:1–6; Luke 4:16–24.

4. The ten perfections outlined by Gautama in this book are: Alms, The Precepts, Renunciation, Wisdom, Courage, Patience, The Mother, Truth, Resolution, Goodwill and Indifference. Gautama explains that the tenth perfection, Indifference, is built on the foundation of the other nine. It is "the balance between desire and desirelessness." The aim is "to show indifference alike to mockery and praise, to pleasure and pain, to poverty or riches, adulation or indignation." See Elizabeth Clare Prophet, *Quietly Comes the Buddha* (Corwin Springs, Mont.: Summit University Press, 2000).

5. 1 Cor. 11:24.

6. Jesus, "The Mystery of the Mother Flame within Thee," April 19, 1981, *Pearls of Wisdom,* vol. 24, no. 24.

7. John 9:24–33.

8. See the Book of Enoch, chapter 42, in Elizabeth Clare Prophet, *Fallen Angels and the Origins of Evil* (Corwin Springs, Mont.: Summit University Press, 2000), p. 142.

Decrees

Heart, Head and Hand
by *El Morya*

Heart

Violet fire, thou love divine,
Blaze within this heart of mine!
Thou art mercy forever true,
Keep me always in tune with you.

Head

I AM light, thou Christ in me,
Set my mind forever free;
Violet fire, forever shine
Deep within this mind of mine.

God who gives my daily bread
With violet fire fill my head
Till thy radiance heavenlike
Makes my mind a mind of light.

Hand

I AM the hand of God in action,
Gaining victory every day;
My pure soul's great satisfaction
Is to walk the Middle Way.

Tube of Light

Beloved I AM Presence bright,
Round me seal your tube of light
From ascended master flame
Called forth now in God's own name.
Let it keep my temple free
From all discord sent to me.

I AM calling forth violet fire
To blaze and transmute all desire,
Keeping on in freedom's name
Till I AM one with the violet flame.

Forgiveness

I AM forgiveness acting here,
Casting out all doubt and fear,
Setting men forever free
With wings of cosmic victory.

I AM calling in full power
For forgiveness every hour;
To all life in every place
I flood forth forgiving grace.

Supply

I AM free from fear and doubt,
Casting want and misery out,
Knowing now all good supply
Ever comes from realms on high.

I AM the hand of God's own fortune
Flooding forth the treasures of light,
Now receiving full abundance
To supply each need of life.

Perfection

I AM life of God-direction,
Blaze thy light of truth in me.
Focus here all God's perfection,
From all discord set me free.

Make and keep me anchored ever
In the justice of thy plan—
I AM the presence of perfection
Living the life of God in man!

Transfiguration

I AM changing all my garments,
Old ones for the bright new day;
With the sun of understanding
I AM shining all the way.

I AM light within, without;
I AM light is all about.
Fill me, free me, glorify me!
Seal me, heal me, purify me!
Until transfigured they describe me:
I AM shining like the Son,
I AM shining like the Sun!

Resurrection

I AM the flame of resurrection
Blazing God's pure light through me.
Now I AM raising every atom,
From every shadow I AM free.

I AM the light of God's full Presence,
I AM living ever free.
Now the flame of life eternal
Rises up to victory.

Ascension

I AM ascension light,
Victory flowing free,
All of good won at last
For all eternity.

I AM light, all weights are gone.
Into the air I raise;
To all I pour with full God power
My wondrous song of praise.

All hail! I AM the living Christ,
The ever-loving one.
Ascended now with full God power,
I AM a blazing Sun!

Lord Michael

In the name of the beloved mighty victorious Presence of God, I AM in me, my very own beloved Holy Christ Self, Holy Christ Selves of all mankind, beloved Archangel Michael, beloved Lanello, the entire Spirit of the Great White Brotherhood and the World Mother, elemental life—fire, air, water, and earth! I decree:

1. Lord Michael, Lord Michael,
     I call unto thee—
     Wield thy sword of blue flame
     And now cut me free!

Refrain: Blaze God-power, protection
     Now into my world,
     Thy banner of faith
     Above me unfurl!
     Transcendent blue lightning
     Now flash through my soul,
     I AM by God's mercy
     Made radiant and whole!

2. Lord Michael, Lord Michael,
     I love thee, I do—
     With all thy great faith
     My being imbue!

3. Lord Michael, Lord Michael
     And legions of blue—
     Come seal me, now keep me
     Faithful and true!

Coda: I AM with thy blue flame
     Now full-charged and blest,
     I AM now in Michael's
     Blue-flame armor dressed! (3x)

And in full faith . . .

Beloved Mighty Astrea

In the name of the beloved mighty victorious Presence of God I AM in me, mighty I AM Presence and Holy Christ Selves of Keepers of the Flame, lightbearers of the world and all who are to ascend in this life, by and through the magnetic power of the sacred fire vested in the threefold flame burning within my heart, I call to beloved Mighty Astrea and Purity, Archangel Gabriel and Hope, beloved Serapis Bey and the seraphim and cherubim of God, beloved Lanello, the entire Spirit of the Great White Brotherhood and the World Mother, elemental life—fire, air, water and earth! to lock your cosmic circles and swords of blue flame in, through and around my four lower bodies, my electronic belt, my heart chakra and all of my chakras, my entire consciousness, being and world.

Cut me loose and set me free! (3x) from all that is less than God's perfection and my own divine plan fulfilled.

1. O beloved Astrea, may God Purity
    Manifest here for all to see,
    God's divine will shining through
    Circle and sword of brightest blue.

1st chorus: Come now answer this my call,
    Lock thy circle round us all.
    Circle and sword of brightest blue,
    Blaze now, raise now, shine right through!

2. Cutting life free from patterns unwise,
    Burdens fall off while souls arise
    Into thine arms of infinite love,
    Merciful shining from heaven above.

3. Circle and sword of Astrea now shine,
    Blazing blue-white my being refine,
    Stripping away all doubt and fear,
    Faith and good will patterns appear.

2nd chorus: Come now answer this my call,
                    Lock thy circle round us all.
                    Circle and sword of brightest blue,
                    Raise our youth now, blaze right through!

3rd chorus: Come now answer this my call,
                    Lock thy circle round us all.
                    Circle and sword of brightest blue,
                    Raise mankind now, shine right through!

And in full faith I consciously accept this manifest, manifest, manifest! (3x) right here and now with full power, eternally sustained, all-powerfully active, ever expanding and world enfolding until all are wholly ascended in the light and free! Beloved I AM! Beloved I AM! Beloved I AM!

Beloved Surya

Beloved mighty victorious Presence of God, I AM in me, my very own beloved Holy Christ Self, Holy Christ Selves of all mankind, beloved Surya, legions of white fire and blue lightning from Sirius, beloved Lanello, the entire Spirit of the Great White Brotherhood and the World Mother, elemental life—fire, air, water, and earth! In thy name, by and through the magnetic power of the immortal, victorious threefold flame of truth within my heart and the heart of God in the Great Central Sun, I decree:

1. Out from the sun flow thy dazzling bright
   Blue-flame ribbons of flashing diamond light!
   Serene and pure is thy love,
   Holy radiance from God above!

Refrain: Come, come, come, Surya dear,
   By thy flame dissolve all fear;
   Give to each one security
   In the bonds of purity;
   Flash and flash thy flame through me,
   Make and keep me ever free!

2. Surya dear, beloved one
   From the mighty Central Sun,
   In God's name to thee we call:
   Take dominion over all!

3. Out from the heart of God you come,
   Serving to make us now all one—
   Wisdom and honor do you bring,
   Making the very soul to sing!

4. Surya dear, beloved one,
   From our faith then now is spun
   Victory's garment of invincible gold,
   Our souls' great triumph to ever uphold!

And in full faith...

Beloved Cyclopea, Beholder of Perfection

Beloved mighty victorious Presence of God, I AM in me, Holy Christ Selves of all earth's evolutions, beloved Cyclopea and Virginia, beloved Helios and Vesta, Lanello and K-17, the entire Spirit of the Great White Brotherhood and the World Mother, elemental life—fire, air, water, and earth! In the name of the beloved Presence of God which I AM and by and through the magnetic power of the sacred fire vested in the threefold flame burning within my heart, I decree:

1. Beloved Cyclopea,
  Thou beholder of perfection,
  Release to us thy divine direction,
  Clear our way from all debris,
  Hold the immaculate thought for me.

Refrain: I AM, I AM beholding all,
  Mine eye is single as I call;
  Raise me now and set me free,
  Thy holy image now to be.

2. Beloved Cyclopea,
  Thou enfolder all-seeing,
  Mold in light my very being,
  Purify my thought and feeling,
  Hold secure God's Law appealing.

3. Beloved Cyclopea,
  Radiant eye of ancient grace,
  By God's hand his image trace
  On the fabric of my soul,
  Erase all bane and keep me whole.

4. Beloved Cyclopea,
  Guard for aye the City Foursquare,
  Hear and implement my prayer,
  Trumpet my victory on the air,
  Hold the purity of truth so fair.

And in full faith . . .

I AM the Violet Flame

I AM the violet flame
   In action in me now
I AM the violet flame
   To light alone I bow
I AM the violet flame
   In mighty cosmic power
I AM the light of God
   Shining every hour
I AM the violet flame
   Blazing like a sun
I AM God's sacred power
   Freeing every one

Glossary

Akashic records. The impressions of all that has ever transpired in the physical universe, recorded in an etheric substance and dimension known as akasha. These records can be read by those with developed soul faculties.

Antahkarana. The web of life. The net of light spanning Spirit and Matter, connecting and sensitizing the whole of creation within itself and to the heart of God.

Ascended masters. Enlightened spiritual beings who once lived on earth, fulfilled their reason for being and have ascended, or reunited, with God. The ascended masters are the true teachers of mankind. They direct the spiritual evolution of all devotees of God and guide them back to their Source.

Ascension. A spiritual acceleration of consciousness that takes place at the natural conclusion of one's final lifetime on earth whereby the soul reunites with God and is free from the round of karma and rebirth.

Astral plane. The lowest vibrating frequency of time and space; the repository of mankind's thoughts and feelings, conscious and unconscious.

Astrea. Feminine Elohim of the fourth ray, the ray of purity, who works to cut souls free from the astral plane and the projections of the dark forces.

Avatar. From Sanskrit *avatara,* literally "descent." A Hindu term for an incarnation of God on earth.

Body elemental. A being of nature who serves the soul as an unseen but constant companion and physician through all the soul's incarnations.

Carnal mind. The human ego, human intellect and human will; the animal nature of man.

Causal Body. Interpenetrating spheres of light surrounding each one's I AM Presence at spiritual levels. The spheres of the causal body contain the records of the virtuous acts we have performed to the glory of God and the blessing of man through our many incarnations on earth.

Chakra. (Sanskrit for "wheel," "disc," "circle.") Term used to denote the centers of light anchored in the etheric body and governing the flow of energy to the four lower bodies of man. There are seven major chakras corresponding to the seven rays, five minor chakras corresponding to the five secret rays, and a total of 144 light centers in the body of man. The seven major chakras, their rays and colors are: First Ray, **throat,** blue; Second Ray, **crown,** yellow; Third Ray, **heart,**

pink; Fourth Ray, **base-of-the-spine**, white; Fifth Ray, **third eye**, green; Sixth Ray, **solar plexus**, purple and gold flecked with ruby; Seventh Ray, **seat-of-the-soul**, violet.

Chela. (Hindi, *cela* from the Sanskrit *ceta,* "slave" or "servant.") In India, a disciple of a religious teacher or guru. A term used generally to refer to a student of the ascended masters and their teachings.

Chohan. (Tibetan, "lord" or "master"; a chief.) Each of the seven rays has a chohan who focuses the Christ consciousness of the ray for the earth and her evolutions.

Christ Self. *See* Holy Christ Self.

Cosmic Clock. The science of charting the cycles of the soul's karma and initiations on the twelve lines of the clock under the twelve hierarchies of the sun (whose names are the familiar names of the signs of the Zodiac). Each of the twelve solar hierarchies focuses a specific God consciousness. The hierarchy of Capricorn is the 12 o'clock line of the clock. The God consciousness of this hierarchy is God-power, and the human perversion of this energy is criticism, condemnation, judgment and black magic. The hierarchy of Aquarius on the one o'clock line focuses God-love, which is perverted in the human consciousness as hatred, mild dislike and witchcraft. Continuing in a clockwise direction, the God qualities are (2) God-mastery, (3) God-control, (4) God-obedience, (5) God-wisdom, (6) God-harmony, (7) God-gratitude, (8) God-justice, (9) God-reality, (10) God-vision and (11) God-victory. The human perversions are: (2) doubt, fear, human questioning and records of death; (3) conceit, deceit, arrogance and ego; (4) disobedience, stubbornness and defiance of the Law; (5) envy, jealousy and ignorance of the Law; (6) indecision, self-pity and self-justification; (7) ingratitude, thoughtlessness and spiritual blindness; (8) injustice, frustration and anxiety; (9) dishonesty, intrigue and treachery; (10) selfishness, self-love and idolatry; (11) resentment, revenge and retaliation. For more information on the Cosmic Clock see Elizabeth Clare Prophet, *The Great White Brotherhood in the Culture, History and Religion of America,* pp. 173–206.

Crystal cord. The stream of God's light, life and consciousness that nourishes and sustains the soul and her four lower bodies. Also called the silver cord.

Cyclopea. Masculine Elohim of the fifth ray, also known as the All-Seeing Eye of God or as the Silent Watcher.

Dark Cycle. The Dark Cycle of the return of mankind's individual and collective karma began April 23, 1969. In this period of transition from the Piscean to the Aquarian age, the Great Law requires that the evolutions of earth deal directly with the momentums of personal and planetary karma set aside for centuries by the grace of God through his Sons incarnate (i.e., Jesus Christ and other avatars). Earth's karma is, therefore, currently being delivered to the people and the nations for balance, according to the cycles of the initiations of the solar hierarchies, through (a) transmutation by the violet flame, and (b) mutual service to life.

Decree. A dynamic form of spoken prayer used by students of the ascended masters to direct God's light into individual and world conditions.

Dictation. The messages of the ascended masters, archangels and other advanced spiritual beings delivered through the agency of the Holy Spirit by a messenger of the Great White Brotherhood.

Divine spark. *See* Threefold flame.

Elemental life. The fiery salamanders, sylphs, undines and gnomes, who are Nature's keepers in the domains of fire, air, water and earth.

El Morya. The ascended master who is the teacher and sponsor of the messengers Mark L. Prophet and Elizabeth Clare Prophet and the founder of The Summit Lighthouse.

Etheric body. *See* Four lower bodies.

Fallen angels. The fallen angels are those angels who followed Lucifer in the Great Rebellion, whose consciousness therefore "fell" to lower levels of vibration. They were "cast out into the earth" by Archangel Michael (Rev. 12:7–12), constrained by the karma of their disobedience to God and his Christ to take on and evolve through dense physical bodies. *See* Watchers

Four Cosmic Forces. The four beasts seen by Saint John and other seers as the lion, the calf (or ox), the man and the flying eagle (Rev. 4:6–8). They serve directly under the Elohim and govern all of the Matter cosmos. They are transformers of the infinite light unto souls evolving in the finite.

Four lower bodies. The four sheaths surrounding the soul; the vehicles the soul uses in her journey on earth: the etheric, or memory, body; the mental body; the desire, or emotional, body; the physical body. The etheric body houses the blueprint of the soul's identity and contains the memory of all that has ever transpired in the soul and all impulses she has ever sent out. The mental body is the vessel of the cognitive faculties; when purified, it can become the vessel of the mind of God. The desire body houses the higher and lower desires and records the emotions. The physical body is the miracle of flesh and blood that enables the soul to progress in the material universe.

Great White Brotherhood. A spiritual fraternity of ascended masters, archangels and other advanced spiritual beings. The term "white"

refers not to race but to the aura of white light that surrounds these immortals. The Great White Brotherhood works with earnest seekers of every race, religion and walk of life to assist humanity. The Brotherhood also includes certain unascended disciples of the ascended masters.

Guru. (Sanskrit) A personal religious teacher and spiritual guide; one of high attainment. A guru may be ascended or unascended.

Holy Christ Self. The Higher Self; our inner teacher, guardian, friend and advocate before God; the Universal Christ individualized for each of us.

I AM Presence. The Presence of God, the I AM THAT I AM, individualized for each of us.

Karma. (Sanskrit) Meaning act, action, work or deed. The consequences of one's thoughts, words and deeds of this life and previous lives; the law of cause and effect, which decrees that whatever we do comes full circle to our doorstep for resolution. The law of karma necessitates the soul's reincarnation so that she can pay the debt for, or "balance," her misuses of God's light, energy and consciousness.

Karmic Board. *See* Lords of Karma.

Keepers of the Flame Fraternity. An organization of ascended masters and their chelas who vow to keep the flame of life on earth and support the activities of the Great White Brotherhood in the establishment of their community and mystery school and in the dissemination of their teachings. Founded in 1961 by Saint Germain. Keepers of the Flame receive graded lessons in cosmic law dictated by the ascended masters to their messengers Mark and Elizabeth Prophet.

Light. The universal radiance and energy of God; the potential of the Christ.

Lords of Karma. The ascended beings who comprise the Karmic Board. Their names and the rays that they represent on the board are: **Great Divine Director,** first ray; **Goddess of Liberty,** second ray; **Ascended Lady Master Nada,** third ray; **Elohim Cyclopea,** fourth ray; **Pallas Athena,** Goddess of Truth, fifth ray; **Portia,** Goddess of Justice, sixth ray; **Kuan Yin,** Goddess of Mercy, seventh ray; **Dhyani Buddha Vairochana,** newly appointed eighth member. The Lords of Karma dispense justice to this system of worlds, adjudicating karma, mercy and judgment on behalf of every lifestream. All souls must pass before the Karmic Board before and after each incarnation on earth, receiving their assignment and karmic allotment for each lifetime beforehand and the review of their performance at its conclusion. Through the Keeper of the Scrolls and the recording angels, the Lords of Karma have access to the complete records of every lifestream's incarnations on earth. They determine who shall embody, as well as when and where. They assign souls to families and communities, measuring out the weights of karma that must be balanced as the "jot and tittle" of the law. The Karmic Board, acting in consonance with the individual I AM Presence and Christ Self, determines when the soul has earned the right to be free from the wheel of karma and the round of rebirth. The Lords of Karma meet at the Royal Teton Retreat twice yearly, at winter and summer solstice, to review petitions from unascended mankind and to grant dispensations for their assistance.

Maitreya. Lord Maitreya ("he whose name is kindness") holds the office of Cosmic Christ and is known as the Great Initiator. He was the guru of Adam and Eve in the Mystery School known as the Garden of Eden and was also the guru of Jesus Christ.

Memory body. *See* Four lower bodies.

Messenger. A messenger is one who is trained by an ascended master to receive by various methods the words, concepts, teachings and messages of the Great White Brotherhood; one who delivers the law, the prophecies and the dispensations of God for a people and an age. Mark L. Prophet and Elizabeth Clare Prophet are messengers of the Great White Brotherhood for The Summit Lighthouse.

Nephilim. (Hebrew) Meaning "those who fell" or "those who were cast down," from the Semitic root *naphal,* meaning "to fall," rendered in the Greek Septuagint, a late translation of the Hebrew scriptures, as "giants" (Gen. 6:4; Num. 13:33). The ascended masters have revealed that the Nephilim are the fallen angels cast out of heaven into the earth (Rev. 12:7–10, 12).

Pearls of Wisdom. Weekly letters of instruction dictated by the ascended masters to their messengers Mark L. Prophet and Elizabeth Clare Prophet for students of the sacred mysteries throughout the world.

Rays. The light emanations of the Godhead. The seven rays of the white light that emerge through the prism of the Christ consciousness are: (1) blue, (2) yellow, (3) pink, (4) white, (5) green, (6) purple and gold flecked with ruby, (7) violet.

Retreat. The spiritual home of an ascended master or heavenly being. Retreats are located chiefly in the etheric plane or heaven-world.

Saint Germain. The ascended master who is Hierarch of the Aquarian Age and sponsor of the United States of America.

Second death. The death of the soul. God's gift of free will carries with it a certain span of consciousness known as the life span, a series of embodiments, and the "bounds of man's habitation." (Acts 17:26) The soul, therefore, is not only confined to time and space during the period of its experimentation with free will, but also limited to a certain number of life cycles. At the end of this opportunity (compart-mentalized in days, years and dimensions), the use that the soul has made of the gift of free will determines its fate. The soul that has chosen to glorify the Divine Ego (Reality) ascends into the Presence of the I AM THAT I AM. The soul that has chosen to glorify the human ego (unreality) passes through the second death, its self-denying consciousness permanently self-canceled. All of its energies, simultaneously passed through the sacred fire, are returned to the Great Central Sun for repolarization. (See Rev. 2:11; 20:6, 11–15; 21:8.)

Sirius. Sirius is the seat of God-government in this section of our galaxy. It is held by astronomers to be a binary star of the constellation Canis Major and is the brightest star in the heavens.

Summit Lighthouse, The. An outer organization of the Great White Brotherhood. Mark L. Prophet founded The Summit Lighthouse in 1958 under the direction of the Ascended Master El Morya to publish the teachings of the ascended masters.

Surya. The Buddha Surya, revered in Hinduism as the Sun god, holds a great balance for the earth from the God Star Sirius and through his disciple Cuzco in the ascended master retreat at Viti Levu in the South Pacific.

Temple, or Body temple. The lower vehicles of man as the dwelling place of the divine potential in the realms of time and space. "Know ye not that ye are the temple of God, and that the Spirit of God dwelleth in you?" (1 Cor. 3:16)

Threefold flame. The divine spark, the flame of God ensconced within the secret chamber of the heart; the soul's point of contact with her Supreme Source.

Twelve solar hierarchies. *See* Cosmic clock.

Two witnesses. The two witnesses are twin flames who come forth in the last days as representatives of Alpha and Omega, the Father-Mother God, to teach and to demonstrate the law of Christ-mastery on both the masculine and feminine rays. They are messengers for the Great White Brotherhood, two prophets who bring the teaching of the ascended masters to the age. (See Rev. 11:3–12.)

Violet Flame. Seventh-ray aspect of the Holy Spirit. The sacred fire that transmutes the cause, effect, record and memory of sin, or negative karma. Also called the flame of transmutation, of freedom and of forgiveness.

Watchers. The Watchers are a class of fallen angels who left their first estate as virgins of God who kept the holy flame of the immaculate matrix of all life. They became the arch-deceivers at the top level of the false hierarchy.

Mark L. Prophet and Elizabeth Clare Prophet
are pioneers of modern spirituality and internationally
renowned authors. For more than 40 years the Prophets
have published the teachings of the immortal saints and
sages of East and West known as the ascended masters.
Together they have given the world a new understanding
of the ancient wisdom as well as a path of practical
mysticism.

Their books, available in fine bookstores worldwide,
have been translated into 20 languages and are sold in
more than 30 countries.